JANE AUSTEN: THE SIX NOVELS

To my Father and Mother

Jane Austen

THE SIX NOVELS

W. A. CRAIK

METHUEN

LONDON and NEW YORK

First published in 1965
Reprinted in 1966 and 1968
First published as a University Paperback 1968 by
Methuen & Co. Ltd
11 New Fetter Lane, London EC4P 4EE
Reprinted four times
Reprinted 1986

Published in the USA by
Methuen & Co.
in association with Methuen, Inc.
29 West 35th Street, New York, NY 10001

ISBN 0 416 29540 1

Printed in Great Britain at the
University Press, Cambridge

Contents

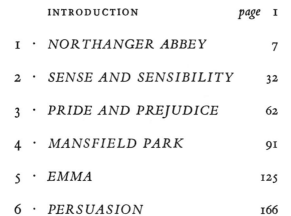

Introduction

'When the eye or the imagination is struck with any un-
common work, the next transition of an active mind will
be to the means by which it was performed.'

Johnson, *Rasselas*, CHAPTER XXX

THE 'ACTIVE MIND', ENGAGED upon a great writer, may study
both the way in which he set about the task of composition and
also the functions fulfilled by the components of his work as we
have it. Both constitute the author's method: 'the means by which
it was performed'. Very little is known of the way Jane Austen
set about her work, and of that little I am concerned only with what
may be deduced from her completed novels; but, since the form
of these novels is inseparable from their substance (being, indeed,
a manifestation of their substance), I mean to discuss not only how
Jane Austen employs the material she has chosen to use, but also
the principles by which she has chosen it.

Some admirers regard Jane Austen as a writer who depicts the
domestic life of the Regency period with photographic realism;
Charlotte Brontë saw her as this kind of writer, but disliked what
she saw:

> What did I find? An accurate daguerreotyped portrait of a common-
> place face; a carefully-fenced, highly-cultivated garden, with neat
> borders and delicate flowers; but no glance of a bright vivid phy-
> siognomy, no open country, no fresh air, no blue hill, no bonny beck.
> I should hardly like to live with her ladies and gentlemen, in their
> elegant but confined houses.
>
> (Letter to G. H. Lewes, 12 January 1848.)

This is really two objections: one to all Jane Austen puts in, the
minutiae of everyday living, and the other to what she omits.
Yet her works are very far from meriting either objection; she

I

deliberately uses her powers and right of selection and arrangement to serve a number of mutually consistent purposes. She carries out the novelist's obvious and elementary duties, to sustain interest in her stories and characters, and to render the events plausible and the characters convincing; she manoeuvres her events and characters into an artistic form that has both proportion and inevitability; and she makes the form embody a moral assessment, first of her characters and their acts, and then, through them, of men's conduct in society. Her greatness lies in the way in which she combines the artist and the moralist; hers is a perfect, because a natural, reconciliation of the two, and in none of her six completed novels does either the artist or the moralist have to give way.

That she is a moralist is beyond dispute, yet it is plain that her characters and situations are not primarily vehicles of moral philosophy, as are those of *Rasselas*. Her novels are so far from being openly didactic that her moral purpose may be overlooked by very superficial readers, or misinterpreted by very ingenious ones. For though she is never obscure, Jane Austen is complex, and though she always writes with great simplicity (her style demonstrating that clarity rather than poise is always her object), she suffers from being known to be an ironist, so that some of her critics have chosen to detect irony in even her plainest and frankest statements.[1] In fact, she combines unusual subtlety of thought and attitude with unusual simplicity of presentation: as Miss Lascelles says, 'The simplicity of Jane Austen's work is the simplicity of a thing made with simple tools.'[2] Naturally this does not mean that she does not use art, but that the art she uses is unobtrusive. This is why there is still something to say about Jane Austen's novels, even though the general tenor of her work has always been

---

[1] The most remarkable and extreme of a number of modern examples is Marvin Mudrick, in *Jane Austen: Irony as Defense and Discovery* (Princeton, 1952). That Jane Austen's statements *are* plain and frank was easily grasped by the appreciative and discriminating among her contemporaries, the outstanding ones being Sir Walter Scott and Archbishop Whately, who reviewed respectively *Emma*, and *Northanger Abbey* and *Persuasion*, in the *Quarterly Review*. Reference to these and other valuable early comments is given in the bibliography.

[2] *Jane Austen and her Art* (Oxford, 1939), p.vi.

evident (except to prejudice or perversity). Her technique has not often been examined, even though it has always been customary to remark on its excellence.

Comparison and analysis have been called the two chief tools of the critic. Although both have, of course, been employed on Jane Austen's work, comparatively few critics[1] have seen fit to use both in conjunction in order to bring out the value of treating a novel as something which develops, where the order in which the writer presents her facts and the amount of time she spends on them are as illuminating as the facts themselves. Even fewer have thought what light each of her novels may throw on its fellows. Although we cannot be certain of the order in which Jane Austen wrote her novels, and although it is probable that there is no clear succession from each novel to the next – she composed and re- vised several of her works concurrently[2] – there is still a clear line of development in them which corresponds generally to the order in which they were published.[3] It is therefore valuable to apply to the whole body of her completed novels the methods which work so well on them separately. As far as I know, this has not been done. While one can scarcely hope to say anything entirely new and original about any classic writer, particularly one so lucid and so generally known as Jane Austen (unless, that is, one is both perverse and eccentric about a writer who appeals to all the reasonable and rational qualities in her reader), one can still hope to illuminate: if not to detect a different kind of excellence, then to reveal more clearly the essential nature of known excellences. Miss Lascelles says: 'I am sure that while quotations from Bradley's essay might well head most parts of this book I should not have realized all that they meant if I had not written it.'[4] As Miss Lascelles to Bradley, so I to Miss Lascelles. It is not part of her

---

[1] Among the most successful and distinguished are Mary Lascelles, *Jane Austen and her Art*, and Edgar F. Shannon, '*Emma*: Character and Construction', *P.M.L.A.* (1956), LXXI, pp. 637–50.

[2] See Q. D. Leavis, 'A Critical Theory of Jane Austen's Writings', *Scrutiny*, X, 1, 2, 3 (1942), and XII, 1 (1944).

[3] *Sense and Sensibility* 1811, *Pride and Prejudice* 1813, *Mansfield Park* 1814, *Emma* 1816, *Persuasion* 1818.

[4] *Jane Austen and her Art*, p.v, alluding to A. C. Bradley, 'Jane Austen', *Essays and Studies*, II, 1911; reprinted in *A Miscellany*, Macmillan, 1929.

scheme to bring out this line of development from *Sense and Sensibility* to *Persuasion*, even though it is implicit in her book, just as the substance of her book is implicit in Bradley's essay. I hope, in my turn, to further the understanding of Jane Austen, both by analysing each of the novels and by treating each novel in relation to those which precede and follow it.

Northanger Abbey causes some difficulty by standing outside the obvious sequence. Published with *Persuasion* after her death, it resembles that novel in being too short for the customary three volumes in which novels were published, and in having about it an air of incompleteness. It is much closer to the small pieces written for her own family than is any of the other complete novels. It is clearly an early work,[1] and the high spirits which impel its burlesque are like those which impel the juvenilia. It is usually dealt with in between *Pride and Prejudice* and *Mansfield Park*;[2] but it is clearly inconvenient and misleading to treat this short, early, unpublished piece in the midst of the finest and most finished works: it interrupts a perceptible line of development and appears (unnecessarily) to its own disadvantage by comparison with their finished excellence. It is too important to omit, however, since (unlike the apparently complete *Lady Susan*) it shows its author working with the materials most congenial to her, in what is clearly coming to be her characteristic way. I feel I have no choice therefore but to deal with *Northanger Abbey* first of all, even though an analysis of this novel must be less interesting as well as less comprehensive than an analysis of *Sense and Sensibility*.

I must explain also why I have not seen fit to deal with all of Jane Austen's writings. Of a writer whose published output was so small, about whom so little is known, it would seem at first sight both reasonable and practicable to consider all that survives. Clearly, however, her letters offer little that can be to my purpose; the letter is to her what it was to Byron: an overflow of spirits and

---

[1] Sir Frank MacKinnon (quoted by Chapman) thinks it is based on the calendar for 1798, and the Mr King mentioned in Chapter III ceased to be the Master of Ceremonies of the Lower Rooms in 1805 (*Northanger Abbey*, pp. 27, xiii).

[2] Because it was preceded by the early versions of *Sense and Sensibility* and *Pride and Prejudice* (*Jane Austen: Her Life and Letters*, W. and R. A. Austen-Leigh, Smith Elder and Co., 1913, p. 96).

disposition to understanding friends, not a conscious work of art, as it was, for example, to Horace Walpole. Of her minor works the early burlesques are not much to the point; though they are clever literary parody, and show very often her lively touch with character and her awareness of the difference between the world of reality and the world of illusion, these juvenilia, many of them unfinished, are mostly high-spirited extravaganzas. *Lady Susan*, which is not parody or burlesque, is complete only in so far as the story is complete; it is very summarily brought to its end, and looks like an experiment: writing in letters is a form Jane Austen rejected for finished work when she revised *Elinor and Marianne* into *Sense and Sensibility*. *Lady Susan* also very remarkably lacks high spirits, and – the only time in Jane Austen – the devil has the best tunes, and unrelieved wickedness is artistically more impressive than virtue. The unfinished pieces *The Watsons* and *Sanditon* have their interest in showing how Jane Austen went to work, since no early drafts of completed novels survive.[1] None of these fragments and juvenilia has the serious moral *impulse* which is so essential to the six major novels (even though a moral *attitude* is generally implicit in them); and one cannot observe a writer's principles of selection and organization when the work is unfinished and one is not sure of her intentions.

In discussing the novels I have occasionally used the same quotation or example to illustrate at different times two different critical points. This by no means shows lack of material on Jane Austen's part, but an attempt of mine sometimes to keep clear a line of argument which involves detail not only from several parts of one novel, but often of two or more novels at the same time; and sometimes to elucidate one aspect of her art at a point where many are involved.

In quoting from the novels I have used the text of R. W. Chapman's edition,[2] and my page and chapter references are to this edition. In the footnotes I have given, at the first mention of

[1] The only part of a completed novel of which we have an earlier version is the cancelled 'Chapter X' of *Persuasion*, which was altered and expanded to its final form in Chapters X and XI of the second volume.

[2] *The Novels of Jane Austen*, ed. R. W. Chapman, five volumes, Oxford; third edition 1933, fifth impression 1953.

all other works, the full bibliographical reference, and thereafter used a short title; the full titles are given in the bibliography.

For the use of their facilities I am indebted to the library staffs of Leicester University and of the British Museum; and, for typing the manuscript, to Miss Grace Thorpe. For help in discussing and arranging my ideas I am grateful to Miss M. M. B. Jones and to my husband.

I · *Northanger Abbey*

JANE AUSTEN DID NOT consider the novel we know as *Northanger Abbey* to be fit for publication.[1] After she had bought it back in 1816 from the publisher to whom – as *Susan* – it had been sold thirteen years before, she attempted some revision, but put it, shortly before she died, 'upon the shelve for the present'.[2] One is glad it was brought down again, for besides being an accomplished burlesque of a literary fashion, it contains much of Jane Austen's characteristic strength.

Northanger Abbey is more dated than any other of Jane Austen's major works and less immediately popular. Because it is short, it depends considerably on the reader to fill in the standards of conduct and social behaviour of Regency Bath and well-to-do rural society around its heroine, standards from which she and so many of the people she meets are different kinds of aberration. The aberrations in this novel – the Thorpe family for example and Captain Tilney – are preposterous and grotesque; they cannot, as Miss Bingley, Lady Catherine, and Mary Crawford, and even Mrs Jennings do, show proper conduct precisely by their violations of it. However, *Northanger Abbey* is dated mainly because it is a literary burlesque, and few people now have even read the works of Mrs Radcliffe and her followers, and can certainly not share Catherine's enthusiasm for them. But it is more than a burlesque of the Gothic and Sentimental Novel – which Jane Austen herself had already done superbly in *Love and Friendship*; it shows the same preoccupations as her other novels, and some of the same skill in presenting her conclusions. It is not wholly

[1] It appeared posthumously with the title given to it by her brother Henry; she herself called it *Catherine* (letter to Fanny Knight, 13 March 1817, *Jane Austen's Letters*, ed. R. W. Chapman, Oxford, 1932, p. 484).

[2] Letter to Fanny Knight, 13 March 1817.

satisfactory, because the two intentions – of literary burlesque and of social and moral comment – come eventually into opposition during the events at Northanger. Up to this point nothing happens to Catherine that is supposed to happen to a heroine, and she does not expect it; at Northanger she begins to think herself the centre of sensational events, and is then disillusioned by Henry Tilney; then when the General turns her out we find she was right to suspect him of misconduct, even if not of wife-murder; so although the Gothic conventions are logically used, the moral effect of Henry's reproving her fanciful suspicions of his father is undermined, and the burlesque satire spoiled. Even so, the character of Catherine and the view of society she reveals are greatly extended, and show where Jane Austen's interests really lie.

The handling of the Bath episodes – the part most literary in impulse and most entertaining – is precise, economical, and excellently contrived, but more elementary than in the other novels. Catherine, uncomplicated as she must be for the purpose of the burlesque, is not a heroine like Emma or even Elinor, who can reveal the theme and its progress by what she does and thinks. The author's own voice must direct the reader. Jane Austen's method is both simple and flexible, as the opening makes clear:

> She was fond of all boys' plays, and greatly preferred cricket not merely to dolls, but to the more heroic enjoyments of infancy, nursing a dormouse, feeding a canary-bird, or watering a rosebush. (13)

She advances a romantic convention of the novel, contradicts it, and reinforces the contradiction with facts. The reader will be alert later when the ironic contrast rests in an odd word:

> Neither robbers nor tempests *befriended* them, nor one *lucky* overturn to introduce them to the hero. (19: my italics.)

This is neat, simple, and funny, and when once done definitely, can become even less obtrusive and the reader will still respond:

> It is indeed a street of so impertinent a nature, so unfortunately connected with the great London and Oxford roads, and the principal inn of the city, that a day never passes in which parties of ladies, however important their business, whether in quest of pastry, mil-

linery, or even (as in the present case) of young men, are not detained on one side or other by carriages, horsemen, or carts. (44)

The transposed epithets 'impertinent' and 'important' (in the manner of her early burlesques) make the point as wittily and unobtrusively as anything in the best of her work.

When the scene changes to Northanger, Jane Austen's attitude changes and her methods with it. The action is more within Catherine herself in the kind of reported throught-process which is the triumph of *Emma* and will be dealt with there in more detail. Catherine's reactions to Isabella's letter are an example:

> Such a strain of shallow artifice could not impose even upon Catherine. Its inconsistencies, contradictions, and falsehood, struck her from the very first. She was ashamed of Isabella, and ashamed of having ever loved her. Her professions of attachment were now as disgusting as her excuses were empty, and her demands impudent. 'Write to James on her behalf! – No, James should never hear Isabella's name mentioned by her again.' (218)

This shows the truth about Isabella, and Catherine's naïve grasp of it, at one and the same time. The literary burlesque is now incidental, not integral:

> She trembled a little at the idea of any one's approaching so cautiously; but resolving not to be again overcome by trivial appearances of alarm, or misled by a raised imagination, she stepped quietly forward, and opened the door. Eleanor, and only Eleanor, stood there. (223)

One is too interested in why Eleanor has come so late at night to care for hints of horrors. From here to the end Jane Austen devotes herself to settling Catherine and Henry, the literary parody, the real motive of the book, having been settled in twenty-four of the novel's thirty-one chapters.

Jane Austen shows herself unwilling to take on much personality as a narrator[1] and throws a large part of her function as arbiter of good sense on to Henry Tilney, not to his advantage (as I shall show later). This he is both at Bath and Northanger. His mocking conversations with Catherine are a judgement on Isabella

[1] Compared, for example, with Fielding.

9

(although he never appears with her) and his opinions on muslin reveal Mrs Allen. When at Northanger, the load becomes artistically more than he can bear; Catherine's *naïveté* does not permit her to work out her own disillusionment like Emma, and circumstances cannot do it for her as they do for Marianne; Henry does it, and his ready instruction, and analysis of her conduct and motives, give him more importance than the plot merits, and, while making him more interesting, make him an improbable lover. Although Henry Tilney's opinion often stands for Jane Austen's, the action is never seen through his personality (as it occasionally is through Mr Knightley's or Edmund Bertram's) and Catherine herself is not acute enough to allow the action to be seen through hers. Jane Austen therefore remains detached from Catherine, who always seems younger and less experienced than her creator and her reader.[1] She should seem so, for a burlesque, and Jane Austen makes Catherine an excellent heroine for the events at Bath, immature and ignorant, and also naturally right-thinking and unconsciously perceptive. Jane Austen's attitude changes (as it must) at Northanger, and the shift from burlesque to questions of morals and society, though not a complete success, shows her skill in presenting her material. When Catherine sees Gothic horror around her the narrative interest lies in her mental processes and misapprehensions and the exclamatory method exposes Catherine to ridicule:

> The manuscript so wonderfully found, so wonderfully accomplishing the morning's prediction, how was it to be accounted for? – What could it contain? – to whom could it relate? – by what means could it have been so long concealed? – and how singularly strange that it should fall to her lot to discover it! (170)

After she realizes her errors, the same method can easily be used to reveal her further, and to throw the same unconsciously ironic light on to persons and events around her as is found in the other novels.

Jane Austen's unique and excellent characters are always admired;

[1] A comparison of the way the seventeen-year-old Catherine impresses one with the way Fanny Price does when she gives her careful and valid judgements and reactions to her fellow characters at the same age makes this clear.

she is one of the few English novelists who, while psychologically accurate with most of her women and many of her men, is just as happy with serious as with comic characters, and able to present both kinds in the same scene without incongruity. *Emma* is superior in this way to anything of Dickens's or even Thackeray's (and he is much nearer to her in aims and method): nothing like the incongruity of Captain Cuttle meeting Mr Carker in *Dombey and Son*, or the Dobbin of the opening chapters of *Vanity Fair* marrying Amelia, is felt when Emma is in company with Mrs Elton – who is quite as farcical as Captain Cuttle and Dobbin; novelists who do connect all their characters and have more in common with Jane Austen, like George Eliot and Henry James, never venture so near to farce. The reason for and the result of such combinations of characters is her excellent organization. Characters of serious interest to both author and reader are treated (with certain reservations in the cases of Fanny Price and Anne Elliot) with humour and irony; while comic characters, however much they may exhibit their idiosyncrasy, have always a serious and essential purpose not merely to the plot but to the emotional, social, and moral preoccupations underlying all Jane Austen's major work. This is bound to form a large part of the discussion of *Pride and Prejudice*, *Mansfield Park*, and *Emma*, where the action is so dependent on personality, but it is also true of *Northanger Abbey* and shows the true bent of her genius, despite a plot contrived to travesty Mrs Radcliffe, which to a great extent dictates the characters.

The exception is Isabella Thorpe, who is far more elementary than any of the other creations outside the minor works, and is exhibited as a foil to Catherine, rather than really used in the many ways Jane Austen even here (in Mrs Allen) shows she can use such a character. Although Isabella is a success in her way, she is a product of the literary burlesque alone: she introduces Catherine to the Gothic novels by which Catherine misinterprets events at Northanger; she personifies the follies and insincerities of literary sentimentality; and, as a foil to the untutored and natural Catherine, she shows the vulgarity of mind and speech that may easily accompany such traits:

'. . . I would not dance with him, unless he would allow Miss Andrews to be as beautiful as an angel. The men think us incapable of real friendship you know, and I am determined to shew them the difference. Now, if I were to hear any body speak slightingly of you, I should fire up in a moment: . . . you have so much animation, which is exactly what Miss Andrews wants, for I must confess there is something amazingly insipid about her.' (40–41)

When her burlesque purpose is fulfilled Isabella leaves the story; this, and the fact that once Captain Tilney has been seen flirting with her he is scarcely seen with his family and never seen talking to them, show both Jane Austen's awareness of her immature technique and her skill in rendering it unobtrusive. Isabella, though literary not realistic in both origin and function, is like Henry Tilney in being the result of a naïve heroine (she would be impossible, for instance, as confidante to an acute heroine like Elizabeth Bennet); that she considers *herself* the stuff of heroines and Catherine merely her confidante is a delightful instance of Jane Austen's ironic economy with her material.

There are many signs even in Isabella of Jane Austen's powers of organization. Isabella's love of money is pertinent when she becomes engaged to James Morland, and it points to more serious topics:

'I cannot bear to be the means of injuring my dear Morland, making him sit down upon an income hardly enough to find one in the common necessaries of life. For myself, it is nothing; I never think of myself.' (136)

The repetition and exaggeration make it clear that she thinks of no one *but* herself; and she contrasts with what it is plain will eventually be the unworldly Catherine's similar situation with Henry Tilney. Isabella shows also another important theme of the novel: Catherine's realizing that she can and must make social and moral judgements. Isabella's preposterous exaggerations show that Catherine's minor ones result from innocent thoughtlessness, not from artifice, and show Catherine's naturally sound and proper principles by contrast with her own flexibility. Her last appearance – her letter to Northanger already mentioned – gives the evidence we need that Catherine's perceptions have sharpened and matured. At points Isabella serves both the burlesque and the moral theme at once:

> . . . I suppose Mrs Morland objects to novels.'
> 'No, she does not. She very often reads Sir Charles Grandison herself; but new books do not fall in our way.'
> 'Sir Charles Grandison! That is an amazing horrid book, is it not? – I remember Miss Andrews could not get through the first volume.' (41–42)

This shows her own silliness, the unromantic sense of Mrs Morland, and Catherine's own sense, especially when a few lines later Catherine gives as her opinion of the novel, 'I think it is very entertaining.'

In the same style as Isabella are her sisters Anne and Maria, who although exaggerated and unrealistic, with no part in the action, show that Isabella is in her way acute; for though Catherine trusts *her*, she is not taken in by her sisters. Jane Austen treats them with all the exuberant irrationality of her early work:

> [Miss Thorpe] was loitering towards Edgar's Buildings between two of the sweetest girls in the world, who had been her dear friends all the morning. (114–15)

John Thorpe makes a pair with his sister; her literary pretensions are matched by his boasts about horses, drinking, and riches. His minor exaggerations about these and his first, casual lie about being engaged to dance with Catherine prepare for his really important lies, for he twice influences Catherine's fate by lying to General Tilney about her fortune. The lies themselves are artistically arranged: he claims to have seen Henry and Eleanor Tilney driving out just when they have promised to walk with Catherine, and he circumstantially reveals his lies at the same rate as he convinces Catherine, by accumulated detail:

> 'Does he not drive a phaeton with bright chestnuts? . . . driving a smart-looking girl . . . hallooing to a man who was just passing by on horseback, that they were going as far as Wick Rocks.' (85–86)

His dissociation from serious characters like Mr Allen and Henry

Tilney is positively useful, for it throws into relief his association with General Tilney, another vain and greedy man, and makes the reader uneasy about the General before there is any reason to suspect him, the man being judged by the company he keeps.

These are all of the characters with a strikingly literary origin; the rest – Mrs Thorpe and Mrs Allen, Mr Allen and Mrs Morland, the General, Eleanor, and Henry and Catherine – are Jane Austen's own, showing both the lively humour of all her work, and the restraint of her later novels. Mrs Allen is a rich creation, effective in the burlesque and important to the revelation of Catherine's character; she and Mr Allen are the only characters who belong both to Bath and to Catherine's home at Fullerton, and so they give her a context. As the burlesque chaperon Mrs Allen is a delight: her disposition produces conduct quite the reverse of the expected; she is neither noble adviser nor villainous deceiver, for she gives Catherine no help at all – either on whether it will rain or on whether it is proper to go out in John Thorpe's gig. Her one interest – dress – impresses the point:

> Our heroine's entrée into life could not take place till after three or four days had been spent in learning what was mostly worn, and her chaperon was provided with a dress of the newest fashion. (20)[1]

She is not destroyed as Isabella would be by Henry's delighted comments on her, which enrich them both:

> Mr Tilney was very much amused. 'Only go and call on Mrs Allen!' he repeated. 'What a picture of intellectual poverty!' (79)

She is one of Jane Austen's small triumphs, a delightful portrayal of a stupid woman, like that great triumph Miss Bates: but unlike her in that Miss Bates is always unconsciously relevant, while Mrs Allen is either fascinatingly irrelevant, as here –

> 'Did she tell you what part of Gloucestershire they come from?'
> 'Yes, she did; but I cannot recollect now. But they are very good kind of people, and very rich. Mrs Tilney was a Miss Drummond, and she and Mrs Hughes were schoolfellows; and Miss Drummond

[1] Compare Evelina's arrival in London, when the chaperon Mrs Mirvan spends some time and trouble getting suitable dresses for her protégée.

had a very large fortune; and, when she married, her father gave her twenty thousand pounds, and five hundred to buy wedding-clothes. Mrs Hughes saw all the clothes after they came from the warehouse.' (68)

– or so obviously right as to be uproarious (in which she looks forward to Lady Bertram), as when she has been praising Henry Tilney and Mrs Thorpe says:

'I must say it, though I *am* his mother, that there is not a more agreeable young man in the world.'
    This inapplicable answer might have been too much for the comprehension of many; but it did not puzzle Mrs Allen, for after only a moment's consideration, she said, in a whisper to Catherine, 'I dare say she thought I was speaking of her son.' (58–59)

Her husband and Mrs Morland represent another type of character. Whilst what they say is reasonable, it is humorous by basing itself on a partial comprehension of the situation, or by being distorted by a prevailing habit of mind. This is one of Jane Austen's most fruitful methods, producing her finest and richest comic effects, from the lesser figures of Admiral Croft, Mrs Jennings, and Mr Bennet, to her heroines Elizabeth Bennet, Emma, and even Marianne Dashwood. Mr Allen at Bath, like Henry Tilney throughout, reinforces the reader's and Catherine's opinions, allowing Jane Austen herself to be apparently detached:

'Young men and women driving about the country in open carriages! Now and then it is very well; but going to inns and public places together! It is not right.' (104)

On matters less serious his foibles may be exposed –

Mr Allen not having his own skies and barometer about him, declined giving any absolute promise of sunshine. (82)

– implying that at home he might do so, and that a distance of thirty miles prohibits it. In a similar way Mrs Morland's limited understanding of Catherine's unhappiness at being parted from Henry Tilney – 'our comfort does not depend on General Tilney' (234) – produces a faith in the improving essay in *The Mirror* as a cure for melancholy, and mundane speculations on the charms, not of Henry Tilney, but of French bread.

General Tilney is interesting though unsatisfactory. He is the ancestor of Sir Walter Elliot in self-indulgent vanity, though obsessed with money as well as with rank. His self-satisfaction is entertaining on its own account –

> 'Mr Allen had only one small hot-house, . . . and there was a fire in it now and then.'
> 'He is a happy man!' said the General, with a look of very happy contempt. (178–9)

– while his self-centredness and insincere charm provide just enough grounds for Catherine's behaviour to be not quite outrageous when she detects hypocrisy and deduces crime; but he has not character enough to make the reader believe he would turn her out of the house simply because he had been told that she had no fortune. His daughter Eleanor is lightly drawn, having only a very small part to play, as the pretext for Catherine's visit, and as a familiar rational partner for Henry; but she is a promising example of the useful and sensible minor character, like Mrs Gardiner in *Pride and Prejudice*, Mrs Weston in *Emma*, and Mrs Croft in *Persuasion*.

Jane Austen is notoriously known to show men only in the company of women, and never to reveal their thoughts and emotions as she does women's.[1] Yet Henry Tilney, a slight figure rather through the brevity of the novel than the part he has to play, is generally considered most attractive. Like all the heroes, except Edward Ferrars, he is fully the equal of a charming heroine, both by his part in the action and the force of his personality. Excepting Catherine, he is the most important character in the novel, being equally relevant both to the burlesque and to the growth of Catherine's personality. He is introduced not as a hero but simply as an agreeable young man; but as he is the only agreeable young man in the book his role is obvious. The equal of Catherine (herself *not* a heroine), he is cleverer and more sophisticated than she, giving balance to the story by showing

[1] This is not true of later figures, Mr Darcy and Mr Knightley in particular.

that a sensible person need not be ingenuous like Catherine, nor a sophisticated one deceitful and silly like Isabella and Captain Tilney. Jane Austen makes good burlesque use of him. Being well-informed and witty, Henry can introduce aspects of Catherine's role as romantic heroine which the action does not include. A fictional heroine should, for instance, keep a journal; Catherine, of course, does not: Henry points out this, and also the difference between a literary journal, a probable real journal, and his own burlesque of both:

> 'Yes, I know exactly what you will say: Friday, went to the Lower Rooms; wore my sprigged muslin robe with blue trimmings – plain black shoes – appeared to much advantage; but was strangely harassed by a queer, half-witted man, who would make me dance with him, and distressed me by his nonsense.'
>
> 'Indeed I shall say no such thing.'
>
> 'Shall I tell you what you ought to say?'
>
> 'If you please.'
>
> 'I danced with a very agreeable young man, introduced by Mr King; had a great deal of conversation with him – seems a most extraordinary genius – hope I may know more of him. *That*, madam, is what I *wish* you to say.' (26–27)

He also acts in all seriousness as her guide on matters of propriety and right thinking, and shows her the serious impropriety of her behaviour at Northanger. These functions recall the way Lord Orville is set up as adviser to Evelina, and the reminiscence seems deliberate, for it is supported by particular incidents: John Thorpe's claim that Catherine is engaged to him for the dance she is having with Henry Tilney recalls Evelina's dilemma when she refuses Mr Lovell and then stands up with Lord Orville (*Evelina*, Letter 11). The similarity reveals both Catherine and Henry, for both behave sensibly and rationally, and show neither Evelina's tortures of sensibility nor Lord Orville's huffiness. The reader can feel sure that Evelina would suffer just the same if Lovell were lying like John Thorpe (if her conduct were as straightforward as Catherine's, as it is, in fact, as blameless), for the source of her misery is her own delicacy.

Henry Tilney is useful at Northanger to keep up the literary burlesque when its intrinsic interest is almost at an end, and at the same time to bring out Catherine's real good qualities:

> 'You feel, I suppose, that, in losing Isabella, you lose half yourself: you feel a void in your heart which nothing else can occupy. Society is becoming irksome; and as for the amusements in which you were wont to share at Bath, the very idea of them without her is abhorrent. . . . You feel all this?'
>
> 'No,' said Catherine, after a few moments' reflection, 'I do not – ought I?' . . .
>
> 'You feel, as you always do, what is most to the credit of human nature. – Such feelings ought to be investigated, that they may know themselves.' (207)

Henry reveals Catherine as she herself – a nature not introspective – cannot; and his approval, that of an acute observer, is equivalent to Jane Austen's own.

Henry's acute gauge of characters' probable motives, and Catherine's universal sympathy, together cover all the aspects of the situation necessary for its full understanding; they are complementary, and their association seems credible despite the heavy weight on Henry of his superiority in age, experience, wit, and understanding.

Catherine is a charming heroine, different and differently treated from all other of Jane Austen's heroines. Much has been said of her in dealing with the people who surround her, because the interaction in this novel is almost all between the minor characters and Catherine herself. There is little interplay, for example, between Isabella and John Thorpe, or Isabella and James, such as there is between Mary Crawford and her brother, or Mary and Edmund, who stand in similar relation to each other and to the heroine. With Catherine for a heroine, the reader has more than merely the amusement provided by an ignorant girl in romantic predicaments which are in turn set against the predicaments of real life. In fact, some of the entertainment is deliberately done away with: Catherine has far more control over her circumstances than many of the romantic heroines she stands for: she manages to arrange her walk with the Tilneys (more or less unconsciously) and resists even her brother to carry it through; her one frustration is

18

when General Tilney turns her out, and while this conduct resembles that of the Gothic tyrant, its consequences and Catherine's coping with them are down-to-earth and bear little relation to the burlesque.

Catherine's language, while showing childish simplicity of thought and the direct expression one would expect, reveals the soundness of her own ideas and the moral failings of those around her. She appears first in contrast to Mrs Allen, whose vacuity is revealed against Catherine's natural politeness:

> Mrs Allen did all that she could do in such a case by saying very placidly, every now and then, 'I wish you could dance, my dear, – I wish you could get a partner.' For some time her young friend felt obliged to her for these wishes; but they were repeated so often, and proved so totally ineffectual, that Catherine grew tired at last, and would thank her no more. (21)

Isabella acts like Mrs Allen, showing Catherine's good sense and her own follies; Catherine would be vulgarized by acting as her confidante, and Isabella demonstrates the point, and assumes the vulgarity herself:

> '. . . I prefer light eyes, and as to complexion – do you know – I like a sallow better than any other. You must not betray me, if you should ever meet with one of your acquaintance answering that description.'
>
> 'Betray you!—What do you mean?'
>
> 'Nay, do not distress me. I believe I have said too much. Let us drop the subject.'
>
> Catherine, in some amazement, complied. (42)

Isabella's cliché-ridden speech throws light on Catherine, who, unique among Jane Austen's heroines, herself uses a good deal of cliché; by contrast with Isabella's, it is clear that Catherine's idioms approximate to her real meaning. This is Isabella:

> '. . . I have been waiting for you at least this age! . . . I am sure I have been here this half hour. . . . I have an hundred things to say to you . . . it looked very showery, and that would have thrown me into agonies! Do you know, I saw the prettiest hat you can imagine, in a shop window in Milsom-street just now . . .' (39)

And this is Catherine:

> 'Oh! Mr Tilney, I have been quite wild to speak to you, and make my apologies. You must have thought me so rude . . . I had ten thousand times rather have been with you.' (93)

So when Catherine is with Henry and Eleanor, who are both accurate and literal, her clichés are not to her disadvantage, as might have been feared, but show an uncomplicated and innocent nature. When she deals with John Thorpe's proposal her simple remarks are richly funny and have an irony more subtle than a consciously witty heroine could provide:

> 'And I hope – I hope, Miss Morland, *you* will not be sorry to see me.'
> 'Oh! dear, not at all. There are very few people I am sorry to see. Company is always cheerful.' (123)

This is a very fair estimate of John Thorpe's social value. Catherine's imaginative grasp of moral principle later throws a cold light on his muddled sentiment:

> 'If there is a good fortune on one side, there can be no occasion for any on the other. No matter which has it, so that there is enough. I hate the idea of one great fortune looking out for another.' (124)[1]

These comments are made even more relevant to the topics of the novel they underline – money and matrimony – by being Catherine's answer to a proposal of marriage, even though she does not know she is receiving it.

When Catherine has been simply contrasted with simple characters her subtleties are brought out by the subtle Henry Tilney. With him Catherine often makes the simple comment which is wittier and more apt than she realizes: 'I cannot speak well enough to be unintelligible' (133); this increases her charm for both Henry and the reader (who are on these occasions intellectual equals). Her frank manners lead to occasional delightful advantages over Henry, of which she alone is unconscious – 'Nobody would have thought you had no right [to be angry] who saw your face' (95) –

[1] The passage is a recollection of Congreve (*Love for Love*, I, viii).

such manners, though not within the rules of etiquette, are not at all impolite. In this she resembles Elizabeth Bennet, whose manners are also unconventional, and contrasts with the later heroines Emma and Anne Elliot, who are models of propriety, indicating that Jane Austen was not yet able at this early stage to reveal her meaning in a form mainly dialogue without breaking through the conventions and proprieties of ordinary society. Thus the character and role of Catherine embodies Jane Austen's concern with the moral basis of conduct which will prove to be the true material for her mature genius to work on.

A fault of the plot is that as Catherine's character becomes more psychologically interesting it becomes less so as a literary force. So much of her effect in the Bath scenes is unconscious and ironic that the story becomes thin when the characters at whom the irony was directed have disappeared, and Catherine's own thoughts which replace them are naïve and incapable of subtlety. Yet she is still capable of holding the reader's interest, is not inconsistent with her early self, and is revealed in other ways; her moral growth, begun at Bath, continues more explicitly at Northanger, and Henry, revealing her to the reader, now reveals her to herself as well. The reader sees also more of her thought-processes, both before and after her suspicions of the General. Although her judgement grows firmer, her attractive childish qualities remain with her, mainly shown in turns of phrase: from this (when the Tilneys refuse to receive her call) –

> She could almost be angry herself at such angry incivility; but she checked the resentful sensation; she remembered her own ignorance. (92)

– she progresses only as far as this:

> . . . she need not fear to acknowledge some actual specks in the character of their father, who, though cleared from the grossly injurious suspicions which she must ever blush to have entertained, she did believe, upon serious consideration, to be not perfectly amiable. (200)

This preserves one's pleasure in Catherine and makes her conversion more telling by its restrained expression. Contrast with

Marianne Dashwood shows that Jane Austen, though less serious, is here both more assured and less simple: for Marianne's behaviour is just as excessive, though in a new direction, after her disillusion as it was before it.

Any consideration of Jane Austen is likely to begin with her creation of character, but examination of her workmanship is equally agreeable, necessary, and enlightening. Her skills are conscious, and one of the greatest of them lies in manipulating her plots: no event or character is ever lost sight of or summarily dismissed, no improbable events bring about required conclusions, and no personality is distorted to fit an obviously predetermined fate. But the plot is not a complete success. Parody is by nature static, a rendering of a state of affairs rather than of a course of action, and Jane Austen has the problem that has faced all writers of parody, that of inventing a satisfactory conclusion. She overcomes it by simply emerging from the burlesque into her own kind of comedy, which, because it is itself revealed through irony, is not inappropriate or jarring. Her plot is well thought out: while the early part is obvious parody, it presents at the same time Jane Austen's other theme, the growth of Catherine's character and her moral sense. The points at which the plot breaks down (and the reasons) have already been mentioned: what remains is to considr ethe skill with which she organizes the plot elsewhere.

In Jane Austen the action always appears to rise out of character, and this is true even of the burlesque *Northanger Abbey*. Catherine's visit to Bath is because Mr Allen has gout, and she does not come even upon *The Mysteries of Udolpho* by chance; she is introduced to it by Isabella, to whom such reading is apt. Even when General Tilney expels Catherine he has a plausible if inadequate motive: John Thorpe has lied to him about Catherine's poverty as he lied to him earlier about her wealth. The event is carefully prepared when the General makes his first appearance at the Cotillon Ball: his whispered words to Henry, though they gratify Catherine, also embarrass her; his later actions reinforce his discourtesy, and his association with the unattractive John Thorpe, before we see anything of his own personality, makes him unattractive by association. Jane Austen is consistently careful in smaller matters.[1] She not only marks the passage of time –

'Monday, Tuesday, Wednesday, Thursday, Friday and Saturday have now passed in review before the reader; the events of each day, its hopes and fears, mortifications and pleasures have been separately stated, and the pangs of Sunday only now remain to be described, and close the week.' (97)

– she skilfully reproduces effects of its passage:

. . . the journey began. It was performed with suitable quietness and uneventful safety. Neither robbers nor tempests befriended them, nor one lucky overturn to introduce them to the hero. Nothing more alarming occurred than a fear on Mrs Allen's side, of having once left her clogs behind her at an inn, and that fortunately proved to be groundless.

They arrived at Bath. Catherine was all eager delight; – her eyes were here, there, every where, as they approached its fine and striking environs, and afterwards drove through those streets which conducted them to the hotel. She was come to be happy, and she felt happy already.

They were soon settled in comfortable lodgings in Pulteney-street. (19)

The journey is duly referred to its fictional counterpart and it is represented by the trivial detail (very representative of Mrs Allen) of the clogs;[2] when they arrive Bath is seen concisely through Catherine's eyes as 'fine 'and 'striking'; and the final sentence with its static words 'settled' and 'lodgings' leaves the way clear for new incident. The journey to Northanger is longer, and just as effective: the details make the journey lifelike at the same time as they reflect on the General:

They set off at the sober pace in which the handsome, highly-fed horses of a gentleman usually perform a journey of thirty miles . . . the tediousness of a two hours' bait at Petty-France, in which there

---

[1] 'An artist cannot do anything slovenly' (letter to Cassandra Austen, Saturday, 17 November 1798, *Letters*, p. 30), though spoken lightly of her drawing, is true enough of all she did.

[2] Judging from her later behaviour – 'I really have not patience with the General!' (238) – this would provide her with conversation for the rest of the journey.

was nothing to be done but to eat without being hungry, and loiter about without any thing to see . . . postilions handsomely liveried, rising so regularly in their stirrups. (155–6)

Henry's teasings soon after show the extent of their intimacy, intensify Catherine's romantic apprehensions about the Abbey, and prepare the reader for what is to come.

'But you must be aware that when a young lady is (by whatever means) introduced into a dwelling of this kind, she is always lodged apart from the rest of the family. While they snugly repair to their own end of the house, she is formally conducted by Dorothy the ancient housekeeper up a different staircase, and along many gloomy passages, into an apartment never used since some cousin or kin died in it about twenty years before. Can you stand such a ceremony as this?' (158)

Jane Austen is equally adept at getting over a longer period of time in the shortest possible space, yet showing quite plainly that time has, in fact, passed:

The following conversation, which took place between the two friends in the Pump-room one morning, after an acquaintance of eight or nine days, is given as a specimen of their very warm attachment . . . (39)

This makes the conversation more than a single incident, it represents the eight or nine days passed over. *Northanger Abbey* covers only a short space of time – six weeks at Bath, four at Northanger, and four days at Fullerton, and this shows already Jane Austen's liking for a steady passage through a short time, and the skill which eventually produces her masterpiece *Emma*, which progresses through a whole year in this way. However, the method raises technical difficulties: she must seem to keep the action moving at a steady pace, must select significant detail from trivial events, yet not appear to give any one incident exceptional prominence. Her methods vary. Until the seventeenth chapter – the events at Bath – it is a day-by-day chronicle, and the happenings receive almost equal reading-space (the ball where Catherine meets nobody at all is roughly the same length in print as the one where she meets Henry Tilney, or as her first outing with John Thorpe). Emphasis is not by length but by contrast or connexion with events before or after: the Thorpe family is not agreeable on its first appearance chiefly because it is not Henry Tilney, whom both Catherine and the reader had hoped to meet. At Northanger Catherine's doings are chronicled in the same way, but with longer intervals passed over, the intervals becoming even wider after her disillusionment.

By this method Jane Austen has to show the actual processes by which friendships and intimacies develop; they cannot grow up out of sight of the reader. She circumvents rather than surmounts this problem. The friendship between Catherine and Isabella is full-blown from the start, while that between Catherine and Henry is always unequal and unconventional, so that even the first meeting can be as informal as any other. Increasing intimacy between them is barely indicated: though towards the end (221) 'Catherine did – almost always – believe that Henry loved her', the reader, though convinced she is right, has had very little demonstration of it. Even conceding that fine shades of feeling would be out of place in this novel, it is plain that it is some distance from *Pride and Prejudice*, where she can demonstrate the precise nature and extent of Elizabeth's feelings for Darcy long before Elizabeth herself knows these feelings exist.

Jane Austen uses only a small section of rural society, and the country is the background of all her work; only *Sense and Sensibility* moves to London, though *Pride and Prejudice* passes through; and Bath, which appears here and in *Persuasion*, is still so rural that Catherine and the Tilneys reach open country easily on foot. It has often been remarked that she shows no interest in this country; in fact, she gives remarkably little systematic detail of anything – whether scenery, furnishing, clothes or personal appearance. She never employs inanimate objects – like the wooden midshipman outside Solomon Gills's shop in *Dombey and Son* – which assume almost the importance of characters; or natural features – like the fog in *Bleak House*, or like Egdon Heath in *The Return of the Native* – which symbolize aspects of the main theme. All her use of background detail is determined by what is strictly and immediately relevant to her purpose. It must be remembered also that she can assume a good deal of knowledge in her reader; like most eighteenth-century authors, she writes for contemporaries and assumes an audience of intellectual and social equals. She has no occasion to expatiate on the social or architectural elegance of Pulteney Street, and the humour of Catherine's behaviour when she 'voluntarily rejected the whole city of Bath, as unworthy to make part of a landscape' (111) would be quite clear (as it still is to many) without any effusions from the author. She can also assume with more safety and certainty of agreement than a modern writer that her reader knows what good furniture looks like, or the Staffordshire breakfast set which General Tilney disparages for being 'quite an old set, purchased two years ago' (175).

But she is alert to her surroundings and the impression they make, and by the end of even *Northanger Abbey* (much more of *Emma* or *Mansfield Park*) the observant reader has had all the information he needs for an adequate and very accurate idea of the story's background. The information is given in observations – usually short – in the part of the narrative at which it has most point. While Catherine is thinking of the Abbey's 'long, damp passages, its narrow cells and ruined chapel', the first account of what it really is makes a neat contrast:

> so active were her thoughts . . . that she was hardly more assured than before . . . of its having fallen into the hands of an ancestor of the Tilneys on its dissolution, of a large portion of the ancient building still making a part of the present dwelling although the rest was decayed, or of its standing low in a valley, sheltered from the north and east by rising woods of oak. (141–2)

The house is described for two reasons. The first is to show ironically Catherine's delusions:

> The fire-place, where she had expected the ample width and ponderous carving of former times, was contracted to a Rumford, with slabs of plain though handsome marble, and ornaments over it of the prettiest English china. (162)

This gives way soon to the second reason when the disingenuous General begins to talk of 'the smallness of the room and simplicity of the furniture, where every thing being for daily use, pretended only to comfort, &c.' (162).

Jane Austen treats more personal matters of costume and appearance in the same way. Nice details of Indian muslins and their cost and quality reveal Mrs Allen's and Henry Tilney's idiosyncrasies, rather than the heroine's costume, and Henry's own appearance is merely one of the many causes of Catherine's pleasure on her way to Northanger:

> And then his hat sat so well, and the innumerable capes of his great coat looked so becomingly important! (157)

In fact, this, Isabella's summary, 'a brown skin, with dark eyes, and rather dark hair' (42), and Catherine's remark of Captain Tilney 'that some people might think him handsomer than his brother' (131) (indicating that he is a good deal handsomer) is all the reader ever discovers about this charming hero's appearance. Just as Jane Austen has no need to describe physical features, she has equally little need to describe expression; her power of creating conversation – the actual cadences of the speaking voice – are such that incidental details of gesture or grimace are superfluous.

Her style is easy, unaffected, and professional. She lived at a time when it was still possible for her to draw on the language and standards of the Augustan prose writers and to follow them without being self-conscious or archaic. In her development from her early burlesques to her major works, her struggles are never with her method of expression but only with her subject-matter itself. It is convenient to divide narrative from dialogue for discussion of *Northanger Abbey* (although in *Emma* and *Persuasion* the distinction is lost), for her incisive talent, though showing equally in both, does so by somewhat different methods. The narrative here is, of course, determined by the burlesque, which gives her prose a very obvious irony – almost without wit – which she never again employs:

> Her father was a clergyman, without being neglected, or poor, and a very respectable man, though his name was Richard – and he had never been handsome. He had a considerable independence, besides

> two good livings – and he was not in the least addicted to locking up his daughters. (13)

She soon turns to something much more to her taste and much more original: the journey (already quoted)

> was performed with suitable quietness and uneventful safety. Neither robbers nor tempests befriended them, nor one lucky over-turn to introduce them to the hero. (19)

This is more than a witty turn of phrase; it shows Jane Austen's undeviating intent, to reveal exaggeration by juxtaposition with truth and good sense, and to do it in the structure of the phrase itself, as she does it in the structure of the novel as a whole. With this irony she can combine her own characteristic style and deal with subjects not needing to be touched for the burlesque, and so can relate her literary theme to the truths of real life.

> To look *almost* pretty, is an acquisition of higher delight to a girl who has been looking plain the first fifteen years of her life, than a beauty from her cradle can ever receive. (15)

This is a trivial truth, but the Johnsonian perception of it is very far from trivial. It therefore reinforces the opening sentence – 'No one who had ever seen Catherine Morland in her infancy, would have supposed her born to be an heroine'; it is the forerunner of the brilliant opening of *Pride and Prejudice*, and indicates the subject and tone of the whole novel in the same way. It shows the kind of irony we are to expect here: the description of apparently agreeable artificialities in such a way that a mundane reality proves more attractive. Jane Austen's narrative is rarely a literal retail of fact.

> He remained with them some time, and was only too agreeable for Catherine to be contented when he went away. Before they parted, however, it was agreed that the projected walk should be taken as soon as possible; and, setting aside the misery of his quitting their box, she was, upon the whole, left one of the happiest creatures in the world. (95)

Here Catherine's confused feelings are represented, the cliché is characteristic of her – 'happiest creature in the world' – and the proper attitude for the reader is pointed out by the author's casual but decisive phrase 'upon the whole', showing her own and the reader's customary affectionate amusement at Catherine; such precision does not belittle Catherine's emotions, but shows them in proportion to the rest of her existence.

In this as in her other novels (except *Persuasion*) there is an absence of even casual imagery so complete as to be remarkable. This is no disadvantage, for with such a style as Jane Austen's imagery could have little to do. She is equally sparing of other devices for giving emphasis. Her style is that of the literate eighteenth century, so lacking in personal mannerism that even its precision seems easy. Her rhythms show that precision is her criterion; they are pleasant and not halting, but she never sacrifices accuracy for the sake of an agreeable cadence, and such cadences as she has are the result of meaning not phrasing, and are epigrammatic rather than oratorical.

One of the greatest pleasures in her novels is conversation. There is a great deal, for she uses speech wherever possible to advance the story and make trivial events significant. Her skill is considerable even here, though she never attempts to handle many people (like the entire Bennet family in *Pride and Prejudice*) at the same time, and is usually careful to say who is speaking, not yet relying much on characteristic speech-rhythm and topic alone to show the speaker. The characters who show her true talent are the ones whose speech is based on life not on literature. Of these the best are Mrs Allen and Catherine and Henry. Mrs Allen is a character revealed by methods Jane Austen uses very often for humorous characters; whatever their subject her speeches show fundamental characteristics: she consistently confuses important matters with trivial ones, and she never advances the conversation.

'. . . I told Mrs Morland at parting, I would always do the best for you in my power. But one must not be over particular. Young people *will* be young people, as your good mother says herself. You know I wanted you, when we first came, not to buy that sprigged muslin, but you would. Young people do not like to be always thwarted.' (104-5)

This, while showing that Catherine's conduct is more important than her clothes, creates an entertaining personality consistent in its own folly – this muslin is the same one that Henry Tilney and she agreed in their first conversation would not wash well. Mrs Allen's stupidity is a pleasure because she is an important commentator on the action, the more effective for being unconscious. Towards the end of the story one of Mrs Allen's speeches can even show Catherine's situation as quite pathetic:

'It was very agreeable, was not it? Mr Tilney drank tea with us, and I always thought him a great addition, he is so very agreeable. I have a notion you danced with him, but am not quite sure. I remember I had my favourite gown on.' (238)

This is Jane Austen's best method with comic characters, whose diction appears to be the result of innate ways of thinking and *idées fixes* (the most elaborate example being Harriet Smith), not simply the result of superficial mannerisms or turns of phrase like Isabella's (though with the Eltons she makes good use of these as well).

There is one conversation – that between the Allens and Catherine on the impropriety of her going out with John Thorpe – which is as good as anything in Jane Austen's best work, and superior to anything else in *Northanger Abbey*.

'These schemes are not at all the thing. Young men and women driving about the country in open carriages! Now and then it is very well; but going to inns and public places together! It is not right; and I wonder Mrs Thorpe should allow it. I am glad you do not think of going; I am sure Mrs Morland would not be pleased. Mrs Allen, are not you of my way of thinking? Do not you think these kind of projects objectionable?'

'Yes, very much so indeed. Open carriages are nasty things. A clean gown is not five minutes wear in them. You are splashed getting in and getting out; and the wind takes your hair and your bonnet in every direction. I hate an open carriage myself.'

'I know you do; but that is not the question. Do not you think it has an odd appearance, if young ladies are frequently driven about in them by young men, to whom they are not even related?'

'Yes, my dear, a very odd appearance indeed. I cannot bear to see it.'

'Dear madam,' cried Catherine, 'then why did not you tell me so before? I am sure if I had known it to be improper, I would not have gone with Mr Thorpe at all; but I always hoped you would tell me, if you thought I was doing wrong.'

'And so I should, my dear, you may depend on it; for as I told Mrs Morland at parting, I would always do the best for you in my power. But one must not be over particular. Young people *will* be young people, as your good mother says herself. You know I wanted you, when we first came, not to buy that sprigged muslin, but you would. Young people do not like to be always thwarted.'
(104–5)

This is at first sight most realistically disorganized, another amusing display of Mrs Allen, since Mr Allen and Catherine spend the whole of it trying to keep her to the point. That point is the real point of the conversation: the propriety of Catherine's conduct. Because the three are shown in relation to the one topic the reader can make a moral judgement on all of them at once; Mr Allen, a sensible man with no foibles, states his opinion firmly and first; it is taken up by the others, who show how far they fall short of him; Catherine's judgement is tentative by comparison with his, and sound by contrast with that of Mrs Allen, who though pliable has no sense at all, any ideas she receives being promptly transmuted into her preoccupations. The whole conversation shows how Jane Austen can make the most apparently commonplace topic reveal the discussion of personal principles and conduct, both social and moral, which is at the heart of all her novels.

2 · *Sense and Sensibility*

ALTHOUGH IT IS QUITE clear that *Sense and Sensibility* is less accomplished than *Pride and Prejudice* (though having strong connexions with it: Willoughby and Wickham are similar and the treatment of Elinor resembles that of Elizabeth Bennet), and that it is probably an earlier work, since the deficiencies are both structural and artistic, it is even more clear that *Sense and Sensibility* is both more accomplished and more ambitious than *Northanger Abbey*. It has a serious subject – as its title makes clear – it is generally more technically accomplished, and it is nearly twice as long, being the proper length for the customary nineteenth-century three-volume novel. As in all Jane Austen's novels, the opening sentence is a good guide to the rest:

> The family of Dashwood had been long settled in Sussex. Their estate was large, and their residence was at Norland Park, in the centre of their property, where, for many generations, they had lived in so respectable a manner, as to engage the general good opinion of their surrounding acquaintance. (3)

The book will clearly be about more than one person: Elinor is not the exclusive heroine that Emma or Catherine Morland is; and Jane Austen's attitude to her subject, and through it her intentions, can be perceived. Her manner is serious, a straightforward retail of facts, and it will soon be plain that, although there are plenty of ironic comments and of humorous characters, this is a serious treatment of a serious theme.

All her novels are, of course, serious in intention, and the conclusions put forward are very far from trivial, but *Sense and Sensibility* resembles *Mansfield Park* in being in places not only serious but solemn. Irony as a method of revealing character is kept away from the major figures and confined to the lesser ones.

The story is ironic in itself – Elinor is obliged to support Marianne in her public distress while being obliged to endure secretly a much more complicated misery herself – and consequently Marianne's conduct is, in many scenes, a good comment on Elinor's. Marianne is as near to a humourless character as Jane Austen ever comes; Elinor, of course, is not, but even so the humour of her speeches and that of Jane Austen's comment on her is usually directed away from Elinor, not because Jane Austen fears the effect of ridicule at Elinor's expense, but because she has created a character so fault-less that ridicule is impossible. One wishes Jane Austen had given herself more opportunities like the occasion when Elinor drinks the wine Mrs Jennings has brought to comfort Marianne:

> Elinor, as she swallowed the chief of it, reflected that . . . its healing powers on a disappointed heart might be as reasonably tried on herself as on her sister. (198)

Minor characters, however, can easily expose themselves, in the brilliant way Mr and Mrs John Dashwood do in the first piece of dialogue in the book, where they discuss how much and what kind of assistance the late Mr Dashwood wished them to give to his widow and her daughters; these two and Lucy Steele are weightier than any minor character in *Northanger Abbey* and show how Jane Austen is able to use irony as a method, not an ornament.

The subject, characteristically, is not an easy one, since it is not the simple opposition that it might seem at first glance, of sense, or rational judgement, represented by Elinor, to the sensibility, or exaltation of spontaneous feeling, represented by Marianne. If it were, it would be much more like the early burlesques. Certainly Marianne is at first guided almost wholly by her emotions, the key to her conduct being

> 'if there had been any real impropriety in what I did, I should have been sensible of it at the time, for we always know when we are acting wrong, and with such a conviction I could have had no pleasure'. (68)

But Elinor is always intended – even if the intention is not always perfectly clear – to be an ideal balance of the two qualities, whose emotions, though rationally controlled, are not the less intense. Jane Austen in her own voice – incisive, epigrammatic and ironic – always speaks with authority, showing the precise importance of her topic and directing the reader's attention to its relevant aspects.

This is particularly true of the way she introduces her many characters; the kind of comment she makes shows just how much use each will be to the action and how much and what kind of interest each is likely to provide. Characters who will reveal themselves by their action and words receive only the necessary emphasis on their most relevant traits. Elinor, who is often Jane Austen's mouthpiece,

> possessed a strength of understanding, and coolness of judgment, which qualified her, though only nineteen, to be the counsellor of her mother, and enabled her frequently to counteract, to the advantage of them all, that eagerness of mind in Mrs Dashwood which must generally have led to imprudence. (6)

Such serious speaking shows the author's serious interest. Minor characters who will have the chance to reveal themselves are announced equally briefly, from an attitude that indicates their function and capabilities:

> He was not an ill-disposed young man, unless to be rather cold hearted, and rather selfish, is to be ill-disposed: but he was, in general, well respected; for he conducted himself with propriety in the discharge of his ordinary duties. (5)

This is firm and precise, but mild irony and epigrammatism make one feel, as will prove the case, that John Dashwood is not important. So also Mrs Jennings:

> . . . a widow, with an ample jointure. She had only two daughters, both of whom she had lived to see respectably married, and she had now therefore nothing to do but to marry all the rest of the world. (36)

This shows roughly what she will do, and the kind of amusement she will provide doing it. Characters who will have little chance to speak for themselves are the only ones analysed at length, the most obvious example being Edward Ferrars:

He was not handsome, and his manners required intimacy to make them pleasing. He was too diffident to do justice to himself; but when his natural shyness was overcome, his behaviour gave every indication of an open affectionate heart. His understanding was good, and his education had given it solid improvement. But he was neither fitted by abilities nor disposition to answer the wishes of his mother and sister, who longed to see him distinguished – as – they hardly knew what. (15)

We must have a sound idea of him from the first, as he has little chance anywhere in the novel to demonstrate his worth. Jane Austen's attitude to her subject, then, is clearly shown in her own serious comment. When most of the characters are summed up in this way and measured against her moral standards, Willoughby, although he appears dramatically and romantically, is none the less suspect because Jane Austen makes no such comment on him at all, and so though she suggests an attitude towards him by her silence, we are allowed to see him as Marianne does, and so to decide unbiased whether her behaviour towards him is wrong.

Jane Austen says very little in her own voice besides these introductions. Such firmly based characters can perform many of her functions as narrator for her. She is neither detached nor superior, and her chief mouthpiece is her heroine Elinor, who gives much sound judgement on events and character, and whose opinions coincide with those of Jane Austen and the right-thinking reader. The sympathy between the author and her creation is such that Jane Austen very rarely finds it necessary to add to what she can say through Elinor; when she does, it is something that Elinor cannot deal with and yet remain consistent with her own personality and with the design of the theme:

> . . . so well was she able to answer her own expectations, that when she joined them at dinner only two hours after she had first suffered the extinction of all her dearest hopes, no one would have supposed from the appearance of the sisters, that Elinor was mourning in secret over obstacles which must divide her for ever from the object of her love, and that Marianne was internally dwelling on the perfections of a man, of whose whole heart she felt thoroughly possessed. (141)

Jane Austen will in such circumstances use another character rather than herself:

> Colonel Brandon was only astonished at her sister's composure, who, though attending and nursing [Marianne] the whole day, . . . felt no real alarm. (307)

Anxiety in Elinor at this stage would be too much like the over-sensibility she eschews, but it is very apt for Colonel Brandon to show concern, and enough is known of him by this point for it to be clear that he is to be taken seriously (whereas Mrs Jennings, expecting that Marianne will die, is not).

This method throws the main burden on to Elinor, and, like Henry Tilney, she has too much to do; but in this case the flaw is more serious, partly because Elinor is more important and more elaborate than he, and partly because this is a much better novel. Elinor is never inconsistent, because her point of view as the representative of the right mixture of sense and sensibility is also her author's; but she has to voice this view at times when she would be more effective silent. The explanations of her conduct given to Marianne when Edward's engagement to Lucy becomes publicly known are necessary to both Marianne and the reader, but Elinor comes near to sounding priggish by having to supply them herself:

> 'My promise to Lucy, obliged me to be secret. I owed it to her, therefore, to avoid giving any hint of the truth; and I owed it to my family and friends, not to create in them a solicitude about me, which it could not be in my power to satisfy.' (262)

Similarly her harangues to Marianne displaying the evils which would certainly have accompanied a marriage to Willoughby are hardly necessary for Marianne at this late stage,[1] and would be better for the reader if they came from a dispassionate narrator. Even such a fault, however, shows how Jane Austen already organizes her work, and shows the consistent planning that such an attitude represents.

From consideration of Jane Austen's attitude to her material

[1] Volume III, Chapter XI.

follows naturally consideration of the material itself, of which the characters are naturally the most immediately important. Jane Austen gives the impression of psychological realism, in analysis of her main characters and in observation of her minor ones, at the same time and by the same means as they are all most deliberately contrived to bring out the rival claims of sense and sensibility in individuals and in society, and to bring out what meaning these terms have for the author.

Marianne is obviously the extreme to which a reliance on romantic feeling can go in an intelligent mind:

> She was sensible and clever; but eager in every thing; her sorrows, her joys, could have no moderation. She was generous, amiable, interesting: she was every thing but prudent. (6)

Her enthusiasm is attractive, but from the first we see she is led by it into errors of judgement; the whole of her opening conversation with Elinor in Chapter IV about Edward Ferrars is at cross-purposes: Marianne does not exaggerate what she feels, but she misjudges Elinor for not allowing her own feelings equally free expression. That she herself is willing to let even a mild enthusiasm run away with her is shown in the same conversation:

> 'And you really are not engaged to him!' said she. 'Yet it certainly soon will happen. But two advantages will proceed from this delay. *I* shall not lose you so soon, and Edward will have greater opportunity of improving that natural taste for your favourite pursuit which must be so indispensably necessary to your future felicity. Oh! if he should be so far stimulated by your genius as to learn to draw himself, how delightful it would be!' (22)

This is the type of all Marianne's thought; she attaches such importance to small manifestations of feeling that she ignores the great ones, most conspicuously, of course, in her relations with Willoughby. Elinor sums it up nicely:

> 'You have already ascertained Mr Willoughby's opinion in almost every matter of importance. You know what he thinks of Cowper and Scott; you are certain of his estimating their beauties as he ought, and you have received every assurance of his admiring Pope no more than is proper . . . Another meeting will suffice

to explain his sentiments on picturesque beauty, and second marriages, and then you can have nothing farther to ask.' (47)

Marianne's enthusiasm and aesthetic discrimination, though attractive, emphasize that there is no serious basis for the acquaintance with him: 'every assurance' suggests Pope as a rival for her in Willoughby's affections. The point is especially stressed in the only conversation (in the whole of the novel) between Marianne and Willoughby, where in reply to Elinor's praise of Colonel Brandon, although they are witty, Marianne is rude (and Willoughby positively malicious):

'. . . he has always answered my inquiries with the readiness of good-breeding and good nature.'

'That is to say,' cried Marianne contemptuously, 'he has told you that in the East Indies the climate is hot, and the mosquitoes are troublesome.' (51)

The more intense Marianne's feelings, the more Jane Austen forces us to see that she is led by them into real wrongdoing. At first her transgressions are slight: her visit to Allenham is a social error, and so trivial that Marianne's retort is quite forceful, and we are almost on her side rather than on Elinor's –

'I am afraid,' replied Elinor, 'that the pleasantness of an employment does not always evince its propriety.'

'On the contrary, nothing can be a stronger proof of it, Elinor; for if there had been any real impropriety in what I did, I should have been sensible of it at the time, for we always know when we are acting wrong, and with such a conviction I could have had no pleasure.' (68)

– and the rest of her behaviour to Willoughby is represented as merely imprudent, and inconsiderate to her mother and sisters; but when he has jilted her she behaves much worse, and it becomes clear that such oversensibility is not merely a social wrong to Mrs Jennings and to her family, but a moral one against herself. Her illness is her own doing, caused by overindulging her grief when she still has no reason to believe the absent Willoughby unfaithful, by indulging her real misery still further when she is jilted, and by wilful and deliberate neglect of herself at Cleveland: she walks 'where the trees were the oldest, and the grass was the longest and wettest', and then commits 'the still greater imprudence of sitting in her wet shoes and stockings' (306).

Jane Austen does not underestimate Marianne's real grief – her meeting with Willoughby in London and her reception of his last letter are painful to read – but the details of deliberate self-neglect and folly at Cleveland rightly make it clear that her illness and all its attendant distress to others are her own fault; and her death, as she herself says, would virtually have been suicide.

> 'My illness, I well knew, had been entirely brought on by myself . . . Had I died, – it would have been self-destruction.' (345)

Marianne, attractive as she is meant to be, has been found even more attractive than Elinor, which Jane Austen clearly did not intend. Yet it is true that Elinor – a much more detailed study of a more attractive personality, who says some of the best things in Jane Austen's six novels, in some of the finest scenes Jane Austen ever wrote – is not entirely satisfactory. One of the reasons has been dealt with – that she has too much work to do and is therefore too much an arbiter of other people's conduct – but there are others, partly the result of an unsure technique, but mainly arising from the plot.

Elinor is an isolated heroine; she has no confidante, for the whole plot hinges on her promise not to reveal Lucy Steele's secret engagement. She appears comparatively unfeeling because she has very little chance to show any emotion. The only emotional scenes she has are those where she has to suppress her feelings, such as the talks with Lucy, or the interview in which she offers Edward the living at Delaford. When Elinor reflects we have only Jane Austen's report on it and Elinor's indirect speech, and the emphasis is mainly on her moral position and the principles on which she acts, rather than on her feelings:

> As these considerations occurred to her in painful succession, she wept for him, more than for herself. Supported by the conviction of having done nothing to merit her present unhappiness, and consoled by the belief that Edward had done nothing to forfeit her esteem, she thought she could even now, under the first smart of

the heavy blow, command herself enough to guard every suspicion
of the truth from her mother and sisters. (140–1)

This is an analysis of what Elinor thinks; it is not the exclamatory
style which reproduces both the thought and the way the character thinks it, the method by which Emma and Elizabeth Bennet
reveal themselves. Elinor is also too much the confidante of the
other characters. Plot demands that Colonel Brandon should tell
his history and what he knows of Willoughby, and it is quite in
keeping with Elinor's character that he should tell *her*, and also
that Mrs Jennings should tell her about Miss Williams –

> 'She is a relation of the Colonel's, my dear; a very near relation.
> We will not say how near, for fear of shocking the young ladies.'
> Then lowering her voice a little, she said to Elinor, 'She is his natural
> daughter.' (66)

– even though Elinor, at nineteen, is one of the 'young ladies'
herself. But this weighs Elinor down, and makes her, for being
reasonable, seem unemotional. This is not to say she is a failure;
she is a much more effective creation than any of Fanny Burney's
heroines, and Jane Austen's method makes her less self-conscious
than Fanny Burney's letter-writing makes *her* heroines, or – to
use a later example – Esther Summerson's first-person narrative in
Bleak House makes her. By comparison with Anne Elliot, though,
Elinor is only a partial success. Anne is a confidante, too, but her
correct and restrained conduct is compensated by what we see of
her private feelings in other ways: her advice to the melancholy
Captain Benwick, for instance, is as relevant to herself as to him.

Elinor, is, in fact, an attractive heroine, both as seen in her
opinions on herself and others, and when in conversation. Her
opinions discipline the events: she gives the rational view of them
which the reader should share. When Mrs Jennings teases Marianne for visiting Allenham, 'Elinor found that in her resolution to
know where they had been, she had actually made her own
woman enquire of Mr Willoughby's groom' (67); although everyone present must have found out, too, the fact is already coloured
by Elinor's surprise and disapproval. We see much of Elinor's
thoughts, and although the phrasing of them is impersonal, it is

lightened by a wit which, although lent by Jane Austen, seems
even so to be characteristic of Elinor:

'Good gracious! – In a moment I shall see the person that all my
happiness depends on – that is to be my mother!' –
Elinor could have given her immediate relief by suggesting the
possibility of its being Miss Morton's mother, rather than her own,
whom they were about to behold. (232)

Such wit and other qualities appear in her conversation as well;
and as Elinor has more to say, to a greater variety of people, than
anyone else in the novel, she cannot fail to be the more interesting
herself; she can be sharp –

'I confess,' replied Elinor, 'that while I am at Barton Park, I
never think of tame and quiet children with any abhorrence.' (123)

– and she can be tactful –

'Marianne can never keep long from that instrument you know,
ma'am,' said Elinor, endeavouring to smooth away the offence;
'and I do not much wonder at it; for it is the very best toned piano-
forté I ever heard.' (145)

– and such incidents prepare for her impeccable behaviour in the
two most important scenes in the novel, when she gets the better
of Lucy Steele without herself descending to malice or lies.

The rest of the characters focus on the two heroines, illuminating them and showing the opposing forces of reason and emotion;
they are ranged as symmetrically as the heroines: Marianne, Mrs
Dashwood and Willoughby oppose Elinor, Colonel Brandon,
Edward Ferrars and Mrs Jennings; the Middletons contrast with
each other and so do the Palmers; such an arrangement shows the
preoccupation with design that is to produce *Emma*. Among the
most important secondary characters are Edward Ferrars, John
Willoughby and Colonel Brandon, who are mutually in contrast.

Edward Ferrars has an important part and very little space; he
is Elinor's equal in right thinking, high principle, and properly
regulated sensibility; he supports her in these respects, being at his
most agreeable when ridiculing Marianne's enthusiasm and expressing his own:

'I like a fine prospect, but not on picturesque principles. I do not like crooked, twisted, blasted trees. I admire them much more if they are tall, straight and flourishing. I do not like ruined, tattered cottages. I am not fond of nettles, or thistles, or heath blossoms. I have more pleasure in a snug farm-house than a watch-tower – and a troop of tidy, happy villagers please me better than the finest banditti in the world.' (98)

This shows Edward to be interesting because he is obviously cleverer than Marianne; it is in the style of Henry Tilney, and makes Edward as much Marianne's intellectual superior as Henry is Catherine's. It is also useful support for Elinor, who gets little from the other few intelligent characters: although it would not be out of character for her to tease Marianne she would be in even more danger of seeming priggish if she were to influence Marianne by precept as well as by example. The whole of Edward's visit to Barton contrasts with Willoughby's: whereas Willoughby is seen only once in conversation in a stay of several weeks, and then only with Marianne and Elinor, Edward has several attractive exchanges with the whole family in the course of one week only, in which they discuss such intimate subjects as his own future career, the amount of money needed to live in comfort, and each other's personal foibles; his recurrent melancholy and reserve only emphasize the more the spontaneous friendship between him and the whole family. When Edward Ferrars appears, he is what he should be, but we do not see enough of him for him to seem Elinor's equal in importance as he clearly is in virtue. The plot does not allow it. His role is necessarily inactive: he cannot court Elinor, and he cannot jilt Lucy, and even his resistance to his mother consists in *not* marrying Miss Morton, and in *not* giving up Lucy. A man situated between two women as he is situated between Lucy and Elinor can hardly avoid looking ineffectual, if not ridiculous; the best Jane Austen can do for him is to keep him in the background once Lucy has appeared. Before this there has been an attempt to reveal the restraint under which he acts in the way that Frank Churchill's behaviour is revealed, by oddities of conduct that can be made to indicate different things: his obvious embarrassment over the ring which contains Lucy's hair makes the reader suspect – despite Marianne and even despite Elinor herself – that it is neither Elinor's nor Fanny's; and Marianne's penetrating comment on his reserve, and the discomfort it causes him, do give him an air of mystery which might be romantic if it were not ironic, and which makes a neat contrast to Willoughby.

Edward Ferrars's antithesis is Willoughby, both in function and treatment. Willoughby displays all the passion that Edward does not, and he does jilt Marianne – to whom he is morally engaged – to marry the heiress Miss Grey, who parallels Edward's Miss Morton. Willoughby, without principles though not without feeling, is a full-sized figure and yet keeps his proper place in the novel as a whole. His first appearance is romantic, and his later behaviour agreeable, but given with significant absence of comment from Elinor or Jane Austen. Though his courtship of Marianne causes all her later conduct it occupies only six chapters out of the novel's fifty, and only one conversation between them is given – that one being frivolous, and on Willoughby's part malicious:

> 'Brandon is just the kind of man, whom every body speaks well of, and nobody cares about; whom all are delighted to see, and nobody remembers to talk to.' (50)

When he leaves Barton he is then out of the story – except for his brief scene in London, and except for his past being revealed by Colonel Brandon – until he appears to make his dramatic confession to Elinor when Marianne is ill. His charm is then recalled, while his conduct appears at once more subtle and convincing, and more relevant to the moral theme of the novel. An unprincipled rake proves nothing, but Willoughby at Cleveland is proof that the feelings Marianne so values do not necessarily induce virtue and can indeed thrive alongside vice (for he has seduced and deserted Eliza only just before he meets Marianne).

What his conduct shows, his speech bears out in his explanation to Elinor. It expresses considerable passion; this is one of the very few places where Jane Austen permits violent speech and oaths:

'What a sweet figure I cut! – what an evening of agony it was! – Marianne, beautiful as an angel on one side, calling me Willoughby in such a tone! – Oh! God! – holding out her hand to me, asking me for an explanation with those bewitching eyes fixed in such speaking solicitude on my face! – and Sophia, jealous as the devil on the other hand, looking all that was – Well, it does not signify; it is over now. – Such an evening! – I ran away from you all as soon as I could; but not before I had seen Marianne's sweet face as white as death.' (327)

This is a deliberate violation of her custom; she rarely uses metaphor, advises her niece to alter a character who merely says 'Bless my heart', and when any of her own virtuous characters name their Deity they do so for solemn and vital reasons. Such a display as this with its apparent riot of adjectives and metaphor – 'bewitching', 'speaking', 'beautiful as an angel', 'jealous as the devil', 'white as death' – is a precise and deliberate revelation of Willoughby's moral chaos, especially when he is giving way to a now illicit love for Marianne and does not scruple to abuse his wife.

Between Willoughby and Ferrars stands Colonel Brandon. His part in the plot is important: he reveals Willoughby's past and presents the living which makes it possible for Edward Ferrars to marry – Lucy, as he thinks, and Elinor as it turns out. The way he does these things makes him morally significant as well. When he first appears it is in contrast to Marianne and as an upholder of 'sense':

He was silent and grave . . . he was on the wrong side of five and thirty; but though his face was not handsome his countenance was sensible, and his address was particularly gentlemanlike. (34)

This is confirmed by Elinor's defence of the flannel waistcoat, and by Marianne's strictures, even though these neatly link the Colonel and Marianne together in the reader's mind, long before there is any chance of the plot's connecting them:

'He may live twenty years longer. But thirty-five has nothing to do with matrimony.'
'Perhaps,' said Elinor, 'thirty-five and seventeen had better not have any thing to do with matrimony together.' (37)

Though his subsequent role is as the masculine equivalent to Elinor's self-control, he is linked to Marianne in a number of other ways, so that the marriage is not incredible – despite the difference between thirty-five and seventeen – and, more important, is not unreasonable. In some ways he resembles her: his own history is highly romantic – with near-elopement and forced marriage – and the personal resemblance between Marianne and the girl he loved emphasizes the parallel; this girl's daughter's disgrace at Willoughby's hands increases the romantic coincidence and the connexion. Points of character and conduct link them also: he feels impelled to call Willoughby out for his desertion of Eliza, and a duel is of itself romantic, even without Elinor's disapproval:

> Elinor sighed over the fancied necessity of this; but to a man and a soldier, she presumed not to censure it. (211)

Mrs Dashwood is a mature and light-hearted version of Marianne, since in her situation the faults due to ill-regulated feelings cannot have such serious results; her only real mistake is to fail to exercise her proper authority over Marianne. Her foibles are attractive and confined to a few topics: carelessness about money, embarrassing and unconventional expressions of kindness, and unrealistic plans for the future. When going to London is suggested, for example, she immediately begs, 'Do not let me hear a word about the expense of it' (156), indicating that this may well be an objection; when they leave Norland she presses Edward to visit her, which puts him in an awkward position, since his family disapprove of any association with Elinor; and when she and her daughters arrive at Barton she immediately plans enlargements: 'These parlours are both too small . . . throwing the passage into one of them . . . a new drawing-room . . . and a bed-chamber and garret above': all this, as Jane Austen says, 'from the savings of an income of five hundred a-year by a woman who never saved in her life' (29). This illuminates Marianne, who obviously resembles her mother, and also keeps her subordinate to Elinor, whom she would outshine if she were allowed to show such qualities in her own actions.

The third daughter Margaret is hardly a character at all; she is a faint reflection of her mother and Marianne, and accompanies them when they need it: she is with Marianne when she sprains her ankle and meets Willoughby, and Mrs Dashwood has plans for her education while her elder daughters are in London; she does only two interesting things, one when she sees Willoughby take a lock of Marianne's hair, and the other when she tells Mrs Jennings what Edward Ferrars's initial is.

The other important character is Lucy Steele. She is important to the design as a whole because she brings out the opposite qualities in Elinor from those Marianne does. Where Marianne's conduct shows that Elinor is ruled by reason, Lucy by contrast shows that her reason is a moral guide, that her self-restraint is not hypocrisy, and that her feelings are powerful and sincere. None of this is true of Lucy; her and her sister's toadying to the Middletons contrasts with Elinor's proper tact just as much as Marianne's rudeness does. Lucy is not merely self-seeking (she is, of course, wrong to hold Edward to an engagement against his wishes, apart from the question of her own indifference to him), she is positively malicious; the two scenes in which she tells Elinor of her engagement use this malice to reveal the extent of Elinor's feelings and self-control. After innuendos like

'you must have seen enough of him to be sensible he is very capable of making a woman sincerely attached to him' (130–1)

and

'you must allow that *I* am not likely to be deceived, as to the name of the man on who all my happiness depends' (131)

there is no need (just as there is no chance) for Elinor to speak out. Lucy lets us see Elinor in opposition to an intelligence almost equal to her own; she has wit enough to bring out the wit in Elinor:

'Mrs Ferrars is a very headstrong proud woman, and in her first fit of anger upon hearing it, would very likely secure every thing to Robert, and the idea of that, for Edward's sake, frightens away all my inclination for hasty measures.'

'And for your own sake too, or you are carrying your disinterestedness beyond reason.' (148)

Elinor's replies to Lucy are all defensive – she does not even select her facts, she uses the same ones as Lucy advances against her – and the result is that she and the reader are always aware of the extent of Lucy's malice, while Lucy does not know whether Elinor is jealous or not.[1]

The rest of the characters are less important, though they differ in many ways. It is always difficult in Jane Austen to draw a line between major and minor characters (or events), as the gradations between them are small, and they are all useful, and usually indispensable, to the action or the theme. Among the minor characters here Jane Austen shows much interest in different kinds of vulgarity. Characters' fallings-off from her standards of sensibility and of refinement make them amusing at the same time as they make them throw light on the main theme. Lucy Steele is vulgar both in behaviour – when she corrects her sister ('you can talk of nothing but beaux; – you will make Miss Dashwood believe you think of nothing else') (124) – and in her own speech:

> 'I felt sure that you was angry with me; and have been quarrelling with myself ever since, for having took such a liberty as to trouble you with my affairs.' (146)

So is Mrs Jennings, but she contrasts with Lucy by being good-natured, and her vulgarity consists in expression, and in limitation – rather than actual deficiency – of feeling. Her coarse and vigorous raillery which so offends Marianne is moderated by being set against the insipid over-refinement of her daughter Lady Middleton, and later becomes subordinate to her equally vigorous good nature.[2] Her lively speech is entertaining – 'Lord! we shall sit and

[1] The style and compression of these exchanges is rather artificial than realistic, recalling the style of eighteenth-century comedy with its felicitous retorts and *double entendre*. One may compare, in Sheridan's *School for Scandal*, the scene between Sir Oliver Surface and his nephew Joseph, where Sir Oliver (disguised as Old Stanley) may observe Joseph as Elinor (behind her defence of propriety) does Lucy; one's sympathies, of course, are with Sir Oliver here, but this is much less subtle – as it must be to be able to be acted – for we are able to see in the novel just how much Lucy knows about Elinor, while Joseph Surface can know nothing at all about his uncle's disguise.

[2] Such simple and downright effects have caught the fancy of those who, with Bradley, place this novel 'lowest on the list', and admire 'dear vulgar warm-hearted Mrs Jennings' out of all proportion to her use. This shows partly that they have not properly observed Jane Austen's careful scheme for her novel, and partly that Jane Austen herself has not yet learned to keep perfect proportion between her component parts.

gape at one another as dull as two cats' (280) – so we are prepared
to see her outspokenness put to good use in rebuking Lucy –

> 'What a charming thing it is that Mrs Dashwood can spare you
> both for so long a time together!'
> 'Long a time, indeed!' interposed Mrs Jennings. 'Why, their
> visit is but just begun!'
> Lucy was silenced. (218–19)

– and we welcome this frank comment on Mrs Ferrars in front of
John Dashwood:

> 'Well!' said Mrs Jennings, 'that is *her* revenge. Everybody has a
> way of their own. But I don't think mine would be, to make one
> son independent, because another had plagued me.' (269)

The minor characters fall into groups of similar uses and characteristics; one such includes the John Dashwoods, Mrs Ferrars and
Robert Ferrars. Mrs Ferrars and Robert are not much more than
machinery of the plot, but they are carefully if concisely treated:
Mrs Ferrars being memorable in a few epigrammatic phrases – 'a
lucky contraction of the brow had rescued her countenance from
the disgrace of insipidity, by giving it the strong characters of pride
and ill nature' (232) – and one speech of inspired silliness – 'Miss
Morton is Lord Morton's daughter' (236); while Robert makes his
mark by buying a toothpick, giving Elinor his views on cottages,
and having a preoccupation with Dawlish. All in this group are
insensitive and mercenary, and are joined midway by the insensitive and mercenary Lucy, so that her marriage to Robert is appropriate (though none the less surprising). Another group centres on
Barton. Sir John Middleton and his wife are both limited – 'Sir
John was a sportsman, Lady Middleton a mother. He hunted and
shot, and she humoured her children' (32) – and so are the Palmers,
Charlotte being a reinforcement of her good-natured mother. Of
this group Sir John has most to do: he is the only active man at
Barton when Willoughby is there, and indicates Willoughby's
masculine talents and amusements at the same time as he shows
his own limitations:

> 'And what sort of a young man is he?'
> 'As good a kind of fellow as ever lived, I assure you. A very

decent shot, and there is not a bolder rider in England . . . and has got the nicest little black bitch of a pointer I ever saw.' (43–44)

This is one of Jane Austen's best methods: she uses a few traits and applies them to a wide variety of subjects. Characters who are restricted and repetitive are not boring, because they unconsciously give useful information, and always have a useful function. Only through someone capable of eavesdropping as Anne Steele does can we learn (as we need to) of how Lucy treats Edward, and how she is determined not to release him from the engagement. In Jane Austen such characters are useful all the time; whenever Miss Steele opens her mouth she tells us something about someone other than herself: a hint about Lucy's beau, or an indication of how Lucy behaves in private; she never merely exposes herself, entertaining though this might well be. Her preoccupations are confined to bonnets and beaux – even the beaux being represented solely by Dr Davies, one of that crowd of Jane Austen creations who never actually appear, and whose finest representative is Mr Perry in *Emma*. Such allusions are put to good use:

'I never saw Lucy in such a rage in my life. She vowed at first she would never trim me up a new bonnet, nor do any thing else for me again, so long as she lived; but now she is quite come to, and we are as good friends as ever. Look, she made me this bow to my hat, and put in the feather last night.' (272)

This is how she tells Elinor about letting out the secret of Lucy's engagement; Lucy's fury is important because the aspects of it shown are important to Miss Steele, and it is made comic at the same time. In the same way she pries, significantly, into the details of Marianne's toilette, just when Marianne is significantly neglecting herself. She is the most vulgar and the most stupid person Jane Austen ever uses – she has to be, to eavesdrop on the vital conversation between Edward and Lucy – but she is funny as well as necessary, and useful to show the comparative merits of even Charlotte Palmer, and to give Lucy a background that makes it an artistic impossibility for her to marry Edward Ferrars.

All the characters are drawn from the gentry, and range from the comparatively wealthy John Dashwoods to the comparatively poor heroines. Hence the settings are all country houses, or the town houses owned, or rented for the Season, by people with country estates. Even though this is true of all the novels, one sees a wider view of society in *Sense and Sensibility*. Yet this does not mean that the other novels are inferior: *Emma*, using only the inhabitants of one small village, has wider social grasp and moral implications, because of the use made of these materials. Although there are no aristocrats in *Sense and Sensibility*, like Lady Catherine de Bourgh in *Pride and Prejudice*, Edward Ferrars is a suitable *parti* for the daughter and heiress of Lord Morton; and, though Mrs Dashwood and her daughters are gentry, their poverty makes those who come below them much lower in the social scale than those who come below, for instance, the Bennets, for the Philipses, though vulgar, are respectable and self-supporting, while the Steele girls are neither. Jane Austen's social standards are therefore clearly only a further reflection of her moral and aesthetic ones; rank is not estimable in itself, but only for the opportunities it allows (witness Lady Catherine), and neither is wealth (as John Dashwood shows), while servants never appear in any important way, not because of snobbery, but because Jane Austen's literary scheme (not her social one) has no place for them.

As in all Jane Austen's novels, character and plot are both equally important; although the characters seem to direct the plot, it is obvious, from the way they throw light on each other and advance the action, that it is as much their duty to advance the plot as it is the plot's to display them. Their conduct at important points always seems credible because it has been prepared at a number of trivial ones beforehand. Mrs Jennings, for instance, is quite able to express a proper condemnation of Mrs Ferrars's behaviour to Edward, because we have already seen that good nature directs her own actions, and that she is habitually outspoken. But the plot of *Sense and Sensibility* is more mechanically elaborate, and generally less likely, than any of Jane Austen's others. Elinor's dilemma is contrived, the work of agencies outside herself, and all she has to do is to endure it; this is also Edward's case, and accounts for his dangerously long absences from the action. The conclusion also, though not positively dissatisfying, depends on two gigantic coincidences:[1] the first one is that Colonel Brandon should conveniently have a living to offer Edward, so that he may marry someone or other; the second is that Lucy should marry Robert:

> How they could be thrown together, and by what attraction Robert could be drawn on to marry a girl, of whose beauty she had herself heard him speak without any admiration, – a girl too already engaged to his brother, and on whose account that brother had been thrown off by his family – it was beyond her comprehension to make out. To her own heart it was a delightful affair, to her imagination it was even a ridiculous one, but to her reason, her judgment, it was completely a puzzle. (364)

And a puzzle it remains: even though Robert's is a character quite likely to do something so silly, and it is a most advantageous match for Lucy, and, of course, we are prepared for something of the sort to happen, because Edward must marry Elinor. There are not really more coincidences than a novel may bear – these are trifles compared to what many novels contain – but Jane Austen is habitually so naturalistic that such trifles show up as faults. A further difficulty is that such a plot obliges the most important events to be all on its outskirts; the minor actors do things and the major ones suffer the consequences. A comparison with *Pride and Prejudice*, which though probably earlier in conception is a greater success, shows where the trouble lies: the dilemma there is the natural result of failings in the personalities involved, chiefly in Elizabeth and Darcy, and the problems are solved when these are understood and corrected. Proof of this is the fact that by the time Elizabeth and Darcy do marry there are more serious practical obstacles to their union than ever before, and that these are seen to be actually irrelevant. Therefore there are none of the difficulties that are seen in *Sense and Sensibility*. Conversely, that this plot is mechanically elaborate does not mean that the rest of the novels are simple; *Pride and Prejudice* is intricate and *Emma* more so, but

[1] Gigantic for Jane Austen, that is; *Jane Eyre, Howards End*, and *The Heart of Midlothian* – to name only a few excellent novels – all rely on much worse ones to bring them to their proper conclusion, and they are all works which do not count coincidence as a part of their method, as some other good novels do, like those of Dickens and Hardy.

they are not merely mechanical: they are morally and psycho-logically intricate, the plot being the manifestation of actions and states of mind. A particular point of overemphasis lies in Colonel Brandon. His previous history of his love for his brother's wife (who resembled Marianne) and of her degeneration and death is barely necessary except to introduce the daughter whom Will-oughby seduces; this is explaining two necessary coincidences – the Colonel's love for Marianne and his knowledge of Will-oughby's real character – by one unnecessary one, even though all this past history gives him a romantic air and makes him a suitable husband for Marianne. These are all signs of an originally juvenile piece of work; when Jane Austen revised it she could and obvi-ously did do a great deal to improve her treatment, but the plot itself, naturally, she could not alter without writing a new thing altogether.

The actual handling of the plot is far from immature, and shows a great advance on the methods of *Northanger Abbey*. This is a full-length novel with a wide range of scene, and a wide variety of incident, which is brought about by having two centres of interest and incident, Elinor and Marianne. The way the different threads of narrative are worked together is excellent, and so is the arrange-ment and balance between scene and scene. For instance, it is im-portant that Willoughby's dramatic appearance in the story, his whole courtship of Marianne, and his sudden departure, which together occupy some weeks, take (as I have already mentioned) only six chapters in the telling; they are immediately followed by Edward Ferrars's visit to Barton, which, although containing no remarkable events and lasting only one week, takes up a whole four chapters. The likeness in Edward's and Willoughby's respec-tive relations to Elinor and Marianne, and in their respective situations – both have a secret to conceal, though we cannot yet do more than suspect this – is emphasized by the almost equal length of time spent on them, while their appearing next to each other brings out the essential difference between them. The con-cerns of the sisters are interwoven throughout, and interest is never allowed to flag. The balance between large sections is equally skilful, and the high points are carefully and dramatically placed,

those in the experience of each heroine being balanced and contrasted with those that come before and after. Lucy's revelations
to Elinor are followed by the journey to London which is under-
taken for Marianne's sake; Marianne's misery when jilted is interrupted by what Colonel Brandon tells of Willoughby's character (which is information given when most needed: he has
known this all along, and it is the author's tact which has him tell
it here); and soon afterwards Lucy arrives, and brings our attention back to Elinor's predicament. The sisters' careers are consciously patterned and parallel in the way Jane Austen tells them,
as well as in themselves. Willoughby's startling departure (Chapter
XV) is paired with Lucy's startling confession of her engagement
(Chapter XXII); the news of Willoughby's engagement leads
up to Marianne's misery when he returns her letters, and Colonel
Brandon's account of him reinforces it; this parallels the meetings
of the Dashwoods and Steeles which lead up to the public
discovery of Edward's engagement, and Colonel Brandon's
offer of the living which reinforces it. Marianne's illness and
Willoughby's confession are the climax, in which Marianne suffers
the most, and Elinor has the most impressive and active part.
From here proceeds a steady resolving of problems, during which
Marianne recovers and reforms; and her temporary loss of health,
when Elinor tells her about Willoughby's confession, is neatly
paralleled for Elinor's part of the story by hearing the false news
of Edward's marriage. The conclusion rightly stresses that Elinor
is made immediately happy, while Marianne is only eventually
so.

The background to the events is indicated as precisely as the
events themselves; and it is no mere accompaniment, it is often
almost a part of them. Scenery and weather provide examples:

> The situation of the house was good. High hills rose immediately
> behind, and at no great distance on each side; some of which were
> open downs, the others cultivated and woody. The village of Barton
> was chiefly on one of these hills, and formed a pleasant view from
> the cottage windows. The prospect in front was more extensive; it
> commanded the whole of the valley, and reached into the country
> beyond. The hills which surrounded the cottage terminated the

valley in that direction; under another name, and in another course, it branched out again between two of the steepest of them. (28–29)

This simple and restrained account is put to many later uses, and at every mention becomes more vivid, while being worked into the action: it is the place where Marianne has her fall and so meets Willoughby; it is where she indulges her melancholy after he has left –

> If her sisters intended to walk on the downs, she directly stole away towards the lanes; if they talked of the valley, she was as speedy in climbing the hills, and could never be found when the others set off. (85)

– and it is the subject of her raptures and of Edward's modified praise.

> 'Here is Barton valley. Look up it, and be tranquil if you can. Look at those hills! Did you ever see their equals?' . . .
> 'It is a beautiful country,' he replied; 'but these bottoms must be dirty in winter.'
> 'How can you think of dirt, with such objects before you?'
> 'Because,' replied he, smiling, 'among the rest of the objects before me, I see a very dirty lane.' (88)

The weather also serves Jane Austen's artistic purposes. It is a dramatic accompaniment to Marianne: a high wind and a risk of rain show Marianne's enthusiasm, and are the immediate cause of her sprained ankle; while damp weather at Cleveland combines with her imprudence to cause her illness, and the effect of her recovery is intensified by the storm. Jane Austen's matter-of-fact description of all these is an implicit and effective comment on Marianne.

Changes of scene are not only necessary to the action but put to good use. When Elinor and Marianne go to Gray's in Sackville Street the primary artistic reason for the visit is to reintroduce their brother John Dashwood behaving in an unsympathetic and mercenary way that will recall the way he left the story. The chance meeting in a public place neatly impresses the reader that John Dashwood ought to have called on his sisters formally and announced his arrival, and that his excuses as well as being feeble are characteristically mercenary: he has devoted the day before to his wealthy mother-in-law, and even this morning his 'so much to do' amounts to 'bespeaking Fanny a seal'; but it also gives us a first sight of Robert Ferrars, dallying over his toothpick and delaying Elinor. As neither Elinor nor the reader knows who he will turn out to be, they have a fine chance to dislike him on his personal merits before they find him to be Mrs Ferrars's favourite.

The more general settings are equally an organizing force. Barton is generally agreeable in its scenery, it is inhabited by generally agreeable people (the Steeles are outsiders), and generally agreeable events take place there. When the sisters visit London, characters are in the main unattractive and the events distressing. Jane Austen appears to dislike London as a place where good qualities get submerged in the crowd; in *Pride and Prejudice* also what influence the city has is bad: Jane and Bingley are kept apart there, and both Mr Bennet and Mr Gardiner fail to find Lydia. The dislike seems to cover cities in general (except for the Bath of *Northanger Abbey*), for Fanny Price is unhappy and ill at Portsmouth, and Anne Elliot dislikes Bath. In *Sense and Sensibility* it is in London that we meet the Steeles, the Dashwoods and Mrs Ferrars, that Marianne is jilted, and that Elinor has to endure first the secret and then the public knowledge of Edward's engagement, with only Mrs Jennings and Colonel Brandon for good company. For the climax, Marianne's illness, the scene moves to the Palmers' house at Cleveland, and the number of characters is suddenly reduced, leaving only the comparatively pleasant ones. The happy ending returns to the happy surroundings of Barton.

There is very little detail anywhere in these scenes, but such changes in themselves allow economical and swift changes of tone and atmosphere, and rapid simplifications of elaborate situations.

Transitions between scenes are often almost as important as the scenes themselves, and quite as well made. Jane Austen has as strong a sense of time as of place, unobtrusive though they both are. A new event is usually related to the one before by the way she presents it, as well as by its own context. Edward's arrival at Barton is a good example: as it coincides with Marianne's first walk in company since Willoughby left, it relates the passage to him and economically covers the intervening space of time; the association makes Edward's arrival seem reasonable – being much more likely than Willoughby's return – and, seen through Marianne's eyes, it enforces the connexion, and means that she can show the pleasure that Edward's visit ought to arouse, which Elinor does not show and Edward cannot express. Jane Austen is just as skilful at separating as at linking events. The move to Cleveland, for instance, emphasizes the change from the elaborate and long-drawn-out misery of London, which is compounded of many minor and aggravating external circumstances, to the complete breakdown at Cleveland, which is all internal, and the more poignant because the setting and characters are kindly. In the same way in *Pride and Prejudice* the scene changes from Elizabeth's complicated and unattractive home to Pemberley, where she and Darcy can meet in a setting conducive to their good understanding. Another fine example is the journey to London with Mrs Jennings, which creates an important and excellently managed break in the story. It is too long for quotation, but is astonishingly brief considering what is done and the space Jane Austen takes to do it. It occupies five hundred words at the beginning of Volume II, Chapter IV, a position and a passage long enough to make a clear division between Barton and London. The reader is made to experience the passage of time, by the matters accompanying its passage: Elinor's review of her position, Marianne's behaviour, the physical facts of their journey are all described as a continuous state of affairs lasting the whole of three days, not mere isolated incidents. The passage opens with Elinor's reflections, which show the suspension between two spheres of action: she has time to think and make plans which divide what has happened from what is to come. It shows their relations with Mrs Jennings:

'so wholly unsuited were they in age and disposition, and so many had been her objections . . . a few days before';

it shows Marianne's disposition and hopes:

'the rapture of delightful expectation which filled the whole soul and beamed in the eyes of Marianne';

and Elinor's own:

'How cheerless her own state of mind in the comparison.' (159)

These ideas anticipate, not recollect, and they draw the reader away from events in Barton to what will happen in London. As Elinor's thoughts move from general considerations to specific resolves for the future, so the passage itself moves from a general account to particular details – 'extort a confession of their preferring salmon to cod, or boiled fowls to veal cutlets'; so it is natural for the details of the journey to give way to details of arrival: 'they reached town by three o'clock the third day . . . ready to enjoy all the luxury of a good fire' (160).

An abrupt opening to a scene is therefore clearly deliberate:

'You will think my question an odd one, I dare say,' said Lucy to her one day as they were walking together from the park to the cottage – 'but, pray, are you personally acquainted with your sister-in-law's mother, Mrs Ferrars?' (128)

Jane Austen's own abruptness emphasizes Lucy's awkwardness; the reader feels this is no casual chat and prepares for the shock that follows. Even more skilful is Willoughby's arrival at Cleveland, which comes after someone else's arrival has been prepared for. Elinor's doubts that her mother could arrive so soon, and her rational attempts at explanation, prepare us for something unusual, and Willoughby's entrance is the more startling because the reader's senses have been sharpened by these preliminaries. However, Jane Austen is not yet master enough to vary her effects; the device where one character is expected and another arrives occurs three times: at Barton, Marianne expects Willoughby and we see Edward, in London she expects him again and Colonel Brandon calls, and at Cleveland, Elinor runs to meet her mother and finds Willoughby.

Material within the scene itself is meticulously arranged; an example being the way we hear the story of Lucy's engagement.

This covers two chapters and two separate occasions with a short space between them, a fine balance between demands of character, exigencies of plot, and tactful handling of the reader. The main facts are given in the first dialogue, but though Lucy proves her statements here, more details are obviously desirable – Elinor would wish to know more, nor can she 'deny herself the comfort of endeavouring to convince Lucy that her heart was unwounded' (142). It would not only make Elinor's self-control incredible if all this were in one scene, it would also be more than the reader could take in. The division is quite natural, the story is kept moving, and Elinor and Lucy in their new relationship are firmly put down among the events of common life – Lady Middleton's card-game, Marianne's piano-playing, and the need to finish Anna-Maria's filigree basket. A witty piece of organization elsewhere is the scene in which Colonel Brandon makes the offer of the Delaford living for Edward, which Mrs Jennings overhears and takes for a proposal of marriage; her misunderstandings are illuminating to the full report of the incident, and to later events: they point out that, although Elinor is not in love with the Colonel, her affections are involved in the conversation, and they make an ironic contrast between the proposal Elinor is not receiving and the fact that she is going to provide the means for Edward to marry Lucy. The scene will have its uses later also, by making it reasonable for Edward to be jealous of Colonel Brandon, since Mrs Jennings from her own observation has suspected an attachment between the Colonel and Elinor.

Among the many topics Jane Austen handles with assurance is money; she deliberately emphasizes it as another aspect of her theme. Actual figures are given, showing not only what the characters think they need to live on, but what Jane Austen thinks as well. This is real social assurance and shows a mature knowledge of the world she writes of. Edward Ferrars is wholly dependent on his mother for the means to marry, and this is an impediment almost as serious as his engagement to Lucy. His stipend of £250 a year contrasts strikingly, even to a modern reader, with his brother's £1,000 a year (equivalent, at Jane Austen's customary rate of 5 per cent, to a capital of £20,000); and it may be compared with Mrs Dashwood's £500 a year, on which she contrives to live cheaply at Barton (with three servants). It is only his mother's settlement of £10,000 upon him that enables Edward to marry and provide for a family. Among later novelists, only Trollope gives such exact and illuminating financial detail.

Financial matters, of course, reveal character also: Mrs Dashwood self-consciously disregards money, and through Marianne the family impracticality is related to the theme of unrealistic sensibility:

'What have wealth or grandeur to do with happiness?'

'Grandeur has but little,' said Elinor, 'but wealth has much to do with it.'

'Elinor, for shame!' said Marianne; 'money can only give happiness where there is nothing else to give it. Beyond a competence, it can afford no real satisfaction, as far as mere self is concerned.'

'Perhaps,' said Elinor, smiling, 'we may come to the same point. *Your* competence and *my* wealth are very much alike, I dare say; . . . Come, what is your competence?'

'About eighteen hundred or two thousand a-year; not more than *that*.'

Elinor laughed. '*Two* thousand a-year! *One* is my wealth! I guessed how it would end.' (91)

This is a key to the references to money: Elinor and her author are realistic, but not materialistic, while Marianne is out of touch with reality and at the same time more of a materialist. Elinor shows a rational moderation in this as she does in more abstract matters, and other characters enhance her: Lucy is the antithesis in being both grasping and also able to manage on unreasonably little, while John Dashwood contrasts with Marianne in finding wealth essential, like her, but in being parsimonious as well. It is proper, in fact, that Marianne and Elinor should eventually marry as they do: Marianne on the £2,000 a year she considers essential, and Elinor on rather less than her ideal minimum, so that it is really Elinor who makes the romantic marriage.

Many points of Jane Austen's style have already been mentioned, for the way she presents her material is necessarily part of the material itself. It is a safe generalization that Jane Austen's method is ironic, even in *Sense and Sensibility*, where Elinor is treated so seriously. Irony is beginning to take its place as one of her finest skills, as a most economical means of delineating character, and as an accurate means of revealing states of mind, and of doing both at once, and allowing the presentation itself to be an implicit moral comment. A final example will demonstrate the point:

> 'Pity me, dear Miss Dashwood!' said Lucy, as they walked up the stairs together . . . 'There is nobody here but you, that can feel for me. – I declare I can hardly stand. Good gracious! – In a moment I shall see the person that all my happiness depends on – that is to be my mother!' –
>
> Elinor could have given her immediate relief by suggesting the possibility of its being Miss Morton's mother, rather than her own, whom they were about to behold; but instead of doing that, she assured her, and with great sincerity, that she did pity her, – to the utter amazement of Lucy, who, though really uncomfortable herself, hoped at least to be an object of irrepressible envy to Elinor. (231–2)

Lucy's words show that she is not saying exactly what she feels: 'good gracious!' is the wrong preliminary, 'all my happiness' is misapplied (it would refer better to her fiancé than to her mother-in-law), while 'mother' is impossibly sentimental for a woman whom she has never met and knows to be disagreeable. These points, and the fact that Elinor observes them, are emphasized by Elinor's unspoken comment, which presents the complexity of a mind which glances at this aspect of the matter even while she does 'with great sincerity' pity Lucy; the pity itself is ironic, of course, in meaning more than Lucy can understand (or than Elinor intends her to understand), since Elinor deplores the hypocrisy and ambition which are driving her.

This passage discloses with distinguished brevity an involved situation; it is both elaborate and subtle, revealing the relation between the two women and their individual private feelings, both their habitual ones and the transitory ones aroused by this particular and indeed trivial exchange; in a short passage such as this Jane Austen does not merely analyse a situation, she reproduces it, so that the time it takes the reader to grasp its implications appears to delay the narrative no more than it would arrest the action in real life.

3 · *Pride and Prejudice*

IF NOT JANE AUSTEN's best novel, *Pride and Prejudice* is certainly her most popular one, and has always been so. It has always been a favourite with readers, just as it was a favourite of Jane Austen's own, her 'own darling child':

> I must confess that I think [Elizabeth] as delightful a creature as ever appeared in print, and how I shall be able to tolerate those who do not like *her* at least I do not know.[1]

It is compressed, shorter than *Sense and Sensibility*, with a more active plot, a good deal more conversation, and much more vivacity. Jane Austen herself suggested it was 'rather too light, and bright, and sparkling. It wants shade; it wants to be stretched out here and there with a long chapter of sense, if it could be had; if not, of solemn specious nonsense, unconnected with the story.'[2] We may take the first part of the sentence as her serious opinion, even though the last is in her customary frivolous letter-writing vein. If *Mansfield Park* represents what she then required of a novel, then *Pride and Prejudice* does stand in need of ballast; the sentence sets out quite clearly the general charm of the earlier work and points to one of the failings of the later one.

Though *Pride and Prejudice* is no less serious in intention than any of the others, its method is livelier and more humorous. This is chiefly because Elizabeth is a lively and humorous heroine – unlike Elinor, Fanny, or Anne Elliot – and largely responsible for the tone of the whole novel. But Jane Austen herself appears here as a lively commentator, though only to present material when

---

1 Letter to Cassandra Austen, 29 January 1813, *Jane Austen's Letters*, p. 297.
2 Letter to Cassandra Austen, 4 February 1813, *Letters*, p. 299.

this cannot be done through Elizabeth.[1] She has to appear more as narrator than she did in *Sense and Sensibility*, first because she has a heroine whose judgement has limitations: she has to make clear what the limitations are, and tell us facts, some of which the heroine cannot tell because it would distort her as it almost distorts Elinor, and some which she cannot know either because her limited judgement does not let her perceive them or because she has no chance to perceive them. Charlotte's acceptance of Mr Collins is an example. Elizabeth cannot know that Mr Collins has proposed to Charlotte on the sly, but we must not only know it, but must know why Charlotte accepted him – 'solely from the pure and disinterested desire of an establishment' – then we can see how far Elizabeth has been misled in her estimate of Charlotte. The account is as far as possible through Charlotte herself, but 'pure and disinterested' is a lively, concise and ironic comment from the author. Jane Austen appears as narrator secondly because Elizabeth is only the main interest of the novel, not the sole one; the title itself shows this: 'pride' and 'prejudice' can easily be made to stand for Darcy and Elizabeth. This is, of course, not the whole truth, but it is much nearer the truth than it is to make Elinor and Marianne stand respectively for 'sense' and 'sensibility'.

As usual, the opening of the novel is a deliberate guide to the whole:

> It is a truth universally acknowledged, that a single man in possession of a good fortune, must be in want of a wife.
> However little known the feelings or views of such a man may be on his first entering a neighbourhood, this truth is so well fixed in the minds of the surrounding families, that he is considered as the rightful property of some one or other of their daughters. (3)

This is irony at its best and most useful. We hear what the story will be about – courtship and marriage; we have a hint in 'the surrounding families' that this will be the concern of more than one couple, the concern not only of Elizabeth and Darcy, but of

---

[1] Even so there is no sign of the author as individual, as Trollope or Fielding is, commenting on the characters as creatures of his own creation (as Jane Austen herself does in her letters: 'I think [Elizabeth] as delightful a creature as ever appeared in print'; 29 January 1813, *Letters*, p. 297).

Jane and Bingley, Mr Collins and Charlotte, and of Wickham and Elizabeth, Miss King and Lydia by turns; we see what the deeper preoccupations of the novel will be – the moral weight of material and financial matters in personal affairs; and we see how the sense of the family and the neighbourhood which accompany the action will bear on individuals, for most of Jane's troubles (for example) are caused by her family, and the neighbourhood gossip is one of the trials after Lydia's elopement, and it encourages and intensifies Elizabeth's misrepresentations of Darcy. Jane Austen characteristically finds ways of subordinating her part as narrator; irony is not merely an attitude, it is a method of presentation, organization, analysis and judgement. Her skill in irony is at its greatest here and in *Emma*, where she can be serious without ever being solemn, both in contrast to *Sense and Sensibility*, where the theme is not suitable, while in *Mansfield Park* – particularly the latter half – and in *Persuasion* she is using a different method. Irony is appropriate in *Pride and Prejudice* because the characters are all deficient in some way, even though the intelligent characters may express Jane Austen's judgement for her.

Elizabeth may do so most of all; she is perceptive even when she misinterprets what she hears, and she is herself given to irony. Her understanding of how his sisters may have been able to influence Bingley is an example:

'They may wish many things besides his happiness; they may wish his increase of wealth and consequence; they may wish him to marry a girl who has all the importance of money, great connections, and pride.' (136–7)

Elizabeth's own words show where her prejudice distorts her judgement, as it does in Wickham's case –

'To treat in such a manner, the godson, the friend, the favourite of his father!' – She could have added, 'A young man too, like *you*, whose very countenance may vouch for your being amiable.' (80–81)

– where 'countenance' is very plainly an unsafe criterion.

Elizabeth is – like Elinor, Emma and Anne Elliot, but unlike Fanny and Catherine – the focus of the novel, but other characters are none the less important. Elizabeth does not overshadow all others as Elinor does by her moral position, or as Emma does by the way the novel is presented through her. The persons who reinforce and correct her judgement gain considerable influence although playing small parts; Jane Bennet, for example, excessively and entertainingly good-natured, is yet right in her estimate of Mr Darcy, and no more wrong than Elizabeth in judging Charlotte (she is too generous, while Elizabeth is too harsh). These characters who do what might have been the narrator's work are Jane and Charlotte; Mr Bennet, who sums up his daughters, his wife, Mr Bingley and Wickham; Mrs Gardiner, who is right about Darcy; and Bingley, whose humorous comments so illuminate Darcy; all these show how close this novel is to *Emma*, which has an even longer list of mutually illuminating characters whose deficiencies and prejudices do not invalidate their judgement. Nothing of this kind can be got from *Sense and Sensibility*, where sense is Elinor's prerogative, with a little assistance from Mrs Jennings and Colonel Brandon. These characters are presented in the same way as the major characters, and the novel therefore is moving away from caricature, even though caricatures are used with great effect (and Jane Austen never dispenses with them entirely even in *Mansfield Park*). These caricatures who have no judgement and can excite no sympathy – Mr Collins, Lady Catherine, Sir William Lucas, and Mrs Bennet – are thoroughly worked in and quite acceptable as a commentary on the main theme. Such characters were tactfully kept apart in *Northanger Abbey*, where Henry Tilney never spoke to Isabella or John Thorpe. The discordances in *Pride and Prejudice* embody principles and themes. Charlotte's marriage to Mr Collins shows that her moral sense is deficient; Mrs Bennet shows how Jane's setting and connexions injure her prospects; so does Sir William Lucas, for he (who has no right to mention such a subject on so slight an acquaintance) first suggests to Darcy the possibility of an engagement between Bingley and Jane, and so shows that though Elizabeth and her father may laugh at him, his folly can be a danger; while Lady Catherine shows that by contrast with her own arrogance Darcy's pride is something much more subtle.

Here is an example from Lady Catherine which concerns both of them:

> 'Young women should always be properly guarded and attended, according to their situation in life. When my niece Georgiana went to Ramsgate last summer, I made a point of her having two men servants go with her.' (211–12)

We already know what happened to Miss Darcy at Ramsgate, and so see that Darcy's pride is much less exceptionable, being concerned with ethics rather than etiquette.

Mr Darcy is the first hero Jane Austen tackles seriously or at much length. He develops like Elizabeth from complacency to self-knowledge and reformation. He is her equal, and reforms her in the same process as she reforms him; and although he cannot be seen from inside as she is, and cannot be seen so often, Jane Austen makes all his appearances important and significant. She reveals his states of mind by giving only their external results to himself and to others. This makes Mr Darcy interesting without taking any of the structural emphasis away from Elizabeth; we can interpret him correctly by what Elizabeth sees, even though she interprets it wrongly.

> 'I should never have considered the distance as one of the *advantages* of the match,' cried Elizabeth. 'I should never have said Mrs Collins was settled *near* her family.'
>
> 'It is a proof of your own attachment to Hertfordshire. Any thing beyond the very neighbourhood of Longbourn, I suppose, would appear far.'
>
> As he spoke there was a sort of smile, which Elizabeth fancied she understood; he must be supposing her to be thinking of Jane and Netherfield, and she blushed as she answered,
>
> 'I do not mean to say that a woman may not be settled too near her family. The far and the near must be relative, and depend on many varying circumstances. Where there is fortune to make the expence of travelling unimportant, distance becomes no evil.' (179)

Elizabeth's misinterpretation of Darcy's words and smile point out the true meaning – he is thinking of her and of Pemberley, not of Jane and Netherfield – and her reply constitutes direct encouragement, particularly when accompanied by the blush which he misinterprets in his turn. Compare this with the prolixity of much of Trollope, whose technique and topics are often Austenian; he is forced to describe from inside all the time, giving in *Barchester Towers* (for instance) analyses not only of the sympathetic figures, but even of the completely grotesque Mr Slope:

> He knew that scandal would soon come upon his heels and spread among the black coats of Barchester some tidings, exaggerated tidings, of the sighs which he poured into the lady's ears. He knew that he was acting against the recognised principles of his life, against those laws of conduct by which he hoped to achieve much higher success. But as we have said, he could not help himself. Passion, for the first time in his life, passion was too strong for him. (*Barchester Towers*, Chapter XXVII)

Character, narrative, and conversation are virtually inseparable. Descriptions of the leading characters throw light on others; Elizabeth, for instance, is seen for the first time as Darcy sees her:

> . . . no sooner had he made it clear to himself and his friends that she had hardly a good feature in her face, than he began to find it was rendered uncommonly intelligent by the beautiful expression of her dark eyes. To this discovery succeeded some others equally mortifying. Though he had detected with a critical eye more than one failure of perfect symmetry in her form, he was forced to acknowledge her figure to be light and pleasing; and in spite of his asserting that her manners were not those of the fashionable world, he was caught by their easy playfulness. (23)

Summaries of character are rare, and most of our information comes from conversation, where it inevitably illuminates speaker as well as subject:

> 'From all that I can collect by your manner of talking, you must be two of the silliest girls in the country. I have suspected it some time, but I am now convinced.' . . .
> 'I am astonished, my dear,' said Mrs Bennet, 'that you should be so ready to think your own children silly. If I wished to think slightingly of any body's children, it should not be of my own however.'
> 'If my children are silly I must hope to be always sensible of it.'

'Yes – but as it happens, they are all of them very clever . . . My dear Mr Bennet, you must not expect such girls to have the sense of their father and mother. – When they get to our age I dare say they will not think about officers any more than we do. I remember the time when I liked a red coat myself very well – and indeed so I do still at my heart.' (29)

We see here the ostensible point – the characters of Lydia and Catherine – we see their father's attitude to his children and his wife, and we see her deficiencies and the children's likeness to her – they have, ironically, exactly 'the sense of their mother'. Such information comes only where it is exactly relevant; we hear little more about Lydia until she asks Mr Bingley about the ball at Netherfield:

> Lydia was a stout, well-grown girl of fifteen, with a fine complexion and good-humoured countenance . . . She had high animal spirits, and a sort of natural self-consequence, which the attentions of the officers, to whom her uncle's good dinners and her own easy manners recommended her, had increased into assurance. (45)

This information is necessary to explain such overconfidence in a girl who by the standards of her time ought to have been still in the schoolroom; the whole incident is useful preparation for her much more shameless elopement.

The introductory character-sketch as Jane Austen used it in *Sense and Sensibility* is superseded by more subtle methods which are now worked into the structure of the novel as a whole. When Mr and Mrs Bennet are sketched in at the end of the first chapter it actually reduces their importance; though they speak first and effectively they are not leading characters; a summary makes it clear that they are not capable of development or much subtlety. Although the news that Mrs Bennet does not understand her husband is some preparation for him to behave unexpectedly vigorously when Lydia elopes, he does not really alter; the elements of his nature merely appear in a new way. Jane Austen begins here to use the method which is at its most perfect in *Emma*, the method first attempted in the later parts of *Northanger Abbey* – where her appearances *in propria persona* as narrator are hardly noticeable, and we never feel consciously that she is

68

directing what we shall think. What the author tells us, what the heroine perceives, and the conclusions the heroine then draws, are so mingled that they are hardly separable.

> If he had been wavering before, as to what he should do, which had often seemed likely, the advice and intreaty of so near a relation might settle every doubt, and determine him at once to be as happy, as dignity unblemished could make him. In that case he would return no more. Lady Catherine might see him in her way through town; and his engagement to Bingley of coming again to Netherfield must give way.
> 'If, therefore, an excuse for not keeping his promise, should come to his friend within a few days,' she added, 'I shall know how to understand it. I shall then give over every expectation, every wish of his constancy. If he is satisfied with only regretting me, when he might have obtained my affections and hand, I shall soon cease to regret him at all.' (361)

The first paragraph gives facts, but is just as easily to be read as Elizabeth's assessment of them as Jane Austen's, and it merges easily with Elizabeth's deductions from them which follow. Thus highly ambiguous facts are often put before us, about which we note consciously only what is relevant at the time:

> 'Till I can forget his father, I can never defy or expose *him*.'
> Elizabeth honoured him for such feelings, and thought him handsomer than ever as he expressed them. (80)

We have time to observe only that Elizabeth is thinking illogically, and the idea that Wickham is at this moment 'exposing' Darcy is remarked just sufficiently for the incident to be readily recalled when Elizabeth learns the truth from Darcy's letter:

> She was *now* struck with the impropriety of such communications to a stranger, and wondered it had escaped her before. (207)

The novel thus has the appearance of the inevitability of real life, at the same time and by the same means as it is organized to embody its author's moral plan.

A few of the minor characters only can be discussed in reasonable isolation. These are the farcical characters, whose motives, as far as Jane Austen investigates them, are interesting only as matter for comedy. These – Mr Collins, Lady Catherine and Mrs Bennet – are similar in the way they are presented and the uses they are put to, and are about equally important. Mr Collins obviously functions for our amusement, talking the riotous and illogical nonsense of the minor works:

> 'Do not make yourself uneasy, my dear cousin, about your apparel. Lady Catherine is far from requiring that elegance of dress in us, which becomes herself and daughter. I would advise you merely to put on whatever of your clothes is superior to the rest, there is no occasion for any thing more.' (160)

His proposal to Elizabeth has a literary basis, again like the early works, and its humour derives from literary conventions; Mr Collins assumes that he should be 'run away with by his feelings' and that her refusal is a romantic convention. He also has a serious purpose and many uses to justify his literary existence, and is kept in his place among more subtle delights. As soon as he has arrived, he is eclipsed at Mrs Philips's evening party by another new and interesting visitor, Wickham; after his magnificent proposal he appears but little, and at Hunsford he is in the background to Lady Catherine, and to Elizabeth and Darcy; thereafter he appears only in two letters, one of cousinly consolation for Lydia's downfall, and the other of warning to Elizabeth and her 'noble admirer' not to 'run hastily into a marriage that has not been properly sanctioned' (363). A little of Mr Collins goes a long way, though he is useful as well as memorable; he is a link between Longbourn and Rosings, between Elizabeth's family surroundings and Darcy's, and therefore helps to balance Darcy's objections to Elizabeth's family with Elizabeth's objections to Darcy's, while his proposal to Elizabeth gives a chance to see that she acts according to her principles, and that her judgement is sound:

> 'Mr Collins is a conceited, pompous, narrow-minded, silly man; you know he is, as well as I do; and you must feel, as well as I do, that the woman who marries him, cannot have a proper way of thinking.' (135)

Lady Catherine is a fit patron for him; she is introduced through him, again saving Jane Austen from introducing her in person, and doing it more effectively because she takes on character from what we know of Mr Collins before she appears in person. As she has no prominent habits of speech – being vulgar in more essential ways – she can be subordinated by appearing through what Elizabeth observes of her:

> She enquired into Charlotte's domestic concerns familiarly and minutely, and gave her a great deal of advice, as to the management of them all; told her how every thing ought to be regulated in so small a family as her's, and instructed her as to the care of her cows and her poultry. Elizabeth found that nothing was beneath this great Lady's attention, which could furnish her with an occasion of dictating to others. (163)

The replies and reactions she produces are the important thing:

> 'Upon my word,' said her Ladyship, 'you give your opinion very decidedly for so young a person. – Pray, what is your age?'
> 'With three younger sisters grown up,' replied Elizabeth smiling, 'your Ladyship can hardly expect me to own it.' (165–6)
> 'She is very welcome, as I have often told her, to come to Rosings every day, and play on the piano forte in Mrs Jenkinson's room. She would be in nobody's way, you know, in that part of the house.'
> Mr Darcy looked a little ashamed of his aunt's ill breeding, and made no answer. (173)

Such remarks prepare for the splendid scene in which she attempts to browbeat Elizabeth into refusing Darcy. Though just as striking as Mr Collins, she is less useful; her only function to the plot is to precipitate Darcy's proposal by trying to prevent it. But she has other uses; she makes Darcy seem interesting and romantic after a bad start, because she embodies the wealth and power of his connexions even before we see his own at Pemberley, but at the same time her indecorous behaviour puts him and his family much more on a level with Elizabeth and hers.

Like Lady Catherine, Mrs Bennet has many of the features of Jane Austen's early work. Her practical use is to be the direct cause of Jane's misfortunes, and of Lydia's as well. She appears almost entirely through her own words, and says some of the funniest irrational things in Jane Austen. She is based on a few strong traits given in her first appearance:

> She was a woman of mean understanding, little information, and uncertain temper. When she was discontented she fancied herself nervous. The business of her life was to get her daughters married; its solace was visiting and news. (5)

These traits are exercised mainly on Jane's prospects of marrying Bingley, her neighbour Mrs Long and her nieces (no one else ever mentions them), and the entail. Her actions are always consistent with herself, but always surprising because she is consistently irrational: 'There is no knowing how estates will go when once they come to be entailed' (65); 'How any one could have the conscience to entail away an estate from one's own daughters I cannot understand' (130). She is useful to the reader because she is invariably wrong where there is visible evidence, and can therefore be assumed to be wrong where there is none:

> 'I beg you would not put it into Lizzy's head to be vexed by his ill-treatment; for he is such a disagreeable man that it would be quite a misfortune to be liked by him.' (19)

This, for the reader, is as good as praise. These three, Mr Collins, Lady Catherine and Mrs Bennet, show how Jane Austen can use humour, as opposed to wit, for satiric purposes, an unusual talent.[1]

---

[1] Thackeray's satire, for instance, can be acute, as in the description of the Crawleys' house in London:

> . . . the marble bust of Sir Walpole Crawley looking from its black corner at the bare boards and the oiled fire-irons, and the empty card-racks over the mantel-piece: the cellaret has lurked away behind the carpet: the chairs are turned up heads and tails along the walls; and in the dark corner opposite the statue, is an old-fashioned crabbed knife-box, locked and sitting on a dumb-waiter. (*Vanity Fair*, Chapter VII)

But his humour is often of the most elementary kind: jibes at the corpulence of Joseph Sedley or the gaucheries of young William Dobbin. George Eliot has a vein of humour similar to some of Jane Austen's; Mr Brooke in *Middlemarch* is a pleasant instance:

> 'Well now, Sir Humphrey Davy; I dined with him years ago at Cartwright's, and Wordsworth was there too – the poet Wordsworth, you know. Now there was something singular. I was at Cambridge when Wordsworth was there, and I never met him – I dined with him twenty years afterwards at Cartwright's. There's an oddity now. But Davy was there: he was a poet too. Or, as I may say, Wordsworth was poet one, and Davy was poet two. That was true in every sense, you know.' (*Middlemarch*, Chapter II)

George Wickham and Lydia are like these farcical characters in being seen wholly from the outside, but they are not as detailed, and have no entertaining qualities apart from their services to the plot. Lydia's elopement is tactfully prepared for in the presentation of Lydia herself. She is the most striking of the sisters after Elizabeth and Jane, which is what her part in the action is, and she makes an impression before either of them:

> 'Lydia, my love, though you *are* the youngest, I dare say Mr Bingley will dance with you at the next ball.'
>   'Oh!' said Lydia stoutly, 'I am not afraid; for though I *am* the youngest, I'm the tallest.' (8)

After Elizabeth and Jane come home from Hunsford and London she comes more to the fore, until she leaves for Brighton and disgrace: she orders a salad she cannot pay for and buys a hat she does not like because she 'might as well buy it as not' and because 'there were two or three much uglier in the shop' (219), revealing the same carelessness of consequence and irresponsibility (on a small scale) as eloping with Wickham will do. When Elizabeth tries to persuade her father to forbid the Brighton visit, this, as well as showing the growth of Elizabeth's feeling of moral responsibility, prepares us to expect some kind of disaster. Wickham is treated like Lydia. What is heard of his actions before the elopement – that he has tried to elope with Georgiana Darcy when he has failed to sponge on her brother – is enough to make his conduct there credible, while he is charming, like Willoughby, not so much by his own acts as because another character, Elizabeth, thinks him so. While Willoughby never says or does anything admirable, Wickham is even more emphatically presented as an obvious hypocrite, and the reader always has the evidence for making the true estimate of him that Elizabeth only makes much later. When he first appears his unprompted confidences to Elizabeth are as improper as she later sees them to be, but because the reader tends to see through Elizabeth's eyes and even more because the sudden confidence is in any case a conventional part of the novelist's stock-in-trade, distrust is not roused at the time. His words always contradict his conduct:

'It is not for *me* to be driven away by Mr Darcy. If *he* wishes to avoid seeing *me*, he must go.' (78)

It is then Wickham who stays away from the ball at Netherfield. Elizabeth herself unconsciously indicates suspicious circumstances, at a point already mentioned:

> Elizabeth honoured him for such feelings, and thought him handsomer than ever as he expressed them. (80)

The illogical reaction invites suspicion of both, and the situation here looks forward to that between Frank and Emma, where it is made clear that Frank's conduct is suspect, by the difference between the reasons he gives for it and the reasons Emma suspects, his real reasons being different from either.

There is a definite pattern in relationships between characters. What Wickham does for Elizabeth, Miss Bingley does for Darcy: Miss Bingley, another hypocrite, while displaying Darcy's wit and right thinking, makes him seem a desirable *parti*, just as Wickham's attentions are proof of Elizabeth's charm.

Bingley and Jane, as well as being like each other, each perform a similar function towards Darcy and Elizabeth. Intelligent and right-thinking, both reveal the greater intelligence and subtlety of the more important character. The exchanges between the two men at Netherfield establish – as Jane Austen has already remarked – that 'Bingley was by no means deficient [in understanding], but Darcy was clever.' (16)

> '. . . upon my honour, I believed what I said of myself to be true, and I believe it at this moment. At least, therefore, I did not assume the character of needless precipitance merely to shew off before the ladies.'
> 'I dare say you believed it; but I am by no means convinced that you would be gone with such celerity. Your conduct would be quite as dependant on chance as that of any man I know; and if, as you were mounting your horse, a friend were to say, "Bingley, you had better stay till next week," you would probably do it.' (49)

The incident does for Darcy what the various conversations with Jane do for Elizabeth. Bingley's weakness also matches Jane's, he being too easily influenced, while she is too good-natured. He is redeemed as a husband fit for her – the plot has put him in a position where he does not seem to be, when he has allowed Darcy to influence him – when he renews his attentions to her *before* Darcy has confessed to using his influence to separate them.

Most of the other characters are handled in the same way as Mr Collins and Lady Catherine, but in less detail. Kitty, Mary, Mr Hurst, and Sir William Lucas are the chief ones. Kitty is not much more than an appendage to Lydia, demonstrating Lydia's vitality by her own lack of it. Mary is more entertaining than she is usually given credit for, another literary burlesque whose language is a delight. One can enjoy 'we must stem the tide of malice, and pour into the wounded bosoms of each other, the balm of sisterly consolation' (289) without perceiving its origin (in sentimental fiction and drama), but not this:

'In point of composition, his letter does not seem defective. The idea of the olive branch perhaps is not wholly new, yet I think it is well expressed.' (64)

This is *Lives of the Poets* with the good sense left out, Dr Johnson mounted and stuffed. Mr Hurst is the gentlemanly bedrock below the gold of Bingley and Darcy. Sir William is the dressing-up of several essential pieces of plot, in particular when he awakens Darcy's suspicions about Bingley and Jane, and he is another type of social and moral ineptitude.

This is the earliest novel to have comically treated characters capable of serious conduct, who are limited only by what the plot lets them do. These are Mr and Mrs Gardiner, Colonel Fitzwilliam, Charlotte Lucas, and Jane. These characters are like Mrs Weston in *Emma*, and the pleasant group of naval figures in *Persuasion*. That their personalities are not at all alike shows how Jane Austen can use a deliberately limited method for a wide variety of effects. Though Mr and Mrs Gardiner are slight their judgement is to be respected, and Mrs Gardiner gives Elizabeth necessary and prudent advice about Wickham. Colonel Fitzwilliam tells Elizabeth how Darcy separated Jane and Bingley; he is seen just enough to be a trustworthy witness to the truth of Darcy's letter, and, by being rational and agreeable, shows that

Elizabeth is attractive to a man of better sense than Mr Collins or Wickham, and that Elizabeth herself is ready to be attracted by a suitable person – 'Elizabeth was reminded by her own satisfaction in being with him, as well as by his evident admiration of her, of her former favourite George Wickham' (180); he therefore provides the necessary step between Wickham and Darcy. Charlotte Lucas and Jane, both standing in relation to Elizabeth, are more important. They both show up some deficiency in her while their own deficiencies show up her virtues. Charlotte is an acute observer; she sees that Jane's feelings may be too well concealed:

> 'Bingley likes your sister undoubtedly; but he may never do more than like her, if she does not help him on.'
> 'But she does help him on, as much as her nature will allow. If *I* can perceive her regard for him, he must be a simpleton indeed not to discover it too.'
> 'Remember, Eliza, that he does not know Jane's disposition as you do.' (22)

More important, she sees a good while before his proposal that Darcy is paying attentions to Elizabeth, a circumstance which Elizabeth ought to have seen, too. She follows her own precepts when she marries Mr Collins –

> 'Happiness in marriage is entirely a matter of chance . . . It is better to know as little as possible of the defects of the person with whom you are to pass your life.' (23)

– and although the marriage is a surprise to the reader as well as to Elizabeth, it has been prepared for, and so is not at all incredible. Charlotte, like Mrs Gardiner, shows that though Jane Austen's subjects are romantic, her view is a practical one, and she most fairly presents the extenuating circumstances in Charlotte's case, though these do not at all undermine our respect for Elizabeth's standards:

> Without thinking highly either of men or of matrimony, marriage had always been her object; it was the only honourable provision for well-educated young women of small fortune, and however uncertain of giving happiness, must be their pleasantest preservative from want. (122–3)

Jane, like Charlotte, contrasts with and interprets Elizabeth; but she regulates her conduct by a prejudice in favour of people rather than against them. Her engagement to Bingley and their whole courtship – except for its one artificial interruption from Darcy – progresses quickly and agreeably, in sharp contrast to Elizabeth's and Darcy's. She has, however, very little to say and not much to do; she is seen mainly through Elizabeth's opinion of her, and most of what she says is to Elizabeth.

Mr Bennet resembles Charlotte, an acute and rational person warped into moral irresponsibility, she by materialism, he by disillusion and lethargy:

'For what do we live, but to make sport for our neighbours, and laugh at them in our turn?' (364)

Wit warps his judgement as it does Elizabeth's, but warps it more.

'Lydia will never be easy till she has exposed herself in some public place or other, and we can never expect her to do it with so little expense or inconvenience to her family as under the present circumstances.' (230)

This is the same kind of argument, though worse, as that with which Elizabeth defends Wickham's paying court to Miss King:

'If it was not allowable for him to gain *my* affections, because I had no money, what occasion could there be for making love to a girl whom he did not care about, and who was equally poor?' (153)

Mr Bennet is seen just fully enough for his penitence to be convincing, when Lydia elopes:

'Let me once in my life feel how much I have been to blame. I am not afraid of being overpowered by the impression. It will pass away soon enough.' (299)

The emotion, convincingly mingled with his customary cynicism, makes him a more solid figure, fit for his coming association with Bingley and Darcy; for the question of his consent to their respective engagements, though a formality, must not be a farce. Mr Bennet's attitude of *laissez aller* not only makes him an obvious foil for Mrs Bennet, but also forces on the two heroines a freedom of moral choice and conduct which they must have for Jane

Austen's purpose, and which all her heroines have. The minor characters are all therefore clearly patterned to bring out the central theme embodied in them and in the two main characters.

Elizabeth Bennet is the key to *Pride and Prejudice*, both for the personality Jane Austen gives her and the way she uses it. Elizabeth is a much more accomplished piece of work and a much more subtle character than any preceding her. Like Elinor before her she is a lens through which the action is seen, and like Emma after her she is a lens with a flaw. The flaw, Elizabeth's faulty judgement, itself, ironically, interprets the events. She does not emerge as the main character until midway through the third chapter, after we have made the acquaintance of all the Bennets, Lady Lucas, the Bingleys and Mr Darcy. She therefore makes her first important appearance in her most important position, in relation to Mr Darcy, when she overhears him slight her ('not handsome enough to tempt *me*'). The scene is presented through her eyes, or, rather, through her ears, showing how the greater part of the novel will be done. We see from it that she is acute and attractive, that she has a personal basis for her prejudice, and a strong inclination towards a perverse estimate, even at the risk of being wrong; as she eventually admits

> 'I meant to be uncommonly clever in taking so decided a dislike to him, without any reason. It is such a spur to one's genius, such an opening for wit to have a dislike of that kind.' (225–6)

This is her own accurate statement of the case. She therefore may discriminate quite properly on other matters not connected with Darcy or with Charlotte (whom her prejudice favours) and she can be Jane Austen's mouthpiece just as Elinor was. Yet there is no danger of her being overwhelmingly clever: her successes against Lady Catherine, Miss Bingley and Mr Collins cannot counterbalance her failure to understand Wickham, her close friend Charlotte, or Mr Darcy.

Her experiences, and the novel, fall into two parts, the first ending with Darcy's letter which follows his first proposal of marriage.[1] In the first part events reveal themselves through con-

[1] Volume II, Chapter XII.

versation and Jane Austen's comment, Elizabeth's reactions being given with two objects: first, to limit what the reader sees and to regulate what he is to think, as in the opinions on Wickham already mentioned; and second, to show her incorrect conclusions, and direct the reader to the true ones, as in her conversation with Colonel Fitzwilliam:

> 'I do not know any body who seems more to enjoy the power of doing what he likes than Mr Darcy.'
>
> 'He likes to have his own way very well,' replied Colonel Fitzwilliam. 'But so we all do. It is only that he has better means of having it than many others, because he is rich, and many others are poor. I speak feelingly. A younger son, you know, must be inured to self-denial and dependence . . . There are not many in my rank of life who can afford to marry without some attention to money.'
>
> 'Is this,' thought Elizabeth, 'meant for me?' (183)

Indeed it is, and although it may refer on one level to the Colonel's interest in Elizabeth, it undoubtedly refers on another to what we have seen of Darcy's, which Elizabeth entirely ignores, although he is paying her just as much attention as the Colonel. In the second part of the novel, after she has realized the errors her prejudice has led her into, her judgement is directed inwards on herself rather than outwards on to other people, and more of the action takes place in her own mind, less in actual events. Compare the lively conversations which take place at Netherfield while Jane is ill (Volume I, Chapter VIII) with those which take place during the stay at Pemberley (Volume III, Chapter III), which involve most of the same people. In the latter the emphasis is all on what Elizabeth feels and perceives, and not on what anyone else says or does, because the interest here is in her moral reform and emotional maturity. During and after her stay in Lambton, Elizabeth is presented – like Catherine Morland after her dis-illusion, and like Emma as a whole – by the kind of reported thought-process which is Jane Austen's most original method. This method imposes organization on the events and relates Elizabeth's changing feelings firmly and unsentimentally to their context:

The present unhappy state of the family, rendered any other excuse for the lowness of her spirits unnecessary; nothing, therefore, could be fairly conjectured from *that*, though Elizabeth, who was by this time tolerably well acquainted with her own feelings, was perfectly aware, that, had she known nothing of Darcy, she could have borne the dread of Lydia's infamy somewhat better. It would have spared her, she thought, one sleepless night out of two. (298–9)

Darcy parallels Elizabeth. Like her, he is deluded about his own character: 'It is I believe too little yielding' (58) is his first and favourable way of putting what he finally admits: 'I have been a selfish being all my life, in practice, though not in principle' (369). Elizabeth is the means of reforming him, as he is of her. Like her also, he is presented differently before and after his first proposal of marriage, and the way it is done is almost the reverse of the way Jane Austen treats Elizabeth. At first Jane Austen gives his actual thought to mark the progress of his attachment, concisely noting its growth and quality:

No sooner had he made it clear to himself and his friends that she had hardly a good feature in her face, than he began to find it was rendered uncommonly intelligent by the beautiful expression of her dark eyes. (23)

Darcy had never been so bewitched by any woman as he was by her. He really believed, that were it not for the inferiority of her connections, he should be in some danger. (52)

. . . they went down the other dance and parted in silence; on each side dissatisfied, though not to an equal degree, for in Darcy's breast there was a tolerable powerful feeling towards her, which soon procured her pardon, and directed all his anger against another. (94)

She is forced to use this method by having a remote hero whom she cannot reveal through the heroine – as Mr Knightley is revealed through Emma, or, rather differently, Edmund through Fanny. But for the most part Darcy is seen only through what he does and says and through Elizabeth's interpretation of him, with help from occasional unprejudiced observers like Colonel Fitzwilliam and Mrs Gardiner. Since his language is always correct and often formal, and since Jane Austen herself eschews strong language for worthy characters, small details of facial expression must often reveal strong emotion, particularly when Darcy's thoughts cannot be retailed like Elizabeth's. This is specially the case during his first proposal, where his language is restrained and correct (though his sentiments may not be). Such phrases as 'his complexion became pale with anger', 'he changed colour', 'a smile of affected incredulity', 'an expression of mingled incredulity and mortification' (191-3) all make an account of his feelings as unnecessary as, if given alongside Elizabeth's, it would be confusing. The irony and a good deal of the comedy of the first part come from the difference between what Mr Darcy means and what Elizabeth thinks he means, and between what Elizabeth's replies intend, and how they appear to Mr Darcy. The misunderstanding is all Elizabeth's doing, though the speeches of both are most skilfully ambiguous.

Jane Austen makes Mr Darcy interesting by the same means as she makes Elizabeth charming, which makes them artistically suited to one another, and imposes a pattern on the novel as a whole. Just as Wickham's attentions show Elizabeth's attractions, so Miss Bingley's show Darcy's; Elizabeth is witty in her exchanges with Jane and Colonel Fitzwilliam, and so is Darcy in his with Bingley and Caroline; Elizabeth sensibly refuses to be involved with Wickham, and Darcy deftly extricates himself from Miss Bingley's schemes;[1] and Darcy is seen as the friend and intellectual superior of Bingley just as Elizabeth is of Jane. External events also connect them, even those which, as far as the action is concerned, seem to separate them. Elizabeth rightly thinks

[1] He only once verges on rudeness towards her, roused by her own excessive rudeness:

'I particularly recollect your saying one night, after they had been dining at Netherfield, "*She* a beauty! – I should as soon call her mother a wit." But afterwards she seemed to improve on you, and I believe you thought her rather pretty at one time.'

'Yes,' replied Darcy, who could contain himself no longer, 'but *that* was only when I first knew her, for it is many months since I have considered her as one of the handsomest women of my acquaintance.' (271)

It is essential here to have an explicit statement from Darcy, to support the Gardiners' opinions, and Miss Bingley provides a good pretext.

Lydia's elopement is an obstacle to any possible engagement with Mr Darcy; but their common feelings of responsibility for the disaster set them apart from the other characters and strengthen the artistic connexion between them. Darcy is as good a match for Elizabeth as Mr Knightley is for Emma; the novel is therefore better balanced than *Northanger Abbey* or *Sense and Sensibility*, where the hero and heroine are unequal in intellect and role.

Around these main characters Jane Austen constructs a recognizable society. It does not embrace so many different elements as *Sense and Sensibility* did – only rural gentry with a glance at the London of the Gardiners – but it shows much greater skill and uses new methods. She makes much use of background characters, those who never appear in person in the action, or who, if they do appear, never speak. This kind, which appeared in *Sense and Sensibility* with Miss Steele's Dr Davies ('the Doctor', used to throw light on one character only), appears here better regulated in Mrs Long and her nieces, who are a barometer of Mrs Bennet's humours:

'. . . Mrs Long has promised to introduce him.'

'I do not believe Mrs Long will do any such thing. She has two neices [*sic*] of her own. She is a selfish, hypocritical woman, and I have no opinion of her.' (6)

'I do think Mrs Long is as good a creature as ever lived – and her nieces [*sic*] are very pretty behaved girls, and not at all handsome: I like them prodigiously.' (342)

Other background characters are not the property of one character but represent a kind of society; such are Colonel Forster and his wife with whom Lydia is 'such friends', who take her to Brighton and epitomize military society; and Mrs Yonge, who chaperoned Georgiana Darcy on her ill-fated visit to Ramsgate, and who hides Lydia and Wickham in London, embodying the shabby and shifty milieu from which Wickham has emerged. This is a new use for characters and looks forward to *Emma* and *Mansfield Park* because it reveals situation rather than personality: the Forsters stand for Lydia's Brighton, just as Mary Crawford's

London is shown by what she tells us of Lady Stornaway and Mrs Fraser.

Two other devices are practically exclusive to *Pride and Prejudice*; first, the character who appears but never speaks, like Lady Lucas and Mr Philips, who therefore merely gives an impression of a type of company; and second the localized but disembodied public opinion. This latter is necessary because of the public nature of many of the events; Lydia's elopement and subsequent reclamation are things that cannot be kept secret:

> The good news quickly spread through the house; and with proportionate speed through the neighbourhood. It was borne in the latter with decent philosophy. To be sure it would have been more for the advantage of conversation, had Miss Lydia Bennet come upon the town; or, as the happiest alternative, been secluded from the world, in some distant farm house. But there was much to be talked of, in marrying her; and the good-natured wishes for her well-doing, which had proceeded before, from all the spiteful old ladies in Meryton, lost but little of their spirit in this change of circumstances, because with such an husband, her misery was considered certain. (309)

Other events could be kept secret, but are not; Wickham's slanders become public and 'every body was pleased to think how much they had always disliked Mr Darcy' (138).

Pride and Prejudice has a main plot admirably suited to Jane Austen's purposes. There is no dissociation here between characters and the things they have to do, as there is in *Sense and Sensibility*, and events always appear to be the natural consequence of the personalities involved. Lydia's elopement is the only event seriously influencing the relations between Darcy and Elizabeth which is not the direct result of the behaviour of one of them. Though adequately prepared by her own previous behaviour and Wickham's, it is a stumbling-block for some readers; but it is not as important as it seems, for it has no direct effect on their relationship, except to let us see Darcy actually behaving as the revised character Elizabeth's reproofs have made him. The always very minor clumsinesses in handling are all on the fringes, and are such as in almost any other novelist would pass unobserved; it is only beside the standard of perfection that Jane Austen sets for herself with *Emma* and (where technique is concerned) with *Mansfield Park* that they are noticeable. Colonel Fitzwilliam appears only at Rosings – as a companion for Darcy and a witness to his letter, and as an admirer for Elizabeth; he is never mentioned elsewhere, and this is a casual use of character which she does not usually permit herself even in her early work.[1] A more striking *gaucherie* is Georgiana Darcy. There is no reason why she should not be at Netherfield, particularly as Darcy hopes she will marry Bingley: she is two years older than Lydia and has already had an 'establishment' in Ramsgate. She seems to be deliberately kept out of the action to satisfy the exigencies of the plot: Wickham can tell irrefutable lies about an absent person, and Darcy can show his esteem for Elizabeth and the Gardiners by introducing them to a hitherto unknown sister.

The events are handled with the same kind of skill as those of *Sense and Sensibility*; Jane Austen's art shows, here as in that novel, in the varying amounts of emphasis she gives to different events, and the way in which she arranges her time-scheme. She wastes no space between episodes, but the impression of time passing is accurately produced, especially by details of the weather:

> . . . from the day of the invitation, to the day of the ball, there was such a succession of rain as prevented their walking to Meryton once. No aunt, no officers, no news could be sought after; – the very shoe-roses for Netherfield were got by proxy. Even Elizabeth might have found some trial of her patience in weather, which totally suspended the improvement of her acquaintance with Mr Wickham; and nothing less than a dance on Tuesday, could have made such a Friday, Saturday, Sunday and Monday, endurable to Kitty and Lydia. (88)

This represents tedium humorously, and Elizabeth's state of mind at the same time (and suggests that it bears some likeness to her silly sisters'). The intervals in time enlarge as the novel progresses, and days and months are handled with equal assurance:

---

[1] *Persuasion* is a different matter, and shows signs of being intended to be eventually longer and considerably revised.

With no greater events than these in the Longbourn family, and otherwise diversified by little beyond the walks to Meryton, sometimes dirty and sometimes cold, did January and February pass away. March was to take Elizabeth to Hunsford. (151)

This leads neatly into an account of Elizabeth's feelings about her visit, and to the journey and visit itself. The matters by which passing time is measured are strictly relevant to what follows, as in the period between Lydia's holiday in Brighton and Elizabeth's in Derbyshire:

> When Elizabeth had rejoiced over Wickham's departure, she found little other cause for satisfaction in the loss of the regiment. Their parties abroad were less varied than before; and at home she had a mother and sister whose constant repinings at the dulness of every thing around them, threw a real gloom over their domestic circle; and, though Kitty might in time regain her natural degree of sense, since the disturbers of her brain were removed, her other sister, from whose disposition greater evil might be apprehended, was likely to be hardened in all her folly and assurance, by a situation of such double danger as a watering place and a camp. (237)

Longbourn is gloomy and its inmates foolish, and signs of cheerfulness – 'health, good humour, and cheerfulness began to reappear at Longbourn' (238) – bring another disappointment, that the tour of the Lakes is to be curtailed to just that part of it – Derbyshire – which will most affect Elizabeth. This curtailment intensifies the gloom that Pemberley is to burst upon, and is a neat manoeuvre: a tour to the Lakes is a probable event; a tour of Derbyshire as the original plan would look far too much like a deliberate use of coincidence.

The action is organized not only by what happens, but by where it happens; the place itself is relevant to what occurs. Though all are rural gentlemen's estates (except London, which is rather passed through than used), Longbourn, Rosings and Pemberley – in ascending order of magnitude as well as in order of appearance – are distinguished by significant physical characteristics. Longbourn itself is not described, except when it is too late to affect our view of it, when we hear that it has a hermitage, and 'a prettyish kind of a little wilderness' (352) for Lady Catherine to inspect. It is one of a group of small estates, including Netherfield and Lucas Lodge, in a neighbourhood of small gentry and of trade, as Sir William Lucas and the proximity of Meryton bear out. Rosings is clearly superior socially:

> [Mr Collins] was so much struck with the size and furniture of [Mrs Philips's drawing-room], that he declared he might almost have supposed himself in the small summer breakfast parlour at Rosings. (75)

But its real attractions are moderate:

> Every park has its beauty and its prospects; and Elizabeth saw much to be pleased with, though she could not be in such rapures as Mr Collins expected the scene to inspire. (161)

This is a background in sympathy with Lady Catherine and with Darcy, who shows at Rosings the unattractive qualities he shares with his aunt. The well-arranged parsonage emphasizes the pomp and suggests the lack of taste of the mansion. After this, Longbourn seems a setting not out of keeping with the folly and vulgarity Elizabeth recognizes in her family, though the place is not in itself vulgar, being a residence fit for the gentleman Mr Bennet is. Pemberley is all the more splendid by contrast; its natural beauty shows the combination in Mr Darcy, as in his house, of nature and taste:

> It was a large, handsome, stone building, standing well on rising ground, and backed by a ridge of high woody hills; – and in front, a stream of some natural importance was swelled into greater, but without any artificial appearance. Its banks were neither formal, nor falsely adorned. Elizabeth was delighted. (245)

The general organization of material also resembles *Sense and Sensibility*. The plan seems less skilful but is more so, because the manipulation is not obtrusive in itself; a good many of the points of construction have therefore been dealt with in discussion of character. The whole novel, by being more assured, appears more spontaneous and natural. There are no *tours de force* like Lucy's two long conversations with Elinor about her engagement to Edward Ferrars. The longest dialogues occur at Mr Collins's proposal – a

glorious exhibition of himself and not much more than a monologue – and at Lady Catherine's attempt to forbid Elizabeth to
marry Darcy. This, although greatly heightened, is a real exchange
of personalities, not merely a giving of information, which is what
Lucy's disclosures really are. Elizabeth scores a practical triumph
over Lady Catherine, unlike Elinor, who can only be said to score
a moral one over Lucy. The exchanges between Elizabeth and the
other characters are all brief; the one chance for a long one, where
Darcy might explain away Elizabeth's prejudices against him (as
Willoughby explains himself to Elinor) is deliberately put aside by
the device of the letter. This is less obviously dramatic, but
essentially more probable and satisfactory. The reader, like Elizabeth, needs time to take in all this information, and if it were given
in person the interview would require most improbable self-
control in Mr Darcy. Willoughby's confession by contrast tells
nothing new, but gives a new aspect of what we know already,
while the violence and incoherence with which he tells it make
him more attractive (though no more estimable). The longest of
the conversations are those between Darcy and Elizabeth after
their engagement, which are merely a review of what has gone
before, giving an agreeable view of the relationship between them,
which is necessary since they have been at cross-purposes or under
some restraint for the whole of their acquaintance. This represents
an advance on *Sense and Sensibility*, where we have no such
evidence of the good understanding between Elinor and Edward
Ferrars, which is merely assumed to exist. Such an account of a
developing relationship is a new technique; it is even more necessary in *Emma*, where a number of minor dilemmas are still to be
resolved even after Emma and Mr Knightley have come to an
understanding, and Elizabeth teasing Darcy sounds very like
Emma teasing Mr Knightley.

A new thing in *Pride and Prejudice* is the handling of groups of
characters. There are almost twice as many characters in this novel
as in *Sense and Sensibility*,[1] and Jane Austen handles larger groups
of them at a time, with the minimum of directives from herself.

---

[1] Twenty-six speaking characters in *Pride and Prejudice*; fourteen in *Sense and
Sensibility*.

The second chapter of the novel introduces the whole of the Bennet family in conversation, without superfluous exchanges, giving useful information not only about themselves by what they say, but also about their neighbours. The scene is really a conversation between Mr and Mrs Bennet, with the daughters' remarks interpolated, which makes it clear and easy to follow. The interpolations themselves are in a significant order. Elizabeth is most important and speaks first:

> 'I hope Mr Bingley will like it, Lizzy.'
> 'We are not in a way to know *what* Mr Bingley likes,' said her mother resentfully, 'since we are not to visit.'
> 'But you forget, mama,' said Elizabeth, 'that we shall meet him at the assemblies, and that Mrs Long has promised to introduce him.'
> (6)

This shows that she shares her father's sense. Lydia is last and therefore in a position second in importance only to Elizabeth:

> 'I am not afraid; for though I *am* the youngest, I'm the tallest.' (8)

Kitty's cough brings forward Mrs Bennet's nerves as a force to be reckoned with, and a 'fretful' reply ranges her with her mother. Mary makes clear the force of Mr Bennet's irony; she brilliantly says nothing:

> 'What say you, Mary? for you are a young lady of deep reflection I know, and read great books, and make extracts.'
> Mary wished to say something very sensible, but knew not how.
> (7)

Mr Bennet's comments and introductions are as efficient as any from a narrator could be, and are more dramatic, so the scene goes as briskly as if one were reading a play, though more clearly, and with more information, in a shorter time, than any play could bear. This same method is used to give the effect of large parties of people in conversation, of which we hear only the interesting parts out of several exchanges taking place simultaneously; the evenings at Netherfield are excellent examples. While all that is said is relevant to the characters and to how they will behave later, neither the order in which they speak nor what they say is logical, but gives the impression of casual and often interrupted chat. On Elizabeth's second evening there, Miss Bingley, bored with her book, opens the conversation by asking her brother about the proposed ball; the subject soon drops, because from Mr Bingley's words it is clear that no one either agrees with Caroline or cares to argue with her:

> 'I should like balls infinitely better,' she replied, 'if they were carried on in a different manner . . . It would surely be much more rational if conversation instead of dancing made the order of the day.'
> 'Much more rational, my dear Caroline, I dare say, but it would not be near so much like a ball.' (55–56)

What this exchange does is to show that Caroline will be aiming all her behaviour at Mr Darcy (who, we know, dislikes dancing), and that as even Mr Bingley is a match for her Darcy will never be taken in. The talk goes on between Miss Bingley and Elizabeth, and it is only when Elizabeth teases him, not when Miss Bingley flatters him, that Mr Darcy speaks himself:

> 'As to laughter, we will not expose ourselves, if you please, by attempting to laugh without a subject. Mr Darcy may hug himself.'
> 'Mr Darcy is not to be laughed at!' cried Elizabeth. 'That is an uncommon advantage, and uncommon I hope it will continue, for it would be a great loss to *me* to have many such acquaintance. I dearly love a laugh.'
> 'Miss Bingley,' said he, 'has given me credit for more than can be.' . . . (57)

For a few lines there is a rational though still light-hearted exchange between Elizabeth and Darcy, which Miss Bingley's interruption emphasizes by seeming merely a frivolous intrusion:

> 'Your examination of Mr Darcy is over, I presume,' said Miss Bingley; – 'and pray what is the result?' (57)

In fact, it has no effect on the topic at all, because Mr Darcy simply goes on talking to Elizabeth. The conversation is intimate, but the setting is quite public; we feel Bingley to be ready to speak because we have already heard him, and we assume Mrs Hurst to be listening because we know she is 'principally occupied in playing with her bracelets and rings' (55). The remarks we hear do not follow logically from the remarks of each previous speaker, but indicate the drift of each speaker's private thoughts, without holding up the conversation with an account of them.

Despite its romantic accessories, its chief one being a remote hero who is fantastically rich, by Jane Austen's standards, with £10,000 a year[1] – *Pride and Prejudice* is to be grouped with the least romantic of all her novels. In most of its features: in ironic presentation through a faulty heroine whose dilemmas are of her own making, and who is witty, independent and charming none the less; in having many humorous but never dangerous minor characters; and in having an air of great gaiety over a serious subject; in all these ways *Pride and Prejudice* is clearly to be grouped with *Emma*; while *Sense and Sensibility*, despite its many things in common with *Pride and Prejudice*, looks forward rather to *Mansfield Park*, where a serious subject is treated with a good deal more seriousness, where the heroine is consciously virtuous and influenced by circumstances which she cannot control, where the hero is a less impressive person both in himself and his part in the action, and where minor characters are either very much deluded or positively ill-natured.

[1] *Emma* by contrast is wealthy with £30,000 *gross*, and Mary Crawford has only £20,000.

4 · *Mansfield Park*

Mansfield Park is wholly the work of Jane Austen's maturity, written when she was between thirty-six and thirty-nine years old. While her novels are essentially serious in intention, this comes closest of them all to being sober in treatment. There are, as well as the obvious great resemblances between this and Jane Austen's other novels, many differences as well, which attract to it those whose interest is in something other than Jane Austen's characteristic offering, differences which show a feeling towards another kind of novel-writing. Jane Austen herself, in a letter to her sister, says that this is an attempt at something new, and is to be about 'ordination'.[1] Like most authors' comments on their work, this is not the whole truth, but this is undoubtedly what forms the central dilemma, for though Fanny is the heroine, her fate depends on whether Mary Crawford, hating the office and status of clergyman, will marry Edmund. This makes the novel quite different from *Pride and Prejudice* or *Emma*, where the central interests, the heroine's delusions and enlightenment, though they involve social and moral problems, are essentially entertaining; *Mansfield Park* has a subject that is solemn in itself, and therefore much less susceptible of humorous treatment. That the action is out of the heroine's control and that it is not capable of much humour show how this novel is like *Sense and Sensibility*. Yet the way Jane Austen handles her material shows how her interests have changed and her skill has increased. The problem in *Sense and Sensibility* of having a heroine with too large a burden of narration and judgement is avoided here, and Jane Austen herself as narrator plays a – for her – very large part indeed. The heroine Fanny is not a lens through which the action is seen, like Elizabeth and Emma and

[1] Letter to Cassandra Austen, 29 January 1813, *Letters*, p. 298.

Elinor: there are many important scenes in which Fanny does not appear at all, such as that in which Henry Crawford tells his sister of his plan to flirt with Fanny, and the later ones where he confesses that, caught in his own trap, he intends to marry her; there is much analysis of the motives and emotions of people other than Fanny herself, such as Maria's reasons for marrying Mr Rushworth, Mrs Norris's attitude to Fanny, and Sir Thomas Bertram's principles and rules of conduct; and a great deal of time and emphasis is given to events in which Fanny has only a very minor part. Therefore Jane Austen is clearly organizing this novel on different principles from her others, indicating a much wider range, and a power to handle a good many more different kinds of topic. The subject is no longer the reform of a single heroine (Fanny has really no faults to lose); it is the breakdown and the subsequent reform of a whole highly organized society – the society formed by those who live at Mansfield Park. This stable and apparently integrated and impregnable order on which Fanny's good qualities and example have no effect is assailed in the absence of its leader Sir Thomas by the worldly Crawfords, who corrupt by degrees almost all the members of that society. They corrupt first Maria and Julia and precipitate Maria's disastrous marriage with Mr Rushworth; then secondly Edmund, who succumbs to Mary Crawford enough to act in a play he totally disapproves of and to have his judgement of Henry's courtship of Fanny distorted by his own love for Mary; then thirdly Sir Thomas, who having found Mr Rushworth a fit husband for Maria, now finds Henry a fit match for Fanny; and finally Fanny herself, who begins to weaken towards Henry when she is unhappy at Portsmouth, and when she thinks Edmund will marry Mary. Maria's elopement is not merely a convenient and melodramatic disaster, it is the final stroke which brings down the whole structure of evil, leaving Sir Thomas reformed, and Edmund and Fanny in a position to become as happy as they may be considered to deserve.

As usual the opening chapter states the themes of the whole novel: it begins with the Ward sisters' various marriages and their consequences; it indicates how they will behave in future by tell-

ing how they behaved when Miss Frances married Captain Price;
it continues with Mrs Norris's proposal that Sir Thomas should
educate Fanny; the consequent discussions first of all raise the
obvious and inevitable point that Fanny will fall in love with one
of her cousins, although all that is actually considered at the time
is whether one of the cousins will fall in love with *her*; and
secondly they show the different intentions of Sir Thomas and
Mrs Norris, and make it clear that even though his motives are
sound their results for Fanny will be very much the same as the
results of Mrs Norris's.

> 'There will be some difficulty in our way, Mrs Norris,' observed
> Sir Thomas, 'as to the distinction proper to be made between the
> girls as they grow up; how to preserve in the minds of my *daughters*
> the consciousness of what they are, without making them think
> too lowly of their cousin; and how, without depressing her spirits
> too far, to make her remember that she is not a *Miss Bertram*.' (10)

This neatly indicates the very injurious effect of such a distinction
on Maria and Julia.

As such an introduction indicates, Fanny is much less of a
heroine than any of the other heroines. Because she is young,
weak and helpless, her judgement, though usually sound, is
limited, and Jane Austen does not make the mistake she made with
Elinor of putting too old a head on her young shoulders. Jane
Austen here is in a position of evident superiority to all her characters. Fanny is always junior to author and reader, a result of the
author's own attitude to her and to all the people Fanny meets.
The reader can never feel Fanny an equal as he does Elizabeth aged
twenty, Elinor aged nineteen, Emma aged twenty-one, or Anne
Elliot aged twenty-eight. Even when Henry is flirting with the
Miss Bertrams – that is, all through the Sotherton visit and the
play rehearsals – when Fanny is the only unbiased observer, Jane
Austen modifies what Fanny tells us by telling things Fanny either
cannot know or is too unsophisticated to see: thus we have enlightening glimpses of Maria –

> When they came within the influence of Sotherton associations,
> it was better for Miss Bertram, who might be said to have two strings

to her bow. She had Rushworth-feelings, and Crawford-feelings, and in the vicinity of Sotherton, the former had considerable effect. (81)

– and equally enlightening ones of Henry Crawford:

> For a day or two after the affront was given, Henry Crawford had endeavoured to do it away by the usual attack of gallantry and compliment, but he had not cared enough about it to persevere against a few repulses; and becoming soon too busy with his play to have time for more than one flirtation, he grew indifferent to the quarrel, or rather thought it a lucky occurrence, as quietly putting an end to what might ere long have raised expectations in more than Mrs Grant. (160–1)

Such comment does occur in the other novels, but only rarely; here it is the common method, in particular when the interest settles on Henry's courtship of Fanny and Edmund's of Mary, when all their motives are equally important and Fanny is in no position to judge of any but her own. So there are accounts of what Henry Crawford feels such as there are of none even of the heroes of the other novels:

> Love such as his, in a man like himself, must with perseverance secure a return, and at no great distance; and he had so much delight in the idea of obliging her to love him in a very short time, that her not loving him now was scarcely regretted. (327)

This, and similar accounts of Mary, recall Emma, who is allowed to reveal her own faults like this, even though neither Henry nor Mary is the leading character, or even a very sympathetic one.

All this shows that Fanny is the pivot of the action rather than an active heroine. Such an attitude to her heroine means that much of Jane Austen's characteristic humour disappears. Where even secondary characters are analysed, the opportunity is, rather, for a biting and humourless irony, displayed both in analysis and conversation.

> In all the important preparations of the mind [Maria] was complete; being prepared for matrimony by an hatred of home, restraint, and tranquillity; by the misery of disappointed affection, and contempt of the man she was to marry. (202)

[Mrs Norris] was very glad that she had given William what she did at parting, very glad indeed that it had been in her power, without material inconvenience, just at that time to give him something rather considerable; that is, for *her*, with *her* limited means, for now it would all be useful in helping to fit up his cabin. (304–5)

Such a method shows that the concise conclusion, however summary, is still perfectly just, whether disposing of minor characters like the Rushworths –

The indignities of stupidity, and the disappointments of selfish passion, can excite little pity. (464)

– or of major ones like Henry Crawford:

. . . without presuming to look forward to a juster appointment hereafter, we may fairly consider a man of sense like Henry Crawford, to be providing for himself no small portion of vexation and regret – vexation that must rise sometimes to self-reproach, and regret to wretchedness. (468–9)

This is a strikingly different conclusion; the seducer Wickham is allowed a degree of prosperity, while the dismissal of Willoughby is almost the reverse of Crawford's, for the corresponding summary is this:

That his repentance of misconduct, which thus brought its own punishment, was sincere, need not be doubted; . . . But that he was for ever inconsolable, that he fled from society, or contracted an habitual gloom of temper, or died of a broken heart, must not be depended on – for he did neither. He lived to exert, and frequently to enjoy himself. (*Sense and Sensibility*, p. 379)

These judgements bring us to the real problem of *Mansfield Park*, which despite its wide range of character and topic, its excellent planning, and its episodes as brilliant and incisive as any ever written, is yet not as completely satisfying even as *Sense and Sensibility*, though its parts are so much superior. It is uncertain just where Jane Austen is usually most sure: in the moral judgement implicit in her presentation of material. This shows most in the episode devoted to the acting of *Lovers' Vows*. Performing a play, as we find from its consequences, is obviously wrong:

Henry Crawford is given his chance to trifle with Maria and Julia and all their baser passions are let loose; Edmund is forced to abandon his principles, to agree to act, and to appear to succumb to Mary Crawford; Fanny is made miserable, the house is thoroughly disorganized just in time for Sir Thomas's return, and general disorder results. Yet it is not clear at first, before these consequences can be seen, why a play as such is a wrong thing. Certainly Sir Thomas is away, and so Edmund's objections – 'It would be taking liberties with my father's house in his absence which could not be justified' (127), and 'My father would totally disapprove it' (126) – have weight, while Edmund's and Fanny's protests at the play actually chosen are very proper:

> Agatha and Amelia appeared to her in their different ways so totally improper for home representation – the situation of one, and the language of the other, so unfit to be expressed by any woman of modesty, that she could hardly suppose her cousins could be aware of what they were engaging in. (137)

These, however, are all questions of expediency and social decorum, and Jane Austen's usual genius for making social decorum a practical manifestation of moral value seems to fail her here; it is difficult to see these considerations as reinforcing the rather vague condemnations of Fanny and Edmund:

> For her own gratification she could have wished that something might be acted, for she had never seen even half a play, but every thing of higher consequence was against it. (131)

> 'In a *general* light, private theatricals are open to some objections, but as *we* are circumstanced, I must think it would be highly injudicious, and more than injudicious, to attempt any thing of the kind.' (125)

Edmund is here put in a position of seeming to try to prevent an evil consequence (Maria's passion for Crawford) which, in fact, he knows nothing about, as he has already told Fanny he is sure that Crawford is interested only in Julia. Some readers have seen in this difficulty a change of attitude in Jane Austen towards her characters, Henry Crawford in particular being interpreted as a personality who nearly escapes from his creator to become the hero of the novel. Yet although he is obviously more attractive in the latter part, when paying court to Fanny, he is always firmly controlled both by Fanny's opinion of him and, when her judgement begins to falter, by Jane Austen's own.

Fanny's judgement is important to the novel as a whole and is a reliable guide through the difficult shifts of emphasis and the changing events of the story. She is not a heroine in the sense that Jane Austen's others are, and there is plenty of proof of a generally different function; as we have seen, the novel opens with a view of Mansfield society in which for the first four chapters Fanny is the youngest member and only a child; even when she is grown up she is inferior socially to her cousins, and mentally and emotionally apart from them, being therefore passive by inclination and personality as well as by her status; even when she acts decisively it is only to resist, to repel others' actions, not to initiate her own: she refuses to act in the play, and refuses to marry Henry Crawford; in fact, the only initiative she shows is when she buys a penknife for her small sister Betsey so that Susan can have back the one that is hers by right. Added to this is her physical weakness, which is another aspect of her helplessness. She becomes ill when she cannot go riding because Mary has the horse, and Jane Austen suggests that a longer stay at Portsmouth might have killed her:

> Though Sir Thomas, had he known all, might have thought his niece in the most promising way of being starved, both mind and body, into a much juster value for Mr Crawford's good company and good fortune, he would probably have feared to push his experiment farther, lest she might die under the cure. (413)

She is remarkable among Jane Austen's heroines also for a reliable judgement in a very young person, and for rarely showing any humour herself or allowing Jane Austen to show any at her expense. She has none of the delusions of Elizabeth or Emma or Catherine Morland, and has no past errors to guide her like Anne Elliot; like Elinor's her opinion is reliable, but because at the same time she is both timid and ineffective in conduct she does not seem either staid or mature, and she is even more solemn than Elinor. Because of these characteristics Fanny is used – until after Sir Thomas's return and Maria's marriage – through all the events which concern the whole group of young people at Mansfield, as a means by which the reader may observe the actions of the group, and discern how much they are in the wrong, a means by which he is able to judge their true value and see how important they will be in the rest of the novel. Edmund, for instance, has no more to do in the play and at Sotherton than either Tom or Maria, but he is kept up as a main character, ready for the more severe trials that Mary will inflict, because he is always the most important person to Fanny. In contrast Mr Rushworth, who is farcical in everything he does and says, is seen, briefly, as a really injured man because Fanny pities him. In this way Fanny looks forward to Anne Elliot, another charming and right-thinking character who has no authority, but who is an even greater triumph because she is not even young.

Such a role as Fanny's, for such a character, and with Jane Austen's usual habit of letting characters make their own effect by acts and speech, somewhat distorts what we feel about what Jane Austen lets us see; this is not a serious fault like the uncertain ethics involved in the play-acting, but it is remarkable in a writer so sure of herself as Jane Austen usually is. Fanny is unduly sensitive to Mrs Norris, as Edmund points out:

> 'I can say nothing for her manner to you as a child; but it was the same with us all, or nearly so. She never knew how to be pleasant to children.' (26)

But as we often see Mrs Norris slighting Fanny, and see what Fanny suffers, Mrs Norris seems – though not more evil or powerful than she should – more immediately painful, despite very welcome corrections from William and Sir Thomas. Edmund, also, comes to seem more noble and charming – simply because Fanny thinks him so – than he ever actually appears in himself and in what he does.

Even after Maria's marriage, when Fanny becomes much more

important, she is still seen as one part of that whole Mansfield household to which Crawford and his sister are directing their attentions. It is Henry and Mary who decide what will happen, as Jane Austen makes plain by the amount of time she spends on what Henry feels about Fanny. In contrast, the growth of Edmund's affection for Fanny is discussed only in the very last chapter; while what Fanny thinks and feels towards Crawford is, because more subtle, more interesting than what she feels towards Edmund.

Putting Fanny in a subordinate place does not prevent her being interesting; once she is seen in her proper place she is the more attractive because she no longer seems too feeble or too passive for a heroine. Her childishness forces Jane Austen to implement Fanny's judgement with her own, which greatly enriches the later part of the novel, as, for example, when Fanny puzzles over Mary:

> She may be forgiven by older sages, for looking on the chance of Miss Crawford's future improvement as nearly desperate, for thinking that if Edmund's influence in this season of love, had already done so little in clearing her judgment, and regulating her notions, his worth would be finally wasted on her even in years of matrimony.
>
> Experience might have hoped more for any young people, so circumstanced, and impartiality would not have denied to Miss Crawford's nature, that participation of the general nature of women, which would lead her to adopt the opinions of the man she loved and respected, as her own. (367)

Such a realistic grasp of probabilities is not demonstrated in any of her other novels, and shows that even though we see Fanny's sufferings most acutely, they are part of the larger pattern formed by Mansfield society, and the Crawfords' relations with it. This is still true at Portsmouth, where Fanny certainly seems to be on her own, working out her own fate; but Mansfield still predominates in the comparisons Fanny is forced to make, which give Mansfield back its proper moral value, which she and the reader have lost sight of because Fanny has been unhappy there:

> At Mansfield, no sounds of contention, no raised voice, no abrupt bursts, no tread of violence was ever heard; all proceeded in a

regular course of cheerful orderliness; every body had their due importance; every body's feelings were consulted. If tenderness could be ever supposed wanting, good sense and good breeding supplied its place. (391-2)

The three Miss Wards – in the novel Mrs Norris, Lady Bertram and Mrs Price – are a powerful organizing force although they are only minor characters; they embody the theme of the effect of environment and upbringing on character. Because Mrs Price is very like her sisters, Portsmouth is seen as an off-shoot of life at Mansfield, and as such it is kept in mind all through the novel; in the opening chapter Miss Frances's marriage to Captain Price gets just as much attention as her sisters', and the frequent mentions of William and his three visits prevent us from forgetting her. Lady Bertram, though made of the same stuff as Mrs Price, is respectable because of her constant association with Sir Thomas: 'Lady Bertram did not think deeply, but, guided by Sir Thomas, she thought justly on all important points' (449). In her own character she is useful because she has a sound grasp of fact and no personal prejudices. Because she says little, what she does say is telling, and she gives delightful because always unconscious comments. This is a method Jane Austen has used before, of letting a character be much more relevant than she knows, and we can interpret the following (as we should) as proof that Fanny, though depressed, is not stupid at all:

> As for Fanny's being stupid at learning, 'she could only say it was very unlucky, but some people *were* stupid, and Fanny must take more pains; . . . she saw no harm in the poor little thing – and always found her very handy and quick in carrying messages, and fetching what she wanted.' (20)

Lady Bertram is often used like this: when Edmund has almost persuaded Maria that it is improper for her to act as Agatha in the play, Lady Bertram quite unconsciously suggests the one thing – Julia's taking the part – that will make Maria act whatever the consequences:

> '. . . All who can distinguish, will understand your motive. – The play will be given up, and your delicacy honoured as it ought.'

'Do not act any thing improper, my dear,' said Lady Bertram. 'Sir Thomas would not like it. – Fanny, ring the bell; I must have my dinner. – *To be sure Julia is dressed by this time.'* . . .

'If I were to decline the part,' said Maria, with renewed zeal, 'Julia would certainly take it.' (140–1: my italics)

She is an excellent and necessary antidote to Mrs Norris; quite impervious to her, she not only points out where Mrs Norris is deluded, but also where she actually distorts fact:

'It will be an education for the child, said I, only being with her cousins; if Miss Lee taught her nothing, she would learn to be good and clever from *them*.'

'I hope she will not tease my poor pug,' said Lady Bertram; 'I have but just got Julia to leave it alone.' (10)

Mrs Norris is one of Jane Austen's most striking creations. She is presented by the same methods as the farcical characters in the other novels, but we are not allowed to dissociate ourselves from her as we do from Lady Catherine or Mrs Elton, for unlike both of these she has a personality strong enough to influence so right-thinking a man as Sir Thomas. Mrs Elton never deludes anyone, and Lady Catherine cannot influence even her own nephew Darcy, but Mrs Norris easily does away with very sensible objections to adopting Fanny, by a mixture of flattery and verbosity:

He debated and hesitated; – it was a serious charge; – a girl so brought up must be adequately provided for, or there would be cruelty instead of kindness in taking her from her family. He thought of his own four children – of his two sons – of cousins in love, &c.; – but no sooner had he deliberately begun to state his objections, than Mrs Norris interrupted him with a reply to them all whether stated or not. (6)

Jane Austen gives reasons why Mrs Norris is disagreeable:

Having married on a narrower income than she had been used to look forward to, she had, from the first, fancied a very strict line of economy necessary; and what was begun as a matter of prudence, soon grew into a matter of choice, as an object of that needful solicitude, which there were no children to supply. (8)

We hear this in the very first chapter, and when at the end
Maria elopes Mrs Norris's distress is emphasized, and we are
forced to pity a character we would gladly despise. Jane Austen
does not excuse her – explanation is not extenuation – but the way
she treats all three of the sisters looks forward to the way George
Eliot treats faulty, grotesque, but yet suffering characters such as
the banker Bulstrode in *Middlemarch*; the reader is made to understand and judge them in the same way as the heroes. Unlike anything of George Eliot's, though, Mrs Norris is a witty and satiric
creation:

> Miss Ward, at the end of half a dozen years, found herself obliged
> to be attached to the Rev. Mr Norris, a friend of her brother-in-law,
> with scarcely any private fortune, and Miss Frances fared yet worse.
> Miss Ward's match, indeed, when it came to the point, was not
> contemptible, Sir Thomas being happily able to give his friend an
> income in the living of Mansfield, and Mr and Mrs Norris began
> their career of conjugal felicity with very little less than a thousand
> a year. (3)

'Obliged to be attached' shows that affection is not in question,
and the cliché 'conjugal felicity' – suspect in itself – is neatly tied
to that chief source of Mrs Norris's felicity, money, in 'a thousand
a year'. She shows how Jane Austen, less light-hearted and less
given to mere entertainment here than elsewhere, is preoccupied
with the social and moral aspects of personality. Mrs Norris is
always a figure fit to be what she becomes when Sir Thomas is
away, his deputy, the person with the greatest nominal authority,
who contributes to the moral chaos by encouraging Maria's
marriage and by not disapproving the play. She is an excellent
creation, but she appears rather out of proportion even so, because
she is painful to Fanny; Fanny is so often the standard of judgement
that, though it is always clearly stated, it cannot always be clearly
perceived that Mrs Norris is not as fearful as Fanny thinks her.

An important person, though absent for the fifteen vital
chapters in which the Crawfords first appear, is Sir Thomas
Bertram. He embodies the best principles and authority of his
society at the very first – 'Sir Thomas was fully resolved to be the

real and consistent patron of the selected child' (8); but his principles are theoretical, so that his not improper interest in 'the distinction proper to be made between the girls' (10) never lets him see the very wrong way he and Mrs Norris go to work to bring the distinction home to Fanny and her cousins. He is impersonal, and indeed absent for a long time, so that his children may regulate themselves by their own moral sense (as Jane Austen likes her characters to do) without any external discipline. When he comes home from Antigua he regains some of our sympathy, partly because of his disappointment with Maria, and partly because of Fanny's changed feelings towards him:

> His kindness altogether was such as made her reproach herself for loving him so little, and thinking his return a misfortune; and when, on having courage to lift her eyes to his face, she saw that he was grown thinner and had the burnt, fagged, worn look of fatigue and a hot climate, every tender feeling was increased. (178)

When Fanny refuses to marry Crawford the situation is the more painful because we are forced to approve of the motives of both of them. Sir Thomas is the most upright and powerful person in the story, and is rightly the last to succumb to the Crawfords' charm; when he has done so all that remains is for Fanny to go to Portsmouth and their various disasters to come upon the rest.

The division between major and minor characters, always a difficult one in Jane Austen, is even more so when all characters are given this kind of consideration, the only difference being how large a part they play. The Bertram children all have a serious purpose in the novel. Tom occupies the least space and is the least essential; he is a link between the Crawfords and the Bertrams, resembling the former in his careless sentiments – 'I have quite as great an interest in being careful of his house as you can have' (127) (being the heir to it) – and since he is the heir he is the first object of Mary's attentions; he is a neat foil for Henry Crawford, being careless and pleasure-loving like him, but shows up Crawford's worse faults by not having them himself. He has, significantly, no interest in emotions or in women: he is merely casually gallant to Mary and wants to act a comedy, or at least to have a comic part himself. Crawford sets out to injure Maria and Julia deliberately while Tom only injures Edmund indirectly when his extravagance forces his father to dispose of the living kept for Edmund. Tom's repentance and reformation, which contribute to the abrupt and tidy ending, are surprising but not improbable in someone who has been guilty of nothing worse than thoughtlessness, and who has provided so much very welcome comedy. He is nearly always revealed in his own words, and is a relief because Jane Austen has little occasion to analyse his thoughts or question his motives. Maria and Julia are more integral and impressive, though they take up no more space; their always appearing together brings out the superficial unity that their training in manners and etiquette has given them. They are the first to suffer when the Crawfords arrive, and at Sotherton they are sharply estranged by their repressed rivalry, which Jane Austen reveals in analysis of each, to make the little they are able to say more telling. Maria is the stronger and more interesting character, because the more important; her occasional acute remarks are illuminating, the following allusion to Mary Crawford reminding us of Edmund's faults as well as her own:

'I am perfectly acquainted with the play, I assure you . . . I can see nothing objectionable in it; and *I* am not the *only* young woman you find, who thinks it very fit for private representation.' (140)

We see little of her association with Henry Crawford, because Jane Austen deliberately prevents any sympathy for her passion. What we do see is therefore very significant, and Jane Austen makes the forms of polite speech and ambiguous remarks and situations act almost as symbols, in a most unusual way. Both Maria and Crawford light-heartedly use the locked gate and the ha-ha at Sotherton to represent her engagement to Mr Rushworth:

'You have a very smiling scene before you.'
'Do you mean literally or figuratively? Literally I conclude. Yes, certainly, the sun shines and the park looks very cheerful. But unluckily that iron gate, that ha-ha, give me a feeling of restraint and hardship . . . Mr Rushworth is so long fetching this key!'

'And for the world you would not get out without the key and without Mr Rushworth's authority and protection, or I think you might with little difficulty pass round the edge of the gate, here, with my assistance.' (99)

For the reader it has much more significance: each remark applies exactly to Maria's elopement, which is indeed without Mr Rushworth's 'authority and protection'. The end of the story is anticipated completely with Julia's angry words, 'I am not obliged to punish myself for *her* sins' (101); this is exactly what she fears will happen at Maria's elopement, 'imagining its certain consequence to herself would be greater severity and restraint' (466), and it is exactly what does happen when she chooses to marry Mr Yates.

The young people Tom, Maria, Julia, Fanny and Mary are attended by various minor characters. Mary has friends in London, Mrs Fraser and Lady Stornaway, who, although they never appear, are proved to be mercenary, frivolous, and worthless. If they were seen in greater detail it would probably be much more difficult to speak so decisively of them. They contrast sharply with the characters Fanny attracts; William and Susan, far from having false standards like Mary's friends, have been given none at all; they are agreeable for being natural, ingenuous, and wholly worthy, and, though relations, are so divided from Fanny by circumstance that they may be said actually to choose to be friends. The amber cross William gives Fanny illustrates his position; this alone gives her pure pleasure, since the necklace Mary (more properly Crawford) gives her, and Edmund's chain, both cause her different kinds of distress. While Portsmouth has given William no false values, it has given Susan nothing; it is left to Mansfield training embodied in Fanny to bring out the good in her.

Between these extremes of warped and sophisticated wit and uncultured virtue, the Rushworths and Mr Yates reinforce the Mansfield characters. They are welcome because they are entirely comic. Yates is frivolous but not vicious; during the play which he initiates he is simply amusing, and even when the serious in the form of Sir Thomas is forced on him he is still merely ludicrous, not firmly condemned. It is quite possible to accept his final reformation when he has married Julia – 'he was not very solid; but there was a hope of his becoming less trifling – of his being at least tolerably domestic and quiet' (462) – when his follies are dealt with so lightly. Mrs Rushworth is one of Jane Austen's collection of exact and unforgettable characters based on one trait and even on one sentence. 'Those who have not more, must be satisfied with what they have' (118), as she says of Crawford's fortune, is worthy to rank with Mrs Ferrars's 'Miss Morton is Lord Morton's daughter', as one of the most amusing truisms ever thought of. Mr Rushworth, like his mother, states the obvious, but produces the effect of amiable stupidity:

> 'For if,' said he, with the sort of self-evident proposition which many a clearer head does not always avoid – 'we are *too* long going over the house, we shall not have time for what is to be done out of doors.' (89)

He is often wildly funny, and, although Fanny is sympathetic and never amused, he is never allowed to be pathetic, though his situation is serious enough.

The Grants, the other associates of the Crawfords, are rather on the edges of Mansfield society, minor and amiable; they are the reason the Crawfords come to Mansfield and they exemplify another kind of marriage – 'Dr Grant does shew a thorough confidence in my sister . . . which makes one feel there *is* attachment' (361) – and Dr Grant is the source of some Mr-Collins-like comedy; Mrs Grant like Tom is a relief from the tangled emotions of the young people, a useful confidante to the Crawfords. She is easy and a little vulgar herself –

> She had not waited her arrival to look out for a suitable match for her; . . . and being a warm-hearted, unreserved woman, Mary had not been three hours in the house before she told her what she had planned. (42)

– so her earnest objections to Crawford's behaviour to Maria and Julia show how much worse he must be:

> 'If he means nothing, we will send him off, though he is Henry, for a time.' (162)

Mary and Henry Crawford are two of the most important characters of all, and all readers feel their charm. They and the Grants contrast with the Bertram family to show the kind of power they have over the Bertrams. There is real family feeling and affection between Mary and Henry and their half-sister, and there are many pleasant scenes between them; no such scenes are imaginable between Maria and Julia and Tom or Edmund, even if the situation allowed them. Maria's and Julia's behaviour is therefore more furtive and less apparently attractive than Henry's flirting, even though they are driven by feeling and he only by vanity. Both he and his sister have an energy and vivacity of expression which is superficially charming, as it should be if persons with the social polish of the Miss Bertrams and the discrimination of Edmund are to be taken in by them. They are introduced attractively because they bring out agreeable feelings in others. But they are introduced in the very contexts that will condemn them: Mary is seen with the two brothers, and Henry with the sisters. Jane Austen herself interposes so that there shall be no mistake:

> He did not want them to die of love; but with sense and temper which ought to have made him judge and feel better, he allowed himself great latitude on such points. (45)

Henry is entertaining but reprehensible when teasing Mrs Grant – 'I like Julia best' (45) – and so is Mary when thinking about the brothers:

> She had felt an early presentiment that she *should* like the eldest best. She knew it was her way. (47)

They often appear together, especially at first, which emphasizes their parallel functions.

Henry's role falls into two parts: the first is his flirtation with Maria and Julia, which continues – with Maria at least – until Sir Thomas comes home; the second is his flirtation with Fanny and the courtship which grows out of it. Thus Crawford seems at first to be a character very like Willoughby or Wickham, whose conduct is the result of vanity, though his motives are always dealt with much more thoroughly than theirs from the start; but he is a much more developed character than either of them: at Sotherton his exchanges with Maria show a subtle wit that neither of the other seducers has:

> 'I could not have hoped to entertain *you* with Irish anecdotes during a ten miles' drive.'
> 'Naturally, I believe, I am as lively as Julia, but I have more to think of now.'
> 'You have undoubtedly – and there are situations in which very high spirits would denote insensibility. Your prospects, however, are too fair to justify want of spirits. You have a very smiling scene before you.' (99)

This neatly turns affront into compliment, and brings on a consciously ambiguous conversation, in which he never commits himself to any indiscretion, again very much unlike Willoughby or Wickham, but looking forward to the equally sophisticated (though less detailed) Mr Elliot.

Crawford leaves Mansfield as socially unblemished as he came, able to return and pay court to Fanny, which shows that he is not merely an instrument of the plot like the other seducers, but an embodiment of the theme of the influence of upbringing and environment. The sections devoted to Sotherton and the play both do more than just interpret character; the first symbolizes what will follow, and the second shows the sisters as eager to act with Crawford, not as the lovers Amelia and Anhalt but as the mother Agatha and her illegitimate son Frederick, so that an abnormal situation in the play points to their improper feelings. This shows much greater technical assurance; the violent passions which provoke disaster – here as in *Sense and Sensibility* and *Pride and Prejudice* – are much more immediately and vividly rendered than was the growth of Marianne's passion for Willoughby, while Lydia's for Wickham was always out of sight. In those we can never guess (at the time) the man's motives, but Crawford's are as important and intelligible as the women's. This Crawford of the first part – not analysed much by the author, revealed through what he says and does and by what the observant Fanny thinks – can enlarge in the latter part without changing at all, and without any honest change of opinion about him being possible in the reader. We may find him more absorbing, but we cannot cease to disapprove of him; it is much more improper to undertake to make Fanny in love with him than to encourage the Miss Bertrams in an interest they already feel. Jane Austen condemns him inescapably, in his own words:

> 'My plan is to make Fanny Price in love with me . . . I cannot be satisfied without Fanny Price, without making a small hole in Fanny Price's heart.' (229)

This comes immediately after discussing Edmund's ordination, and makes the reference to 'the bread of idleness' (229: from Proverbs xxxi. 27) a bitter condemnation. On such a basis his kindnesses to William, lending him a hunter and arranging the lieutenancy, are plainly self-seeking, and his falling in love with Fanny is no extenuation. Even his expressions of feeling remind us of his vanity and what it has done:

> 'What are you waiting for?'
> 'For – for very little more than opportunity. Mary, she is not like her cousins; but I think I shall not ask in vain.' (293)

There are no artistic grounds – of construction or treatment – for thinking he may marry Fanny; Jane Austen has made it impossible. Having done so she can allow him considerable psychological accuracy, and can even risk facing the probability – new to her work – that in reality, such a woman as Fanny might marry such a man as him.

> Would he have persevered, and uprightly, Fanny must have been his reward – and a reward very voluntarily bestowed – within a reasonable period from Edmund's marrying Mary. (467)

As he is more subtle and in many ways so much more estimable than any of the other villains, his punishment is greater in proportion to his capacity for feeling it:

> . . . we may fairly consider a man of sense like Henry Crawford, to be providing for himself no small portion of vexation and regret – vexation that must rise sometimes to self-reproach, and regret to wretchedness – in having so requited hospitality, so injured family

peace, so forfeited his best, most estimable and endeared acquaintance, and so lost the woman whom he had rationally, as well as passionately loved. (468-9)

The conclusion is harsh; and *Mansfield Park* is a harsher novel than the others, because it considers deeper questions than any of the others.

The part Henry plays for Fanny, Mary plays for Edmund, and she is treated very much the same. There is the same very subtle mixture of limited attractiveness and undeviating moral disapproval, and a degree of psychological interpretation not attempted before in a secondary character. Her speech is lively and arch and is itself a comment:

> 'Cannot you imagine with what unwilling feelings the former belles of the house of Rushworth did many a time repair to this chapel? The young Mrs Eleanors and Mrs Bridgets - starched up into seeming piety, but with heads full of something very different - especially if the poor chaplain were not worth looking at - and, in those days, I fancy parsons were very inferior even to what they are now.' (87)

This is cleverly said - she catches an antique air with the choice of names and the phrase 'did many a time repair' - but the idea behind it is commonplace and cynical. Although she is intelligent, Mary is wilfully perverse in a way Elizabeth Bennet never is in the face of inescapable truth, a significant example being the way she argues with Edmund about the length of the wilderness at Sotherton:

> 'I am sure it is a very long wood; and that we have been winding in and out ever since we came into it; and therefore when I say that we have walked a mile in it, I must speak within compass.'
> 'We have been exactly a quarter of an hour here,' said Edmund, taking out his watch. 'Do you think we are walking four miles an hour?'
> 'Oh! do not attack me with your watch. A watch is always too fast or too slow. I cannot be dictated to by a watch.' (95)

This foreshadows the way she will later refuse to come to terms with Edmund's being ordained. Mary is, in fact, easier to judge than Henry, because his speech is more correct than hers; though her faults are more elaborate, she condemns herself with everything she says. Her language is often such as Jane Austen has only used for really vulgar persons. 'A horrible flirt', 'very detestable', the idea of 'the address of a Frenchwoman' (42–43), and her foolish puns such as the notable ones on 'Rears and Vices' (60), though they would hardly be striking in a less precise writer, in Jane Austen recall Isabella Thorpe rather than Elizabeth Bennet, and anticipate Mrs Elton rather than Emma.

Mary's good qualities can never alter the author's or reader's estimate of her, but they make her a lively and often agreeable element in the story: her sentiments are open and frank, and make an agreeable change from the restraint of Fanny and the hypocrisy of Mansfield as a whole. She makes Fanny a more interesting character: the friendship which develops between them throws more light on Fanny's character by providing different situations to see her in; it also lets us see in detail the progress of the affair between Mary and Edmund by making Fanny, ironically, the confidante of both. Mary's chief function is in relation to Edmund, of course, and her frivolity shows up his virtue, her false estimates of his conduct making it clear that, though rigid and humourless, he is not priggish. Jane Austen displays their mutual affection in the very terms which make their marriage artistically impossible:

'My sister and Mr Bertram – I am so glad your eldest cousin is gone that he *may* be Mr Bertram again. There is something in the sound of Mr *Edmund* Bertram so formal, so pitiful, so younger-brother-like, that I detest it.' (211)

Her frivolity from this point onwards extends to her conduct; before this it was confined to her opinions. During Henry's courtship of Fanny, which follows, Mary always makes it clear that Jane Austen will never have her marry Edmund: she treats Fanny casually (cheating her about the necklace which is really a present by proxy from Henry), while we constantly hear Edmund's praise of her, most of which can be seen to be untrue and to point in another direction: 'I know her disposition to be as sweet and faultless as your own' (269) shows that Edmund's

unconscious standard of perfection is Fanny herself. Mary's reaction to the elopement – though it shocks Edmund – is in keeping
with what has gone before: 'it was the detection, not the offence
which she reprobated' (455). But Jane Austen's estimate of how a
marriage between Mary and Edmund would have turned out is
in keeping, too:

> Impartiality would not have denied to Miss Crawford's nature, that
> participation of the general nature of women, which would lead
> her to adopt the opinions of the man she loved and respected, as
> her own. (367)

A good deal about Edmund Bertram has been said in discussion
of Fanny and Mary, for it is one of his deficiencies that he, like
Edward Ferrars, appears more through what effect he has on the
heroine than through what he is in himself. He is not the hero in
the sense that the other novels have a hero (just as Fanny is not the
heroine), but is a part of the pattern formed by Fanny, Mary and
himself, and it is always difficult for a novelist to portray the
somewhat undignified position of a man between two women
who are both in love with him. Like Fanny he is almost without
humour either in himself or in what Jane Austen does with him.
Like the other characters, he appears in most detail in the latter
part of the book, chiefly through confiding to Fanny his fluctuat-
ing feelings for Mary. Though his personality is a quiet one, his
part in the novel is important. He assists Jane Austen by being a
man of sound sense expressed at the right times:

> Miss Crawford must not misunderstand me, or suppose I mean to
> call [the clergy] the arbiters of good breeding, the regulators of
> refinement and courtesy, the masters of the ceremonies of life. The
> *manners* I speak of, might rather be called *conduct*, perhaps, the
> result of good principles; the effect, in short, of those doctrines
> which it is their duty to teach and recommend.' (93)

This immediately shows up Mary, who ignores this serious and
proper idea, and tries to persuade him to take up the law. At a
longer view the speech emphasizes Jane Austen's concern for the
relationship between social manners and private morals, here as in
all her novels. His part links him with Fanny, for like hers his

judgement – except in the play – is never contradicted by his conduct; therefore he is unlike his father, who unconsciously acts quite against what he knows to be right. Edmund persists in taking orders despite Mary, and even his agreeing to act is not done to please her (as she thinks) but to prevent worse:

> 'When I have put them in good humour by this concession, I am not without hopes of persuading them to confine the representation within a much smaller circle than they are now in the high road for.' (155)

He also gives what reasons there are for thinking play-acting wrong. He and Fanny together generally direct the reader's opinion, a conjunction necessary because on several points one of them errs, he because he is deluded and she because she is immature: when Fanny fears she may have to go and live with Mrs Norris he gives a proper idea of the aunt and not the over-terrible one that Fanny has;[1] conversely we see where he overpraises Mary, when Fanny is more cautious.

Although Edmund and Fanny eventually marry, and the novel therefore has a superficially conventional shape, the story is not about this in the way the other novels are about the events leading to the heroine's marriage. The courtship indeed never happens in the novels at all, but only in a brief summary on the last page but one of the last of three volumes. The story could more fairly be said to be about a young man's escape from marriage with an unsuitable woman, and his cousin's from an unsuitable man. The handling of the story therefore shows considerable differences from the other novels, whether the author is concerned with characters, with incident or with her own narrative.

When characters are introduced they come in by degrees, and in relation to every other important character, not merely to the heroine (as is generally the case even – on the surface – in *Emma*);

---

[1] 'Mrs Norris is much better fitted than my mother for having the charge of you now. She is of a temper to do a great deal for any body she really interests herself about.' (27)
She does indeed do a great deal for Maria, and the irony that what she does is mostly wrong does not invalidate what Edmund says.

they show that their relevance is to the whole of the society they are part of. When Maria and Julia first appear their speeches are not even distinguished from each other:

> They thought her prodigiously stupid, and for the first two or three weeks were continually bringing some fresh report of it into the drawing-room. 'Dear Mamma, only think, my cousin cannot put the map of Europe together – or my cousin cannot tell the principal rivers in Russia – or she never heard of Asia Minor – or she does not know the difference between water-colours and crayons! – How strange! – Did you ever hear any thing so stupid?' (18)

They show not much learning (and that pointless), and only social accomplishments – 'she does not want to learn either music or drawing' (19) – and they show how, as outspoken children, they think of Fanny and how, as restrained adults, they will still think of her; Mrs Norris's interruptions bring in the novel's moral basis –

> 'If you are ever so forward and clever yourselves, you should always be modest; for, much as you know already, there is a great deal more for you to learn.' (19)

– and show how bad her own moral influence is: 'I know there is, till I am seventeen' is neither a clever nor a modest reply. Lady Bertram's comments show her own limited sense:

> '. . . except her being so dull, she must add, she saw no harm in the poor little thing – and always found her very handy and quick in carrying messages, and fetching what she wanted.' (20)

This comment shows that she always sees facts,[1] that she is kind to Fanny, that she is an inadequate parent (parental control being another theme of the novel), and that she has a welcome lack of respect for Mrs Norris. These characters are introduced gradually, with help from the author about their natures, because they need to be seen correctly whatever their context. Mrs Norris, for instance, meddles with Sir Thomas, with the play and the Craw-

---

[1] Like Miss Bates, another valuable and stupid woman, Lady Bertram could say 'what is before me, I see'.

fords, with the Rushworths, and would like to meddle with Fanny's refusal of Crawford. This is as though Mrs Bennet were to go to Rosings and to Pemberley: that would destroy the shape of *Pride and Prejudice*, but Mrs Norris is essential to all these parts of *Mansfield Park*.

The Portsmouth episode is Jane Austen's first attempt at a very late introduction of new characters, comparable to the theatrical hazard of a new character in the third act. In *Sense and Sensibility* the only late character was Mrs Ferrars; *Pride and Prejudice* has only Miss Darcy; Portsmouth here includes a whole group of new personalities, and looks forward to *Persuasion*, with the Harvilles and Captain Benwick, who appear for the first time at Lyme. The Portsmouth episode is entirely successful, not only because she is perfectly at home with new material which is much lower in the social scale than any she has used before, but because it is an essential part of the whole novel. It allows the climax to happen and to be retailed to Fanny and to the reader, in the right order; it allows Mary to give herself away completely in her letters to Fanny, for 'if [Tom] is to die, there will be *two* poor young men less in the world' (434) is a very tasteless and unfeeling pun; it allows Fanny then to come back to Mansfield and be valued as she ought; and most important of all, it makes the reader and Fanny see how important and valuable the standards embodied in Mansfield really are:

> If tenderness could be ever supposed wanting, good sense and good breeding supplied its place. . . . Fanny was tempted to apply to them Dr Johnson's celebrated judgment as to matrimony and celibacy, and say, that though Mansfield Park might have some pains, Portsmouth could have no pleasures. (392)

In the first part of the novel Jane Austen's handling of a large number of almost equally important characters and pieces of plot is something quite new and excellent, and more different from her customary method than the later stages of the story are, where the situations between Henry and Fanny, and Mary and Edmund, though their tone is new, and though they are more serious and analytical than what precedes them, still use methods she has used often before. The excursion to Sotherton and the episode dealing with the play are technical *tours de force*.

The Sotherton visit brings together all the characters and keeps them all before the reader's eyes (with the trifling exceptions of Lady Bertram and Sir Thomas), and this one excellently planned incident shows them at a social gathering, superficially in harmony and apparently enjoying themselves. What they do and say shows how much they are really at odds, and how far from happy they really are. The scene opens, of course, with Fanny, who is a constant point of reference, and we see the scenes she sees, though what she sees is not primarily relevant to her in the way what Emma sees is relevant. Fanny is a convenient moral observer, who herself does very little. The journey to Sotherton sets out the chief oppositions: Maria's and Julia's over Henry, and Mary's and Fanny's over Edmund:

> Happy Julia! Unhappy Maria! The former was on the barouche-box in a moment, the latter took her seat within, in gloom and mortification. (80)

> [Mary] had none of Fanny's delicacy of taste, of mind, of feeling; she saw nature, inanimate nature, with little observation; . . . In looking back after Edmund, however, when there was any stretch of road behind them, or when he gained on them in ascending a considerable hill, they were united, and a 'there he is' broke at the same moment from them both, more than once. (81)

Maria's proprietary pleasure in Sotherton when they arrive sets forth the struggle between her feeling for Henry and her worldly ambitions: Sotherton – a fine place – stands for the latter much more effectively than the foolish Mr Rushworth himself can ever do:

> She could not carelessly observe that 'she believed it was now all Mr Rushworth's property on each side of the road,' without elation of heart; and it was a pleasure to increase with their approach to the capital freehold mansion, and ancient manorial residence of the family, with all its rights of Court-Leet and Court-Baron. (81–82)

Such terms indicate ironically the way Maria thinks of it, and show that whatever Sotherton stands for, it does not stand for its owner (as Pemberley very clearly does stand for Mr Darcy) at all. The tour of the house concentrates on the chapel, which causes alterations in the relations between both groups of characters. Mary's views on religion and the clergy express themselves quite spontaneously, and they can be equally naturally followed by her finding out that Edmund is to take orders, and by her significant reaction:

> 'If I had known this before, I would have spoken of the cloth with more respect.' (89)

That is, she would have changed what she said, but has no idea that her sentiments remain frivolous and vulgar. While this is going on Julia teases Maria and Mr Rushworth for being so appropriately placed near the altar: this is because she hopes to drive Henry away from Maria, but it brings home to the reader how near and inevitable the marriage is, and it is the beginning of the ambiguous exchanges between Maria and Henry:

> 'I do not like to see Miss Bertram so near the altar.'
> Starting, the lady instinctively moved a step or two, but recovering herself in a moment, affected to laugh, and asked him, in a tone not much louder, 'if he would give her away?'
> 'I am afraid I should do it very awkwardly,' was his reply, with a look of meaning. (88)

Once they get into the garden the party splits up more and more, and gets more and more unhappy; the wilfulness of the young people is brought out when they ignore Mrs Rushworth their hostess, and Mrs Norris their chaperon, to get outdoors. The rest of the disparate events all take place in the wilderness – which is itself significant – and have Fanny as a point of moral reference. She has little to do, but it has been pleasant to see her enthusiasm for the avenue and for her romantic idea of the chapel (where, according to her reading of Scott, a Scottish monarch ought to sleep below), and so by contrast we appreciate her anxiety. The narrative returns to Mary and Edmund, to the question of ordination, and to the moral questions which underlie the whole novel:

'It will, I believe, be every where found, that as the clergy are, or are not what they ought to be, so are the rest of the nation.' (93)

Mary is unalterably frivolous – 'You really are fit for something better. Come, do change your mind. It is not too late. Go into the law' (93) – and the exact quality of Edmund's affection for her is shown when his pleasure at her taking his arm is expressed between this speech of hers and his refusal to alter fact for her pleasure: he knows how far they have walked in the shrubbery, and she cannot alter him; it is a trivial argument, but it is just as significant as the one on ordination. This scene makes it clear that Edmund cannot satisfactorily marry Mary without some change in Mary's character or in Jane Austen's own plans for the story, both of which would make pointless all she has done with both Edmund and Mary so far.

The next chapter deals with Henry and Maria, Julia, and Mr Rushworth. He, Henry, and Maria meet Fanny, Mr Rushworth is sent back to the house for the key into the park, and Maria and Henry climb across the ha-ha while he is gone. As I have already explained, the ambiguous talk of the two characters makes this refer to Maria's engagement, and the author makes it also foreshadow Maria's elopement, which is rightly the more accurate parallel of the two. Fanny's comments reinforce the point:

> Fanny, *feeling all this to be wrong*, could not help making an effort to prevent it. 'You will hurt yourself, Miss Bertram,' she cried, 'you will certainly hurt yourself against those spikes – you will tear your gown – you will be in danger of slipping into the ha-ha. You had better not go.' (99–100: my italics)

Fanny, though naturally nervous, is clearly not thinking much of the possible discomfort of falling into a ditch, and her remarks, offering Maria an excuse to change her mind, are not at all out of proportion to the rudeness Maria is offering her fiancé, or to what significance the event has for author and reader. Julia comes next, and her words – 'I am not obliged to punish myself for [Maria's] sins' (101) – show that her fate is bound up with Maria's not only by their rivalry for Henry, but because they are the same kind of personality. Though Fanny dreads Mr Rushworth's arrival, he is a relief for the reader, but even his humour is sharply relevant:

'Nobody can call such an under-sized man handsome. He is not five foot nine . . . In my opinion, these Crawfords are no addition at all. We did very well without them.' (102)

That reminds Fanny of the other Crawford, Mary, and of Edmund – who are not in Rushworth's mind, of course – so that what Rushworth says is as important to the plot as what Edmund has said about the clergy is important to the theme. The journey home is a relaxation, after Fanny's final disappointment of missing seeing the avenue; Mrs Norris's characteristic chatter brings her back into the general design and reminds the reader of the unfortunate influence she has had on Maria and Julia.

Jane Austen seems to have decided on the method she uses in this episode – a method not altogether characteristic – for several good reasons. A close examination of Henry, Maria and Julia to which this is equivalent would unbalance the story, and make Fanny even less of a heroine than she is; it would make an equally close examination – running concurrently – of Edmund and Mary impossibly cumbrous; and it would demand a style of writing which was not comic or dramatic, and quite alien to Jane Austen, a style which might well have come too close to the play *Lovers' Vows* for that play to make the effect that its mere mention does in the novel as it is now.

In the later sections after Sir Thomas's return, character separates itself from the incidents it should dictate. Even at the end of *Pride and Prejudice*, where incidents do not precisely reveal what Elizabeth and Darcy feel, the things that happen are the basis for Elizabeth's deductions about herself and Darcy. This is not true of *Mansfield Park*. Fanny is obliged to maintain opinions of Henry Crawford that she has formed long before, from how he treated Maria, and shows no sign of those she might form from the way he behaves to her, or from his obtaining a lieutenancy for William and other general kindnesses; she is given no time to react to this before she receives his proposal of marriage. We do not see enough of Edmund and Mary, either, to form an opinion of the situation between them; his confessions to Fanny show his dilemma very well, but they give no idea of what his future conduct will be, and we are not allowed to accept Fanny's deductions: 'He had said enough to shake the experience of eighteen' (270) indicates clearly that Jane Austen and her reader have more experience than this.

The great events of the second part are not vivid or significant: Fanny's coming-out ball is told in a single chapter (the visit to Sotherton took two) with scarcely any conversation – a few words from Sir Thomas and William only – and very little incident: when Fanny dances with Edmund they do not talk, and we are not permitted to hear what Mary said to him earlier:

> The evening had afforded Edmund little pleasure. Miss Crawford had been in gay spirits when they first danced together, but it was not her gaiety that could do him good; it rather sank than raised his comfort; and afterwards – for he found himself still impelled to seek her again, she had absolutely pained him by her manner of speaking of the profession to which he was now on the point of belonging. (279)

The rest of the chapter tells how Fanny worries over Henry's attentions, but even so we see and hear none of them. When Fanny goes to Portsmouth the action all takes place behind the reader's back as well as behind Fanny's, and we find everything out by letter. This is unavoidable, as Jane Austen clearly cannot reintroduce Maria at this point, and the method has some virtues; it gives great emotional and psychological accuracy, and a good deal of suspense. But *Mansfield Park* suffers from great length and a danger[1] that character may become almost dissociated from its surroundings, so that one of Jane Austen's greatest skills, to show the exact relation between material circumstances and emotional states, is suppressed.

Although speech is used less in the latter part of this novel, Jane Austen's rendering of different styles of speech is markedly more assured. Mary's vulgarities have already been pointed out as both

[1] As Henry James's novels do, who himself always prefers psychological accuracy to a dramatic effect, and will interrupt what could be quite lively conversations with paragraphs of analysis of thoughts.

subtle and precise. The Bertram family can have no class-distinctions within it, yet the speech of its different members is quite individual. Edmund speaks the respectable eighteenth-century English natural and customary to Jane Austen's men; so does Sir Thomas, yet he is quite distinct, without being at all mannered like Mr Collins, or witty and eccentric like Mr Bennet.

Although *Mansfield Park* apparently covers a much longer space of time than Jane Austen usually employs, the real events of the story – apart from the introducing of Fanny as a little girl – take place in just over a year, the year in which Fanny becomes nineteen. The childhood chapters are important and memorable because the power of upbringing and environment is an important theme, and the reader must find out about the adolescent years of the girls in particular. Jane Austen wisely makes this adolescent period very short in the telling – only three chapters – because the distresses of childhood in literature are always more intense than those of maturity;[1] Fanny's unhappiness as a child, short as it is, colours one's ideas of Mansfield Park almost too much. I have already mentioned that Mrs Norris appears dreadful even though Maria and Julia and Lady Bertram ignore her; Sir Thomas also seems more frigid than he should – even than Jane Austen describes him – because Fanny cannot communicate with him. Mansfield begins to be seen as it actually is when Fanny thinks she will have to leave it and live with Mrs Norris – in Chapter III – which is a situation a great deal worse than her present one. The Portsmouth household shows the virtues of Mansfield by the contrast it provides, and shows the different and more serious ills of a different kind of upbringing, which would have been Fanny's if she had stayed with her family. Susan, though a distinct personality, shows the best that Fanny might then have been, but her difficulties cannot affect us as Fanny's have done, because Jane Austen keeps herself and the reader at a distance from them, and

[1] Jane Eyre's misery as a nine-year-old girl at Gateshead is just as painful as her misery after leaving Mr Rochester, even though in the latter case she is not only miserable but likely to starve; one feels more strongly the distresses of David Copperfield the boy than those of David Copperfield the man, and one recalls painfully the very secondary plight of Osmond's daughter in *The Portrait of a Lady*, and of Becky Sharp's son Rawdon in *Vanity Fair*.

in any case a character appearing so near the end of a book is not likely to absorb one's attention. Portsmouth is deliberately compared with Mansfield through the Ward sisters:

> Of her two sisters, Mrs Price very much more resembled Lady Bertram than Mrs Norris. She was a manager by necessity, without any of Mrs Norris's inclination for it, or any of her activity. Her disposition was naturally easy and indolent, like Lady Bertram's. (390)

Lady Bertram, the middle sister, occupies a position between Mrs Price and Mrs Norris, just as Mansfield is the laudable medium between the cold-hearted overorganized life of Mrs Norris and the impulsive slovenly one of Mrs Price.

Mansfield is the country setting all Jane Austen's stories have; Portsmouth is a new thing for her to attempt. She has not before shown how any of the permanent residents of a city might live, for the Bath of *Northanger Abbey* is very much an enthusiastic visitor's view, with none of the details of crowd, noise, and dirt, that Anne Elliot notices. Even though the Prices' way of life is down-at-heel, slovenly and deplorable, it is not below Jane Austen's usual social level: they have two servants and room to sleep five children, so are presumably quite as well off financially as Mrs Dashwood, who has the same servants and less expenses. The noise, dirt and discomfort result entirely from Mr and Mrs Price's mismanagement of the income they have. The effect recalls the experiment with a lower-class family in the fragment of *The Watsons*: what would seemingly not make a full-length novel can make a very fine episode in *Mansfield Park*. Portsmouth is handled with as much authority as her customary milieu and by the same methods: brief but adequate details of topography – the dockyards and the ramparts – introduced only where they are relevant to what is going on or to the people involved (such as William's sudden embarkation and Mr Price's exclusively nautical interests), with a few significant details of the weather:

> The sun's rays falling strongly into the parlour, instead of cheering, made her still more melancholy; for sun-shine appeared to her a totally different thing in a town and in the country. Here, its power

was only a glare, a stifling, sickly glare, serving but to bring forward stains and dirt that might otherwise have slept. (439)[1]

The skill she shows here points towards the Bath section of *Persuasion*, which affects Anne in a similar (though less alarming) way to that in which Portsmouth affects Fanny. Portsmouth seems all the worse because Mansfield is a grander place than Jane Austen has been accustomed to use. Sir Thomas, a wealthy baronet and a Member of Parliament, is nearer to Mr Darcy than to Mr Bennet, and plainly very superior to Mr John Dashwood or Sir John Middleton (who is only a knight). This is the first use of the grand and the familiar at once (Mr Darcy is always rather remote), and so points forward to Mr Knightley and also to the very confident handling of Sir Walter Elliot, who, as a baronet with the consequent social obligations upon him, is firmly condemned for being not only foolish but vain.

Mansfield Park, with all its excellences, paradoxically gives the impression both of being very long (though it is not so long as *Emma*) for what it has to do, and also of having almost too much material in it for a single novel (the relations between Edmund and Mary can hardly be seen as clearly as they need); but its most serious fault lies in the feeling of moral insecurity that results when the play-acting is so heavily condemned on what cannot but seem inadequate grounds.

Yet every reader must be impressed with *Mansfield Park*. Its pattern is less mechanical even than that of *Pride and Prejudice*, a pattern of temperaments, emotions, and moral values; Jane

[1] The passage recalls Crabbe, much read and admired by Jane Austen, who has the same use of a disagreeable sunshine.

That window view! – oil'd paper and old glass
Stain the strong rays, which, though impeded, pass
And give a dusty warmth to that huge room,
The conquer'd sunshine's melancholy gloom;
When all those western rays, without so bright,
Within become a ghastly glimmering light,
As pale and faint upon the floor they fall,
Or feebly gleam on the opposing wall:
That floor, once oak, now pieced with fir unplaned
Or where not pieced, in places bored and stain'd.
    (*The Borough*, Letter XVIII)

Austen controls it by her well-tried method of conversation and small precisely noted incident. The heroine is less in control; the latter part of the novel, from Henry's courtship of Fanny, is worked out through the separate characters, and each – in conjunction with Fanny – controls the narrative shape of the sections in which he or she is predominant. Fanny herself is the focus of the Portsmouth scenes, of course, and although the material is different from what Jane Austen usually uses, she handles it in her customary way, so that impressive though it is, it is less interesting from the point of view of organization than the earlier parts. These later sections, though fine, and far more subtle than anything in the preceding novels, seem less satisfactory than one comes to expect of this novel; *Mansfield Park* resembles *Persuasion* in its setting and in its serious tone, but, for its organization of characters, of many styles of speech, of significant words and actions, and of what might be called sub-plots, can only be compared with *Emma*, because in some ways it seems to be on the point of excelling even that perfect work.

5 · Emma

Emma is Jane Austen's best and most misunderstood work. In *Mansfield Park* readers feel difficulties and attempt to explain them; in *Emma* the workmanship is so fine that it conceals itself, and readers find difficulties and imperfections where none exist except what their own preconceptions create. Even though Jane Austen's own forebodings about this novel have proved surprisingly true –

> I am very strongly haunted with the idea that to those readers who have preferred *Pride and Prejudice* it will appear inferior in wit, and to those who have preferred *Mansfield Park* very inferior in good sense.[1]

– nevertheless *Emma* is generally admitted, even by those who do prefer the other two works, to be her finest novel, and as nearly perfect, of its kind, as any work of art can be. She has withdrawn from the larger scene and sensational events of *Mansfield Park*, and in this story of a single year in a Surrey village, a year in which nothing happens so unusual even as an elopement – birth, marriage, and an encounter with gipsies being the most striking events – Jane Austen exhibits at their finest her unsurpassed powers of creating and interpreting human character and motive, and of presenting a series of events which give the impression of real life at the same time as they form a coherent and tenable moral pattern. *Emma* is obviously like *Pride and Prejudice* because it is about the heroine's delusions and her gradual enlightenment, but it shows clearly the lessons learned in the writing of *Mansfield Park* in being, not more assured than *Pride and Prejudice*, but technically a great deal more elaborate. Jane Austen is now capable of handling more closely observed characters, and a much more intricate plot, without the help of any sensational events to reveal the

[1] Letter to James Stanier Clarke, 11 December 1815, *Letters*, p. 443.

former or propel the latter. To present her story she returns to the method, practised in *Sense and Sensibility* and mastered in *Pride and Prejudice* (*Mansfield Park* having taught her the possibilities and deficiencies of another), of letting the heroine herself present as much of the action as possible. Emma is like Elizabeth in being deluded, but instead of one overwhelming delusion she has several allied ones, springing from 'a disposition to think a little too well of herself'; she is a social snob,[1] oversure of her own judgement, and so has a propensity for match-making; and Jane Austen therefore, once she has made these deficiencies clear, can use Emma's judgement, which on other matters is right and rational, anywhere she chooses instead of expressing her own. Jane Austen appears much less in person as narrator because here we need to know scarcely anything that Emma cannot tell us, consciously or unwittingly; the unity of the plot and character is therefore much closer than ever before. Even in *Pride and Prejudice*, Jane Austen had to preserve a balance between two almost equally active characters, Elizabeth and Darcy, which gave her things she must say in her own voice because the reader needed to know facts about Darcy that Elizabeth was in no position to see or to understand. But in *Emma* we see (with very few exceptions) only what Emma sees, just as in *Sense and Sensibility* we see only what Elinor sees; but the whole plot, as well as the character of Emma herself, would be spoilt if we saw any more. This represents a great advance on *Sense and Sensibility*, which might be improved if the reader were permitted to see more, and Elinor a good deal less – if it were more like *Mansfield Park*, in fact. Once it is clear what Emma's limitations are, there are scarcely any facts the reader knows which Emma herself does not know in some sort, and the way Emma misinterprets them is the way the reader is enabled to interpret Emma. The whole of the situation between Frank and Jane, which Emma does not even suspect, is seen by means of her, and richly illuminates her; her mistaken conclusions point towards the true ones. When Emma guesses that Mr Dixon sent Jane the

---

[1] There is no doubt about this; the only doubt for modern readers, Americans in particular, is just how much is snobbery, and how much a true conception of worth and order in eighteenth-century society.

piano the reader knows she is wrong, and therefore begins to look for the likely alternative giver (which Colonel Campbell plainly is not) and so is in a position to notice Frank's ambiguous remarks on the music that comes with the piano:

> 'Very thoughtful of Col. Campbell, was not it? – He knew Miss Fairfax could have no music here. I honour that part of the attention particularly; it shews it to have been so thoroughly from the heart. Nothing hastily done; nothing incomplete. True affection only could have prompted it.' (242)

On first reading, of course, the reader does not, and is not intended to, draw the right inferences, but he is supposed to notice the evidence enough to reconsider it with Emma herself, and enough to see its strength when the truth is told. The virtue of this method is that although Emma's interpretation of what she sees of the relationship between Frank and Jane is wildly wrong, all the moral judgements she herself makes, and leads the reader to make, are strikingly right. She thinks, for instance, that Frank is foolish and inconsiderate to Mrs Weston for wasting a day of his stay by going to London for a haircut; although he has really gone to buy Jane the piano, this also is foolish and inconsiderate, and immediately seen to be so when Jane has all the embarrassment of her friends' speculations and of Emma's suspicions of an improper present from Mr Dixon. Even though this suspicion is as far-fetched as it is uncalled-for, the natural reaction even of reasonable persons like Mrs Weston and Mr Knightley is to disbelieve that the present came from Colonel Campbell. Emma's occasional condemnations of Frank throughout their association hold good in the same way as this early one, even when his real motives are at last found out. Emma, though deluded, is therefore never ridiculous, and the irony of the novel is much more subtle and thorough than in any of the other novels, because it is dependent on and coexistent with the heroine herself.

Like *Pride and Prejudice* again, *Emma* is serious in intention but lively and humorous in tone, primarily because it has a lively heroine, who, though not as verbally witty as Elizabeth, has a good deal of humorous appreciation and natural vivacity, and like Elizabeth (and significantly unlike Fanny) has energy and good health. When Jane Austen does appear as narrator she consciously adapts her tone and attitude to harmonize with Emma's. Although she clearly helps the reader to see just where Emma is unreliable, and to judge her accordingly, Jane Austen appears to be Emma's intellectual and social equal and contemporary just as she is Elizabeth Bennet's. There are none of the reservations on Emma that there are on Fanny, where Jane Austen withholds herself from Fanny's quite sound opinions:

> She may be forgiven by older sages, for looking on the chance of Miss Crawford's future improvement as nearly desperate, for thinking that if Edmund's influence in this season of love, had already done so little in clearing her judgment, and regulating her notions, his worth would be finally wasted on her even in years of matrimony. (*Mansfield Park*, p. 367)

Jane Austen and the reader rank with the 'older sages', but Emma, only three years older than Fanny, is treated as an adult like author and reader, in intellect if not in experience. Jane Austen, as narrator and in her accounts of what Emma thinks, both in reported and direct speech, merges easily into Emma herself; the method becomes increasingly flexible as the novel goes on, as the reader becomes increasingly receptive to the method and to Emma's foibles, and when the course of events and not the mere exhibition of Emma becomes the chief interest:

> The house was larger than Hartfield, and totally unlike it, covering a good deal of ground, rambling and irregular, with many comfortable and one or two handsome rooms. – It was just what it ought to be, and it looked what it was – and Emma felt an increasing respect for it, as the residence of a family of such true gentility, untainted in blood and understanding. – Some faults of temper John Knightley had; but Isabella had connected herself unexceptionably. She had given them neither men, nor names, nor places, that could raise a blush. These were pleasant feelings, and she walked about and indulged them till it was necessary to do as the others did, and collect round the strawberry beds. (358)

The precise mixture of proper feeling and of snobbery is beautifully rendered: the house, which is described as Emma sees it, opens up a proper view of its owner's 'true gentility', 'untainted in blood and understanding', all of which the reader knows Jane Austen approves and (if he is reading properly) approves himself; the hint of overemphasis comes in with Isabella – '*she* had given *them* [the Woodhouses and therefore Emma herself] neither men, nor names, nor places, that could raise a blush' (my italics) – and Emma's overcomplacency is confirmed by the verb 'indulged': one 'indulges' in pleasures that savour of luxury and excess rather than of virtue. Yet all this is done without holding up the narrative, or making a heavy point of what is only a reminder, in a scene which is really devoted to the affairs of all the other characters rather than Emma's own.

Jane Austen as narrator therefore makes her appearances as unobtrusive as possible. These appearances are, of course, bound to be more frequent in the opening chapters where characters have to be introduced, and for this purpose she returns to the very simple and inexhaustibly effective method used in *Sense and Sensibility*, introducing characters herself with the few necessary facts, and then permitting them to be revealed and to reveal themselves in action and conversation. Here, even the first introduction is always as nearly as possible from Emma's point of view, so characters appear in relation to her and therefore to the main theme of the novel; this is Mr Woodhouse:

> She dearly loved her father, but he was no companion for her. He could not meet her in conversation, rational or playful.
>
> The evil of the actual disparity in their ages (and Mr Woodhouse had not married early) was much increased by his constitution and habits; for having been a valetudinarian all his life, without activity of mind or body, he was a much older man in ways than in years; and though everywhere beloved for the friendliness of his heart and his amiable temper, his talents could not have recommended him at any time.
>
> Her sister, though comparatively but little removed by matrimony, being settled in London, only sixteen miles off, was much beyond her daily reach; and many a long October and November evening must be struggled through at Hartfield, before Christmas brought the next visit from Isabella and her husband and their little children to fill the house and give her pleasant society again. (7)

The occasions when characters or events are seen by the reader and not by Emma are very rare, and occur only when the reader must be put in possession of ideas which Emma cannot give. The fifth chapter, in which Mr Knightley and Mrs Weston discuss Emma and her new friend Harriet, is the longest. This is more economical than if Jane Austen herself told the reader what to think, as it shows Mr Knightley and Mrs Weston as reliable judges, and shows the relations between the two, as well as those between them and Emma. The other notable occasion is when Mr Knightley suspects an association between Frank and Jane and observes their behaviour while they are playing at anagrams with Emma and Harriet. The reader needs some definite and trustworthy guide here to be able to assess properly all the clues which Emma has seen and consistently misinterpreted, but Jane Austen cannot conveniently perform the office, because Emma, though misguided, must not seem stupid. Mr Knightley is a suitable guide because he has already been proved right in his prophecy that Mr Elton would not marry beneath him, and we need proof that his judgement is more acute than Emma's to make his rebukes to her tolerable. He also needs some emphasis here to counteract his dislike of Frank. It is quite clear that this dislike is jealousy, but it needs to be made clear that his jealousy is not unreasonable and that his dislike is justified. Mr Knightley and Mrs Weston, therefore, as the only people who show us things when Emma is absent, become second in importance only to Emma (which is what Jane Austen intends), because they consciously reinforce or correct her judgement throughout the novel. They are the only two who do so at all importantly, compared with the many who perform the same office for Elizabeth in *Pride and Prejudice*. This is not because there are fewer characters here who could, but because those who might are in no position to do so; Jane and Frank have too much to conceal, and Mr John Knightley does not appear often enough, although he gives one very useful hint that Mr Elton may be paying court to Emma.

There are many more characters in *Emma*, though, who comment validly and unconsciously (and therefore ironically) than there are even in *Pride and Prejudice*; it would be safer to say that there is not one who does not do so, since all the characters are there primarily for their relevance to Emma herself. This is why Jane Austen's greatest minor characters appear in *Emma*; she is one of the few English writers besides Shakespeare who creates bores who are wholly absorbing and amusing in direct proportion to their relevance to the theme of the work as a whole – Mr Woodhouse, Harriet Smith and Miss Bates have the characteristics of the bore in life rather than in literature, the latter being usually based on a catch-phrase or an *idée fixe*;[1] Mr Woodhouse is certainly absorbed by his own health and judges other people by their effect on it, but his expression is infinitely varied; while the essence of Harriet and Miss Bates is that each is a feather to each wind that blows, with no consciously fixed ideas at all. They are all three richly relevant not to the topic of their own choosing but to an aspect of the situation hidden from them, and often from their hearers as well, so that only the writer and the reader understand their relevance. One of many instances is Miss Bates's rambling remarks when Frank Churchill speaks of Mr Perry's setting up a carriage (which Jane has told him in the course of their secret correspondence):

> 'Mrs Perry herself mentioned it to my mother, and the Coles knew of it as well as ourselves – but it was quite a secret, known to nobody else, and only thought of about three days . . . I will not positively answer for my having never dropt a hint, because I know I do sometimes pop out a thing before I am aware . . . I am not like Jane; I wish I were. I will answer for it *she* never betrayed the least thing in the world.' (346)

These all do what in the other novels has been the narrator's job, and achieve the effect Jane Austen was striving for as early as the latter part of *Northanger Abbey*. The technical achievement is,

---

[1] As they are for Dickens, one of the few great writers who dares to create bores. His bores become funny chiefly by repetition, like bores in farce, although they usually have some incidental relevance to matters of importance – Harold Skimpole in *Bleak House*, for example, shows up how easily John Jarndyce can be gulled. But the chances of failure are enormous; it is an enthusiast who does not become tired of Skimpole, Mr Dick or even Mrs Nickleby before their last appearance.

as always, inseparable from the moral one. Satire is almost absent in *Emma*, the element that made it easy to condemn Isabella Thorpe, Miss Steele or Mrs Bennet for being stupid as well as for being wrong. Such easy condemnation is withheld here; we are forced to judge Harriet and Miss Bates, stupid though they both are, in a way both more rational and more responsible. While the methods which present both them and the conclusions we are to draw from them are the same as in the other novels, the application of them is the result of Jane Austen's experience with the serious and dangerous personalities in *Mansfield Park*. In the following example the effect made by Harriet's own utterances is reinforced by Mr Knightley's opinion, and we are then in a position to accept these two statements, which would be almost irreconcilable at the moral level at which *Northanger Abbey* was working:

> 'I should say she was a good-tempered, soft-hearted girl, not likely to be very, very determined against any young man who told her he loved her.' (473)

> 'From all my observations, I am convinced of her being an artless, amiable girl, with very good notions, very seriously good principles, and placing her happiness in the affections and utility of domestic life.' (474)

The only persons we are permitted to deride in the early way are Mrs Elton and (to a lesser degree) Mr Weston. Both are a necessary relief from the strain of following fine points, and an enrichment of them by contrast.

Characters can be seen also in relation to each other. Jane Austen's art has perfected itself to the point where hints at links between characters seem as inexhaustible as they are in life. This is done partly by what Emma observes and partly by the way characters talk to each other; even more than in *Pride and Prejudice*, narrative, delineation of character and characters' opinions and conversation become inseparable:

> 'I am as confident of seeing Frank here before the middle of January, as I am of being here myself: but your good friend there (nodding towards the upper end of the table) has so few vagaries

herself, and has been so little used to them at Hartfield, that she cannot calculate on their effects, as I have been long in the practice of doing.' (120)

Mr Weston, here proposing Frank's visit, shows the relations between himself and his wife, and the close friendship between her and Emma, while at the same time his overconfidence and our well-founded faith in Mrs Weston's judgement foreshadow the visit's postponement.

Characters in general show only that part of them which Emma brings out. This is a limitation Jane Austen overcomes by another of her well-tried devices: the character who never appears in person. There are more of these here than in any other of her novels, and some of them are brilliant: it is difficult for the reader to realize that he has met William Larkins and Mr Perry only through hearsay. These two are useful examples. Mr Knightley is the most convincing of Jane Austen's heroes, because we see his functions as a landowner and administrator unusually clearly; William Larkins is the embodiment of those functions, of the side of Mr Knightley that Emma cannot reveal:

'However, the very same evening William Larkins came over with a large basket of apples, the same sort of apples, a bushel at least, and I was very much obliged, and went down and spoke to William Larkins and said every thing, as you may suppose. William Larkins is such an old acquaintance! I am always glad to see him. But, however, I found afterwards from Patty, that William said it was all the apples of *that* sort his master had; he had brought them all – and now his master had not one left to bake or boil. William did not seem to mind it himself, he was so pleased to think his master had sold so many; for William, you know, thinks more of his master's profit than any thing; but Mrs Hodges, he said, was quite displeased at their being all sent away. She could not bear that her master should not be able to have another apple-tart this spring.' (239)

This is Miss Bates being useful again; William and Mrs Hodges show precisely and economically and very usefully how Mr Knightley lives at Donwell, for in person he is seen only in the very feminine atmosphere of Hartfield. Lord David Cecil's objection that Jane Austen's men have no life away from their womenfolk[1] is not true of Mr Knightley; in fact, the observation that 'he had been walking away from William Larkins the whole morning, to have his thoughts to himself' (449) shows that his masculine world can be too much with him. Mr Perry brings out Mr Woodhouse in the same way; he is the personification of Mr Woodhouse's valetudinarian habits; but not only this: he and Mrs Perry, along with the Coles, represent the level of society into which Emma does not go, so he automatically places Miss Bates, who does associate with them, and also gives a view of Highbury village as a whole. Some others support him in this: the Martins (whose main purpose is to show the social level natural to Harriet), Miss Nash, the parlour-boarder Miss Bickerton, and the whole group of servants who include the Hartfield coachman James and Miss Bates's maid-of-all-work Patty.

The people Jane Austen mentions who live elsewhere than in Highbury have a social use, not a personal one. The Sucklings, for example, are not necessary to bring out Mrs Elton's evident character or personal manners, but they do make her true social standing quite plainly a good deal lower than her social pretensions. The Churchills show that Frank is socially a suitable *parti* for Emma, and that the only objections to him are moral ones; they do little for Frank as a personality, and, of course, their chief use is to the plot, because Mrs Churchill is the reason why he keeps his engagement secret. The Campbells are more important, for the details of their behaviour and family life and mutual affection make Jane seem more attractive than her role at Highbury gives her the chance to be, and show that she is a most suitable wife for Frank, by upbringing if not by fortune, and a not impossible one for Mr Knightley. Between characters who do not appear and those who do come a small but interesting group of children, used, like the Gardiner children in *Pride and Prejudice*, to fill out the representation of family life. Jane Austen wisely avoids much speech or action, but they are occasionally striking:

> . . . Mr John Knightley returning from the daily visit to Donwell, with his two eldest boys, whose healthy, glowing faces shewed all

[1] *Poets and Story-tellers*, p. 104.

the benefit of a country run, and seemed to ensure a quick dispatch
of the roast mutton and rice pudding they were hastening home for.
(109)

Even babies can have their attractions:

> . . . the youngest, a nice little girl about eight months old, who was
> now making her first visit to Hartfield, and very happy to be danced
> about in her aunt's arms. (98)

It is important that Emma, though wrong-headed, is a good aunt
(the older children make a long stay with her), and that John
Knightley, though moody, is a good father; that Mr Knightley
knows what children like – 'their uncle comes in, and tosses them
up to the ceiling in a very frightful way' (81) – while Mr Woodhouse, for all his grandfatherly pride, knows nothing about it:

> 'They are all remarkably clever; and they have so many pretty ways.
> They will come and stand by my chair, and say, "Grandpapa, can
> you give me a bit of string?" and once Henry asked me for a knife,
> but I told him knives were only made for grandpapas.' (80–81)

These groups of characters, of so many different kinds, so geo-
graphically and socially precise, make this account of a small
section of village life both solid and convincing, and emphasize
that the principles underlying the action are universal in application, and just as far-reaching as those of novels with apparently
wider scope.

Both reported and actual characters alike have something in
common besides their relevance to the heroine. In *Emma* there is
not one of the unsatisfactory or comically disproportionate marriages that appear in the other novels. The couples we see here
are happy: the Westons and the John Knightleys, for instance,
and even the Eltons, though they may not suit anyone else, seem
to suit each other perfectly well; those who are merely heard
about are summed up by the invaluable Miss Bates:

> 'It is such a happiness when good people get together – and they
> always do. Now, here will be Mr Elton and Miss Hawkins; and
> there are the Coles, such very good people; and the Perrys – I
> suppose there never was a happier or a better couple than Mr and

Mrs Perry. I say, sir,' turning to Mr Woodhouse, 'I think there are few places with such society as Highbury. I always say, we are quite blessed in our neighbours.' (175)

Even Mr Churchill says at last, with unconscious irony, that he wishes Frank '[may] find as much happiness in the marriage state as he [has] done' (443). This is not, of course, to say that the marriages in *Emma* all represent Jane Austen's ideal. John Knightley's character, for example, has not been improved by marriage to Isabella. Yet *Emma* undoubtedly produces a much more agreeable atmosphere than the only other novel which treats its subject with such seriousness and at such length: in *Mansfield Park* the only satisfactory matches are those of Sir Thomas and Lady Bertram and of the Grants, which are neither of them perfect, while apart from the very unsatisfactory matches of Mary Crawford's friends, neither the Norrises nor the Prices are well-matched, and Maria Bertram's marriage ends in disaster.

The real characters in *Emma* – those seen both in conduct and speech – are all presented much more fully than in any of the other novels; this is the longest of them and has the fewest active characters (except for *Northanger Abbey*), so it is natural that these characters should be seen more closely and presented more realistically. Mrs Elton is, in fact, the only representative of the kind of farcical character who gives some of the most obvious pleasure in the other novels. She is employed like Lady Catherine as a character who excites no sympathy whatever and a good deal of laughter, but she is presented more by the means used for Mrs Norris, who though funny in the same way is by contrast considerably more painful and potent. Like Lady Catherine, she is an important character who appears late – more than half-way through the story – and is immediately used as relief from the subtleties and elaborations of the plot, and from the confusions in the heroine's mind. It is easy to enjoy Mrs Elton's snobbery and vulgarity, and as she does little to forward the action besides getting Jane a post as governess (which Jane does not take), her snobbery and vulgarity constitute her chief use. Jane Austen has made the reader very conscious of the force of snobbery in Emma

herself by the time Mrs Elton appears, so that he quite properly
disapproves it; Mrs Elton shows how Emma's snobbery, though
a fault, contrasts with the depths to which snobbery in the unintelligent can go, and emphasizes that Emma, though a snob, is never
vulgar. Mrs Elton is useful also to fill in the passages of time
between the more important events which take place during
Frank's visits. She is introduced in the way she is to appear, as
such characters always are: if it were not for news of the future
Mrs Elton, there would be only the smallest of breaks (that made
by Harriet's call on the Martins) between Jane's coming and
Frank's, and the two events might be seen as cause and effect (as,
in fact, they are) before Jane Austen thinks desirable. The traits
we hear of are such as to prepare for what Mrs Elton will be, so
the reader has high hopes of humour and none at all of sense:

> The charming Augusta Hawkins, in addition to all the usual
> advantages of perfect beauty and merit, was in possession of an
> independent fortune, of so many thousands as would always be
> called ten; a point of some dignity, as well as some convenience.
> (181)

Her conversation is realistic and closely observed:

> 'Oh! Mr Weston, do not mistake me. Selina is no fine lady, I
> assure you. Do not run away with such an idea.'
> 'Is not she? Then she is no rule for Mrs Churchill, who is as
> thorough a fine lady as any body ever beheld.'
> Mrs Elton began to think she had been wrong in disclaiming so
> warmly. It was by no means her object to have it believed that her
> sister was *not* a fine lady; . . . and she was considering in what way
> she had best retract, when Mr Weston went on. (306–7)

This is not merely a collection of mannerisms like Isabella Thorpe,
whom her person, tastes and speech recall. It recalls rather the way
Mrs Norris appears, in its mixture of speech and unobtrusive
author's comment. Once all Mrs Elton's qualities are made plain
Jane Austen wastes no time in simply displaying them, even where
such a display could fairly be said to be useful. During the strawberry-picking picnic at Donwell, Mrs Elton represents a whole

episode concerning a whole group of people, in a most abbreviated version of herself:

> . . . strawberries, and only strawberries, could now be thought or spoken of. – 'The best fruit in England – every body's favourite – always wholesome. – These the finest beds and finest sorts. – Delightful to gather for one's self – the only way of really enjoying them. – Morning decidedly the best time – never tired – every sort good – hautboy infinitely superior – no comparison – the others hardly eatable – hautboys very scarce – Chili preferred – white wood finest flavour of all – price of strawberries in London – abundance about Bristol – Maple Grove – cultivation – beds when to be renewed – gardeners thinking exactly different – no general rule – gardeners never to be put out of their way – delicious fruit – only too rich to be eaten much of – inferior to cherries – currants more refreshing – only objection to gathering strawberries the stooping – glaring sun – tired to death – could bear it no longer – must go and sit in the shade.'
> Such, for half an hour, was the conversation. (358–9)

Mr Elton is a fit mate for his wife, sharing a number of her traits in a modified form: his courtship of Emma is merely ambition, and as reprehensible as Emma thinks it:

> He wanted to marry well, and having the arrogance to raise his eyes to her, pretended to be in love; . . . He only wanted to aggrandize and enrich himself; and if Miss Woodhouse of Hartfield, the heiress of thirty thousand pounds, were not quite so easily obtained as he had fancied, he would soon try for Miss Somebody else with twenty, or with ten. (135)

– the last being what he gets with Miss Hawkins. As his wife is more exaggerated than himself, he is rightly seen very little after she appears. His real use is in the first quarter of the novel, when Emma is trying to marry him to Harriet. He needs to be a personality easily understood for us to follow Emma's mistake safely here, so that we thoroughly understand the kind of error she is likely to fall into with the much more elaborate characters and intricate situation of Frank and Jane. But Mr Elton is just ingenious enough for Emma's mistake to seem the result, not of stupidity, but of that freedom from personal vanity which Mr Knightley praises. Mr Elton has the other useful purpose of revealing Robert Martin; Elton is constantly before the reader's eyes, and the constant contrasts between the two of them, instituted by Emma and followed up by Harriet, illuminate both gentlemen without Martin's having to appear in person:

> The most satisfactory comparisons were rising in [Harriet's] mind.
>
> 'It is one thing,' said she, presently – her cheeks in a glow – 'to have very good sense in a common way, like every body else, and if there is any thing to say, to sit down and write a letter, and say just what you must, in a short way; and another, to write verses and charades like this.'
>
> Emma could not have desired a more spirited rejection of Mr Martin's prose. (76)

This shows Harriet's, Mr Elton's, and Emma's follies all at once. From the first mention of him it is clear that Mr Elton will not marry Harriet:

> '. . . it would be a shame to have him single any longer – and I thought when he was joining their hands to-day, he looked so very much as if he would like to have the same kind office done for him! I think very well of Mr Elton, and this is the only way I have of doing him a service.'
>
> 'Mr Elton is a very pretty young man to be sure, and a very good young man, and I have a great regard for him. But if you want to shew him any attention, my dear, ask him to come and dine with us some day. That will be a much better thing. I dare say Mr Knightley will be so kind as to meet him.'
>
> 'With a great deal of pleasure, sir, at any time,' said Mr Knightley laughing; 'and I agree with you entirely that it will be a much better thing. Invite him to dinner, Emma, and help him to the best of the fish and the chicken, but leave him to chuse his own wife.' (13–14)

The extent of his silliness is the extent of Emma's delusion, and the reader learns about both at the same time. She is right about him wishing to be married; she merely mistakes his object. His compliments are inept and therefore ambiguous:

> 'I know what your drawings are. How could you suppose me ignorant? Is not this room rich in specimens of your landscapes

and flowers; and has not Mrs Weston some inimitable figure-pieces in her drawing-room, at Randalls?'

Yes, good man! – thought Emma – but what has all that to do with taking likenesses? You know nothing of drawing. Don't pretend to be in raptures about mine. Keep your raptures for Harriet's face. 'Well, if you give me such kind encouragement, Mr Elton, I believe I shall try what I can do. Harriet's features are very delicate, which makes a likeness difficult; and yet there is a peculiarity in the shape of the eye and the lines about the mouth which one ought to catch.'

'Exactly so – the shape of the eye and the lines about the mouth – I have not a doubt of your success. Pray, pray attempt it. As you will do it, it will indeed, to use your own words, be an exquisite possession.' (43–44)

Emma assesses his artistic taste accurately, and after the woolliness of his first speech she may well take his next as signs of more woolliness, although '*the* eye' and '*the* mouth' are significant: a lover would certainly say '*her* eye' and '*her* mouth'. From such moderate beginnings, where his wish to please Emma restrains him, he progresses easily to his silly behaviour at the Westons' Christmas party, and to his ridiculous proposal –

'Charming Miss Woodhouse! allow me to interpret this interesting silence. It confesses that you have long understood me.' (131)

– which in turn, with its romantic clichés, social ambition and unconscious impertinence, forms a perfect transition to his vulgar behaviour with his even more vulgar wife.

Mr Weston is similar to Mrs Elton in function and treatment, though less striking for having characteristics less pronounced; like her he is a relief from the considerations which absorb Emma and the reader when Jane, Frank, Harriet or Mr Knightley are in question. He is necessary to the plot as the husband of Mrs Weston and the father of Frank; these purposes served, he is chiefly a matter for entertainment, but he shows also the precise limits of Emma's snobbery. He appears in the second chapter with details of his origins in trade, before we have a chance to judge Emma for misjudging Robert Martin, who is no lower socially than Mr

Weston was at the same age. It is easy to see that when Emma objects to Robert Martin it is prejudice, for his own behaviour, and Mr Knightley's good opinion of him, show that in education and intelligence he is Mr Weston's equal. Mr Weston is a good foil for Mr Knightley, representing cheerful over-sociability as John Knightley represents over-retirement:

> [Emma] felt, that to be the favourite and intimate of a man who had so many intimates and confidantes, was not the very first distinction in the scale of vanity. She liked his open manners, but a little less of open-heartedness would have made him a higher character. – General benevolence, but not general friendship, made a man what he ought to be. – She could fancy such a man. (320)

This does not point to Mr Knightley in person, because Emma does not yet know her own feeling towards him, but the description fits no one else. Another parallel also is easy to see: that between Mr Weston – the man who called on his wife

> . . . to agree with him, that, with a little contrivance, every body might be lodged, which she hardly knew how to do, from the consciousness of there being but two spare rooms in the house. (126)

– and Frank Churchill, the son who goes to town for a haircut (really for a piano), being inconsiderate to his stepmother in his professed reason and to his fiancée in his real one; and the parallel is valid even though Mr Weston's easy good nature is based on sound principles such as Frank has never shown.

Mr John Knightley is founded on the exaggeration not of a deficiency but of a good quality that takes on the nature of a fault: Mr Weston is too gregarious, John Knightley too retiring. The two men make an excellent background for Mr Knightley, and Mr John Knightley is useful also to display Emma:

> He was not a great favourite with his fair sister-in-law . . . She was quick in feeling the little injuries to Isabella, which Isabella never felt herself. Perhaps she might have passed over more had his manners been flattering to Isabella's sister. (93)

Despite such feelings, she approves of his good qualities:

'. . . if you could compare him with other papas, you would not think him rough. He wishes his boys to be active and hardy; and if they misbehave, can give them a sharp word now and then; but he is an affectionate father – certainly Mr John Knightley is an affectionate father. The children are all fond of him.' (81)

Mr Woodhouse, Harriet, and Miss Bates are all bores, of whom Miss Bates is the most popular, and probably the best-known person in the novel after Emma herself. Besides being the representative of 'the inferior society of Highbury' (23) – from the Perrys down to John ostler – which she refers to constantly in her chatter, Miss Bates is primarily a mine of indispensable information, chiefly about Jane and Frank. In fact, she does not enter the story herself until Jane is about to come to Highbury. As she herself says, 'what is before me, I see' (176), and she sees it all very clearly. In presenting someone who is apparently a sponge for news, Jane Austen in fact gives relevant information in its most relevant order, and begins with such simple points as this:

'Whenever she is with us, Mrs Cole does not know how to shew her kindness enough; and I must say that Jane deserves it as much as anybody can. And so she began inquiring after her directly, saying, "I know you cannot have heard from Jane lately, because it is not her time for writing;" and when I immediately said, "But indeed we have, we had a letter this very morning," I do not know that I ever saw anybody more surprized. "Have you, upon your honour!" said she; "well, that is quite unexpected. Do let me hear what she says." ' (157)

Emma was unwilling to hear one of Jane's letters, and calculated that the chances were against it, so the reader is in a position to guess that Mrs Cole felt the same. Such passages lead to the eventual subtlety of such as this, which follows after the signs of dispute between Frank and Jane at Donwell, and is, in fact, a perfectly accurate account of the circumstances which decide Jane to accept the post as governess which she has been refusing:

'. . . this is such a situation as she cannot feel herself justified in declining. I was so astonished when she first told me what she had been saying to Mrs Elton, and when Mrs Elton at the same moment

came congratulating me upon it! It was before tea – stay – no, it
could not be before tea, because we were just going to cards – and
yet it was before tea, because I remember thinking – Oh! no, now
I recollect, now I have it; something happened before tea, but not
that. Mr Elton was called out of the room before tea, old John
Abdy's son wanted to speak with him . . . about relief from the
parish: he is very well to do himself, you know, being head man at
the Crown, ostler, and every thing of that sort, but still he cannot
keep his father without some help; and so when Mr Elton came back,
he told us what John ostler had been telling him, and then it came
out about the chaise having been sent to Randall's to take Mr Frank
Churchill to Richmond. That was what happened before tea. It
was after tea that Jane spoke to Mrs Elton.' (382–3)

Since Miss Bates rarely understands the significance of what
she observes, it makes it the more probable that Emma should
misinterpret the same things when she only hears them indirectly.
It also makes our enjoyment very great when we hear that even
Miss Bates has been right once, about Emma and Mr Elton:

'A Miss Hawkins. – Well, I had always rather fancied it would be
some young lady hereabouts; not that I ever – Mrs Cole once
whispered to me – but I immediately said, "No, Mr Elton is a most
worthy young man – but" – In short, I do not think I am particularly quick at those sort of discoveries.' (176)

Her random allusions are usually relevant to some later matter,
though they are conspicuously not relevant to the matter in hand.
In her first speech, for instance, Miss Bates mentions her mother's
deafness and her spectacles, and these will later form Frank's
excuse for a few words with Jane while he mends the spectacles,
virtually *tête-à-tête*, Mrs Bates being deprived of both hearing and
sight. Despite her chatter, Miss Bates keeps the story moving
briskly; she covers in her monologues whole episodes of secondary
importance, bringing scenes vividly before the reader without
giving them the undesirable emphasis they would have if presented in direct narrative. The greater part of the ball at the
Crown is shown in this way with a fine effect of bustle and crowd,
giving useful hints about Jane, and relationships Emma has no
interest in. This is a much richer scene than the one at Netherfield

in *Pride and Prejudice*, where we only see selected incidents that Elizabeth sees, and where the interest is held because she can see more than her prejudices permit her to understand. Therefore, Miss Bates in fact condenses a great deal of assorted information into a small space, even while she seems to be characteristically diffuse.

Harriet Smith, though less popular than Miss Bates, is almost as fine, in very much the same way. Like Miss Bates, she is a constant source of information which she does not know she possesses, but instead of this being facts like Miss Bates's, it is judgements, generally on herself and Emma. She resembles Lady Bertram in the way she states obvious truths without being at all aware how devastating they are:

> 'I shall always have a great regard for the Miss Martins, especially Elizabeth, and should be very sorry to give them up, for they are quite as well educated as me.' (31)

This is as effective an assessment of herself as any of Lady Bertram's are of Mrs Norris. Jane Austen introduces her with merely the necessary facts about her birth and origins, and about her very conventional beauty – 'She was short, plump and fair, with a fine bloom, blue eyes, light hair, regular features, and a look of great sweetness' (23) – making it clear that she is a very inadequate substitute for Mrs Weston, and not at all the romantic figure Emma tries to imagine her. As Jane Austen never tells the reader what Harriet really feels, but only what Emma thinks she must feel, Harriet is revealed only from what she actually says, and the hesitations, contradiction and tautology which make her obviously amusing and inferior to Emma are also always enlightening; they reveal exactly the mind that never opposes an argument, but is never really swayed from its own original opinion: it is not at all incredible, though it is a surprise, when she eventually accepts Robert Martin, despite the intervening attractions of Mr Elton and Mr Knightley. The unfinished sentences which reveal her hopelessly muddled thinking are a convenient shorthand which does not muddle the reader in the least; they make a sharp contrast with her devastatingly simple statements of what she considers to be facts, which vary between the unconscious irony of 'Mr Elton, who might marry any body!' (74) (it is soon clear that he cannot marry Emma for one) and the equally unconscious pro-fundity of 'Nobody cares for a letter; the thing is, to be always happy with pleasant companions' (55).

Mr Woodhouse, like Harriet and Miss Bates, is humorous, unintelligent and largely sympathetic, a bore who is not boring, for the same reasons as they are. Like Mr Weston and Mrs Elton, he is used for comic relief and has little to do with advancing the plot, but the reader has important matters kept before him by Mr Woodhouse's trivial, but usually unconsciously ironic, com-ments on them. Both he and his daughter Isabella draw con-clusions too large from events too small:

> 'But you must have found it very damp and dirty. I wish you may not catch cold . . . for we have had a vast deal of rain here. It rained dreadfully hard for half an hour, while we were at break-fast. I wanted them to put off the wedding.' (10)

The process of mind shown in this can be used on more important matters to be ludicrously wrong (as this is) or strikingly right, like this comment on Frank:

> 'That young man (speaking lower) is very thoughtless. Do not tell his father, but that young man is not quite the thing. He has been opening the doors very often this evening, and keeping them open very inconsiderately. He does not think of the draught. I do not mean to set you against him, but indeed he is not quite the thing!' (249)

Such remarks and his steady preoccupation with the weather, food, personal comfort, and the health of everyone he knows, keep the events at a comfortable unromantic level; his rebuke to Jane for getting wet is a healthy antidote to Emma's romantic fancies about her:

> 'I am very sorry to hear, Miss Fairfax, of your being out this morning in the rain. Young ladies should take care of themselves. – Young ladies are delicate plants. They should take care of their health and their complexion. My dear, did you change your stock-ings?' (294)

'Beloved for the friendliness of his heart and his amiable temper', with 'habits of gentle selfishness' (7–8), Mr Woodhouse has little virtue in himself, but is the touchstone by which the moral worth of others may be tried. Frank's thoughtlessness, Mr John Knightley's short temper, Mrs Elton's dreadful archness – 'Here comes this dear old beau of mine' (302) – all show most strongly against him, who is defenceless against them, while he brings out equally Mrs Weston's tact, Emma's unfailing consideration and affection, and Mr Knightley's kindness. His feeble character (which Isabella inherits) makes one see the reason for Emma's decisive and managing qualities and makes one tolerant of them; and it is proved before the reader's eyes that, as Mrs Weston says, 'I do not think Mr Knightley would be much disturbed by Miss Bates. Little things do not irritate him' (225–6); so while she tries to prove that Miss Bates would be no hindrance to a marriage with Jane, she proves that Mr Woodhouse will be no hindrance to a marriage with Emma.

There remain only Emma, Mr Knightley, Frank Churchill, Jane Fairfax and Mrs Weston. The last two have of necessity very little to do, Mrs Weston because she has a very small part, and Jane because any close consideration of the distress her secret engagement causes her would overbalance the story, which must concentrate on Emma. The engagement is seen therefore only for the trouble it causes Emma and Highbury; Jane's misconduct in agreeing to such an engagement is considered for its social, not its personal, effects. In fact, Jane is usually seen through Miss Bates's outpourings, where amusement at the aunt leaves the reader little space to pity the niece.

Frank himself is in very different case. It is a notable point in the construction of *Emma* that characters are very often seen by means of those most concerned with them: Harriet is always seen through Emma, Jane through Miss Bates, and Mr Elton through Harriet and Emma by turns; Frank therefore stands out by being seen in relation not to one person but to many: to Mr Weston, Mrs Weston, Mr Knightley, Miss Bates and Emma by turns; in fact, in relation to everyone but the one whose relations with him ought to be known, Jane Fairfax. Other people's opinions, being so varied and attributing such different motives to him, make him a puzzling figure, and force the reader to reserve judgement on him. Just as Mr Woodhouse brings out the best in people, Frank Churchill brings out the worst. He encourages Emma's ridiculous suspicions of Jane and Mr Dixon (to divert suspicion from himself), he makes Jane seem disagreeable simply because he puts her under constant strain, and his very existence emphasizes such qualities as Mr Weston's easy carelessness:

> Mr Weston, unasked, promised to get Frank over to join them, if possible; a proof of approbation and gratitude which could have been dispensed with. – Mr Knightley was then obliged to say that he should be glad to see him; and Mr Weston engaged to lose no time in writing, and spare no arguments to induce him to come. (357)

Although we see Frank doing attractive things, judgement on him is never explicitly given, although it is clearly indicated. Even before he appears we are subtly prepared to receive him:

> Now, it so happened that in spite of Emma's resolution of never marrying, there was something in the name, in the idea of Mr Frank Churchill, which always interested her. (118)

As we have just seen her to be hopelessly wrong about Mr Elton, whom she knows, it is easy to suspect here that she will be just as wrong about someone she has not yet seen. Jane Austen never gives any clue to Frank's emotions, and his acts are always variously interpreted: his notorious haircut, for instance, is excused by Mrs Weston and Emma, but Mr Knightley sees him as 'just the trifling, silly fellow I took him for' (206). Even though his manners and social conduct are always superficially charming, just as Crawford's are when he is paying his attentions to Fanny; and even though his bad behaviour, like his bad temper when he arrives at the Donwell picnic, is later explained – it is not the heat but a quarrel with Jane that has upset him – explanation does not excuse him. He deserves Jane's displeasure, so the poor opinion of him that Emma and the reader have formed does not need to be altered. Even Mr Knightley's sharp reproof when Frank makes Jane sing beyond her powers does not need to be softened: 'That fellow thinks of nothing but shewing off his own voice' (229). Although Frank's real motive – his pleasure in performing with Jane – is more than just showing off, he is not the less inconsiderate. Frank is important because he explains Emma herself. He embodies the vital difference between the artistic principles governing Emma – foolish conduct resulting from faulty judgement, but from motives fundamentally irreproachable, invariably honest and as frank as possible – and his own downright wrong actions causing deliberate and consistent deceit, which produce nevertheless some of the same effects as Emma's own.

Mr Knightley stands at the other extreme; his conduct is always irreproachable and his judgement unshakable. As *Emma* is the longest of the novels and has the fewest characters, we are able to see Mr Knightley, out of all the heroes, in the greatest detail. He is the least romantic and the most agreeable. He is the combination of the *savoir-faire* of Darcy with the domestic virtue of Edmund Bertram, while his occasional bluntness shows Jane Austen's mature outlook:

> 'Mr Knightley's downright, decided, commanding sort of manner . . . suits *him* very well; his figure and look, and situation in life seem to allow it; but if any young man were to set about copying him, he would not be sufferable. On the contrary, I think a young man might be very safely recommended to take Mr Elton as a model.' (34)

This, of course, primarily points out that Mr Elton's manners are conventional to the point of insincerity; it also shows the maturity which, in *Persuasion*, allows Anne Elliot to value, as a sign of honesty, Wentworth's occasional tactlessness above Mr Elliot's invariable courtesy. The close intimacy between Mr Knightley and the Woodhouse family, and the sixteen years' difference in age between him and Emma, make him unromantic, and moreover we see Mr Knightley doing things no other hero does, like managing the practical details of his estate and buttoning his gaiters, things which emphasize the familiar acquaintance between him and Emma that is so necessary to the proper development of the novel. His abruptness, his steady and agreeable humour, his tact, and his age, make his invariable good sense agreeable, and his lectures to Emma tolerable, in a way that, by comparison, Edmund's to Fanny are not. Mr Knightley does not seem priggish, because his wit is part of his good sense, while Edmund's is usually confined to extenuating asides or incidental remarks, as when he solemnly advances his reason for taking part in the play, and only afterwards indulges in the mild humour of 'They will not have much cause of triumph, when they see how infamously I act' (*Mansfield Park*, 155). While this is Mr Knightley disagreeing with Emma:

'. . . does not the lapse of one-and-twenty years bring our understandings a good deal nearer?'

'Yes, – a good deal *nearer*.'

'But still, not near enough to give me a chance of being right, if we think differently.'

'I have still the advantage of you by sixteen years' experience, and by not being a pretty young woman and a spoiled child.' (99)

He is one of the few, other than Emma herself, whose thoughts are reported. As with Mr Darcy, this occurs when the heroine herself cannot tell all we need to know; in *Pride and Prejudice* this is at the beginning of the story; in *Emma* it is towards the end. For instance, when Frank, Jane and Emma play at anagrams the scene is presented wholly through Mr Knightley's eyes, and this prepares for his eventual proposal to Emma to be seen through both of them in turn, Jane Austen's own lively style producing an irony not at all at odds with what we have seen to be natural to Mr Knightley himself:

He had found her agitated and low. – Frank Churchill was a villain. – He heard her declare that she had never loved him. Frank Churchill's character was not desperate. – She was his own Emma, by hand and word, when they returned into the house; and if he could have thought of Frank Churchill then, he might have deemed him a very good sort of fellow. (433)

Finally there is Emma herself, 'the heroine' (Jane Austen said) 'whom no body but myself will much like'.[1] Considered as a

[1] J. E. Austen-Leigh, *A Memoir of Jane Austen*, Bentley, 1871 (second edition); reprinted Oxford, 1926, p. 157.

personality apart from the novel in which she appears, this might possibly be true, but this is what one must not, and eventually cannot, do. Emma, like Elizabeth Bennet, is the key to her novel; take away Emma and there is less left than there is of *Hamlet* without the Prince of Denmark. She is not only the main character; she is the shape of the novel as well. The flaw in her character not only interprets events as Elizabeth's does, it here actually decides what the events themselves shall be; nearly all that happens is what Emma herself witnesses, and the few things we see that she does not are all vitally and necessarily connected with her. The great constructive originality of the book is that we see everything through her eyes and yet are able to perceive the progress of matters Emma never suspects, or if not to perceive them on first reading, to be put in unwitting possession of evidence whose relevance we realize later. The eventual shape of the story is clear from the beginning:

> Emma Woodhouse, handsome, clever, and rich, with a comfortable home and happy disposition, seemed to unite some of the best blessings of existence; and had lived nearly twenty-one years in the world with very little to distress or vex her . . . The real evils indeed of Emma's situation were the power of having rather too much her own way, and a disposition to think a little too well of herself. (5)

This tells the deficiency on which Emma's actions will depend, and the circumstances which allow it to appear ('the power of having rather too much her own way'), and it indicates both the pleasant tone of the book – 'the best blessings of existence' is not ironic but one of the valuable facts that Jane Austen provides at the beginning of her stories – and the possibility that things may happen both to distress and to vex Emma, and that they will be very much her own fault. Once this outline is established, Emma's mixture of foolishness and charm shows in her own speech; she is seen to be kind to her father, and happy for Miss Taylor though the marriage brings Emma no advantage, and these good qualities impress themselves at the same time as the topic shows the form in which Emma's vanity will show itself, that of match-making:

'You like Mr Elton, papa, – I must look about for a wife for him. There is nobody in Highbury who deserves him – and he has been here a whole year, and has fitted up his house so comfortably that it would be a shame to have him single any longer – and I thought when he was joining their hands today, he looked so very much as if he would like to have the same kind office done for him! I think very well of Mr Elton, and this is the only way I have of doing him a service.'

'Mr Elton is a very pretty young man to be sure, and a very good young man, and I have a great regard for him. But if you want to shew him any attention, my dear, ask him to come and dine with us some day. That will be a much better thing.' (13–14)

It is clear that Mr Woodhouse is quite right, and Emma hopelessly wrong, but it is also clear that Emma is intelligent and perceptive, and it is soon proved – though not in a way Emma likes – that Mr Elton is indeed eager to marry. From such simple methods Jane Austen moves, when Harriet appears, to the subtle presenting of Emma's own thought-processes:

> She found her altogether very engaging – not inconveniently shy, not unwilling to talk – and yet so far from pushing, shewing so proper and becoming a deference, seeming so pleasantly grateful for being admitted to Hartfield, and so artlessly impressed by the appearance of every thing in so superior a style to what she had been used to, that she must have good sense and deserve encouragement. Encouragement should be given. Those soft blue eyes and all those natural graces should not be wasted on the inferior society of Highbury and its connections. The acquaintance she had already formed were unworthy of her. The friends from whom she had just parted, though very good sort of people, must be doing her harm. (23)

Here is the characteristic progression from Jane Austen's statement of facts to her report of what Emma thinks, and to conclusions of Emma's own which are wholly unjustified by the facts. Harriet's beauty arouses a reasonable reaction, but her manners appeal to Emma's vanity and snobbery – 'so proper and becoming a deference' – and the two together produce the delightful but quite unwarranted conclusion 'she must have good sense and deserve encouragement': that is, she must be sensible because she is pretty and admires Emma, and therefore (another *non sequitur*) should occupy a higher place in society – although with no hope of advantage from the elevation, as Mr Knightley and Mrs Weston point out. The consequence of such reasoning is that Emma, doing more than justice to Harriet, does serious injustice to the Martins, who 'must be doing her harm'. The smooth progression makes Emma much more estimable than the ridiculous figure an analysis of such passages suggests, yet it never lets the reader muddle actual fact with Emma's inferences. Jane Austen can give all the information she needs through Emma, because at the same time as Emma misreads what she sees, she helps the reader to understand it:

> 'This man is almost too gallant to be in love,' thought Emma. 'I should say so, but that I suppose there may be a hundred different ways of being in love. He is an excellent young man, and will suit Harriet exactly; it will be an "Exactly so," as he says himself; but he does sigh and languish, and study for compliments rather more than I could endure as a principal. I come in for a pretty good share as a second. But it is his gratitude on Harriet's account.' (49)

After this, even though it is quite clear to the reader that Emma is indeed the 'principal', it is impossible to feel superior to Emma, entertaining though her delusion may be. She has observed the facts most intelligently and has herself pointed out, though unconsciously, her own mistakes, and the ironic possibilities of the situation: Mr Elton is indeed 'too gallant to be in love' – since his courtship of her is provoked by ambition. Emma has more in common with Mary Crawford than with Fanny, the heroine who immediately precedes her. At her worst Emma wilfully misuses her natural sense as Mary does:

> 'Till it appears that men are much more philosophic on the subject than they are generally supposed; till they do fall in love with well-informed minds instead of handsome faces, a girl, with such loveliness as Harriet, has a certainty of being admired and sought after . . . I am very much mistaken if your sex in general would not think such beauty, and such temper, the highest claims a woman could possess.'

'Upon my word, Emma, to hear you abusing the reason you have, is almost enough to make me think so too. Better be without sense, than misapply it as you do.' (63–64)

Emma's speech here is good enough for wit in some authors, but not good enough for Jane Austen; it is merely a neat generalization, and painfully recalls Mary arguing about the length of the shrubbery at Sotherton, against all the force of Edmund's reason.

The story takes its shape from Emma's progress out of her errors into moral and emotional maturity. She is wilfully wrong about Mr Elton, but quick to acknowledge her mistake, and does not make the same one again. His courtship accounts for about one-third of the novel, has meat enough for a whole novel from many hands, and is dealt with a good deal more skilfully than any other hand could do. It is also a good deal more subtle and skilful than the hints leading up to Lydia's elopement in *Pride and Prejudice*: the latter is merely a not unlikely course for the action to take; the former points towards the only possible one. Jane Austen uses Mr Elton's courtship as preparation for the much more elaborate subtleties which Frank Churchill produces. Emma is not repeating her earlier fault: Frank deliberately misleads her about himself, and gives her good reason to think he is courting her; though she suspects Jane of an affair with Mr Dixon, she is actually right here about there being a good reason for Jane to be reserved and unhappy:

'She is *not* to be with the *Dixons*. The decree is issued by somebody. But why must she consent to be with the Eltons? – Here is quite a separate puzzle.' (285)

Emma is right about both things, and even though she is wrong to tell Frank her suspicions of Jane and Mr Dixon, he is much more wrong to encourage her to do so.

The real disaster, and the climax of the novel, is when Emma realizes that Harriet is in love with Mr Knightley, and in some hopes of a return. Jane Austen, adhering to her plan, has aroused some criticism here because the reader has no chance to detect what is going on in Harriet's mind; there are none of the clues here such as Frank's and Jane's behaviour, Miss Bates's gossip, and Mr Knightley's observations provide. However, as Emma has guessed everyone's feelings wrongly from the beginning, and as she has only the encounter with the gipsies (and her own wishes) to link Harriet and Frank, it is perfectly reasonable for the reader to assume that Emma is going to be wrong this time as well. It is ironically fitting that Emma, who has ruled the action and so made all her own problems, should have those problems solved for her by matters in which she takes no active part at all: Mr Knightley's proposal which she even tries to prevent, Frank's engagement to Jane, and, best of all, Harriet's engagement to Robert Martin – the only point in the whole novel at which Harriet manages to make up her mind for herself.

Jane Austen presents Emma by well-tried methods: her match-making and snobbery are both revealed in a romantic treatment of the commonplace which harks back to the (by comparison) simple burlesque of *Northanger Abbey*:

> It was Miss Taylor's loss which first brought grief. It was on the wedding-day of this beloved friend that Emma first sat in mournful thought of any continuance. (6)

The strain reappears in high-flown ideas of Harriet's parentage – she is merely 'the natural daughter of somebody' (22) in fact –

> 'The misfortune of your birth ought to make you particularly careful as to your associates. There can be no doubt of your being a gentleman's daughter, and you must support your claim to that station by every thing within your power, or there will be plenty of people who would take pleasure in degrading you.' (30)

The whole tendency of this as of all the novels is to ridicule this false literary romanticism, by a deliberate and ironic use of literary and romantic conventions and cliché. Mrs Elton is useful later in this respect to counteract what may be the reader's unduly harsh estimate of Emma's social lapses and romantic impulses, since Mrs Elton's social behaviour is wholly deplorable, and her sensibility all factitious.

Although Emma herself appears to decide absolutely the whole course of the action, this is the farthest from haphazard of all Jane Austen's precisely planned plots. This seems to be – for Jane Austen – the perfect plot, in which there is no need for coincidence to produce the right ending. We see every detail necessary, every step in the relationship between Frank and Jane (which is the one motive force besides Emma herself), even though like Emma we cannot (at first reading) see the indications for what they are. Jane Austen does not intend that we should. When, for instance, Frank stays behind to mend Mrs Bates's spectacles while Miss Bates goes to fetch Emma and Mrs Weston, there is no fact to show that he has stayed so as to speak to Jane, but when Emma arrives there are all the indications of an interrupted conversation – he has not finished the spectacles, Jane has been helping him wedge the leg of the piano, she is not calm enough to begin to play at once, and the visitors are 'at least ten minutes earlier than I had calculated' (240). None of this is proof, but it is circumstantial evidence.

Since in general we know only what Emma knows, we cannot guess Harriet's feelings for Mr Knightley, which are the other main cause of the novel's crisis; but it is quite plain that she is not at all in love with Frank – she never shows any interest in him, and in any case we are now prepared for Emma to be wrong in every one of her guesses – and there are a few faint signs that Mr Knightley is the object of her affections: Harriet always admires Mr Knightley, and very early she compares him and Robert Martin:

'Certainly, he is not like Mr Knightley. He has not such a fine air and way of walking as Mr Knightley.' (33)

She is certainly right to think Mr Knightley's dancing with her a greater service than Frank's happening to rescue her from the gipsies, and he does thereafter begin to show an interest in her, even though this is on Robert Martin's account.

The range of events has closed in from what it was in the other novels; the scene never changes from Highbury, so there can be no use of the atmospheres of different places such as there is in *Pride and Prejudice* and *Mansfield Park*. This is refining to the utmost, and has the paradoxical advantage that where even the high points are so commonplace the most casual event and the apparently idlest chat become very significant indeed, and the reader becomes unusually alert to their significance. The only event in the plot which might be called a fortunate coincidence is Mrs Churchill's death, and this is as remote from the real action as could well be – she is a character we never even see – and her death is foreshadowed from the very beginning; she is always an invalid, and it is only because she is such an unconscionable time a-dying, and therefore suspected of being not ill at all, that her death comes as a surprise.

Such a method means that a steady progression is made through the period the story covers. Events are emphasized by the amount of space given to them, and though this is no day-by-day account, the blending of events is almost imperceptible; there are no long periods so lightly passed over as the two months in *Pride and Prejudice* which are covered (neatly enough, however) in two sentences:

> With no greater events than these in the Longbourn family, and otherwise diversified by little beyond the walks to Meryton, some-times dirty and sometimes cold, did January and February pass away. (*Pride and Prejudice*, 151)

This movement from one event to the next is effected particularly by unlocalized comments. Thus Harriet first appears in person in the midst of Emma's private opinions about her –

> Harriet certainly was not clever, but she had a sweet, docile, grateful disposition; was totally free from conceit; and only desiring to be guided by any one she looked up to . . . Altogether she was quite convinced of Harriet Smith's being exactly the young friend she wanted. (26)

– which leads easily into the midst of a particular but representative dialogue:

> Emma encouraged her talkativeness – amused by such a picture of another set of beings, and enjoying the youthful simplicity which could speak with so much exultation of Mrs Martin's having 'two parlours, two very good parlours indeed; one of them quite as large as Mrs Goddard's drawing-room'. (27)

The conversation arises out of the general situation to which it is relevant, the absence of any detail of time or place emphasizing that this is a typical as well as a significant exchange. The next chapter is a sharp contrast. Mr Knightley and Mrs Weston discuss this friendship between Emma and Harriet; this conversation also is given neither time nor place, but it is all direct speech even though Emma has no part in it.

Against such economical and effective methods of subordination, the main scenes, carefully documented in every particular, and with every particular significant, are brilliantly effective.[1] The strawberry-picking party at Donwell arises out of Mr Knightley's casual remarks to Mrs Elton:

'The year will wear away at this rate, and nothing done. Before this time last year I assure you we had had a delightful exploring party from Maple Grove to Kings Weston.'
'You had better explore to Donwell,' replied Mr Knightley. 'That may be done without horses. Come, and eat my strawberries. They are ripening fast.' (354)

But in Jane Austen it is the rule that 'great event from trivial causes springs' and that this is a great event the careful preparation shows. Mrs Elton's plans are elaborate though preposterous:

'It is to be a morning scheme, you know, Knightley; quite a simple thing. I shall wear a large bonnet, and bring one of my little baskets hanging on my arm. Here, – probably this basket with pink ribbon. Nothing can be more simple, you see . . . a sort of gipsy party. – We are to walk about your gardens, and gather the strawberries ourselves, and sit under trees; – and whatever else you may like to provide, it is to be all out of doors.' (355)

This conversation is again unlocalized, showing that it prepares for something more important than itself. It does introduce one important new idea:

'There is but one married woman in the world whom I can ever allow to invite what guests she pleases to Donwell, and that one is –'

[1] The ball at the Crown and the picnic at Donwell are as memorable and significant in relation to the events around them as such stirring matters as the Battle of Waterloo in *Vanity Fair* or Bill Sikes's death in *Oliver Twist*.

157

'– Mrs Weston, I suppose,' interrupted Mrs Elton, rather morti-
fied.

'No – Mrs Knightley; – and, till she is in being, I will manage
such matters myself.' (354–5)

But apart from this, we hear merely who will be coming to the
party – Miss Bates, Jane, Emma, Harriet and Mr Woodhouse –
and the party itself begins through him, the person who makes
the most fuss about going to it:

> Under a bright mid-day sun, at almost Midsummer, Mr Wood-
> house was safely conveyed in his carriage, with one window down,
> to partake of this al-fresco party; and in one of the most comfortable
> rooms in the abbey, especially prepared for him by a fire all the
> morning, he was happily placed, quite at his ease, ready to talk with
> pleasure of what had been atchieved, and advise every body to come
> and sit down, and not to heat themselves. (357)

Jane Austen makes use of every physical fact at her disposal:
the weather is favourable to Mr Woodhouse, sharply localizes
the scene, and is later the excuse Frank Churchill gives for his bad
temper. The setting also is important: a clear picture of Donwell
is built up in the course of the chapter, which gives a background
for Mr Knightley, and shows Emma's feelings – which are a nice
mixture of almost proprietary pleasure and a proper estimate of
Mr Knightley's social worth. Thus the event is felt to be important, although the reader cannot at first reading know just
why it is so: Mr Knightley talks to Harriet, and so, as is later
discovered, makes her think he may be in love with her; Jane,
pestered beyond endurance by Mrs Elton's offers of a post as
governess, breaks down and goes home, to meet Frank and
quarrel with him, as it turns out; Frank's arrival, the next thing to
happen, is – if Mr Knightley's suspicions in the previous chapter
have been noted – significant by its proximity to Jane's departure,
while the weather which he blames for his temper is a no more
adequate explanation than his haircut was of his going to London.
The details therefore which make the scene realistic are an essential part of the whole structure of the novel. The gradually mount-
ing discomfort of the whole party prepares for the disastrous

events at Box Hill the next day, when everyone, Emma especially, is unhappy and disagreeable.

The story as a whole is as well balanced as individual scenes. It is in a way a similar shape to *Mansfield Park*, about the same length, with two distinct parts, of which the first, Mr Elton's courtship – corresponding to Crawford's flirtation with Maria and Julia – is about one-third the length of the second, which is devoted to the events surrounding Frank and Jane – corresponding to Crawford's courtship of Fanny. Both novels have a penultimate section in which the heroine undergoes acute distress, Emma when she has offended Mr Knightley and then finds that Harriet has hopes of his affection, and Fanny a more sensational one at Portsmouth, physically distressed, laid siege to by Crawford and unhappy about Edmund. The relation between the sections is much firmer in *Emma*, since all are relevant to common aspects of Emma's character, her match-making and vanity. It is easy to follow the process of her delusions about Mr Elton, so they lead naturally to her more elaborate delusions about Frank, where although she has learned a good deal from her first mistake she is hoodwinked deliberately by Frank, who has his own reasons for deceiving her. Her first error is only finally remedied at the very end, when her own sense and Mr Knightley's influence persuade her to give up her first and strongest illusion, that Harriet is worthy of better things than Robert Martin represents. The balance also between the time spent on the nadir of misery and the ascent from it to happiness is better managed than in *Mansfield Park*. Emma spends only three chapters on her misery, while fifteen are spent on the cheerful detail and disclosures which precede Harriet's, Jane's and her own marriage. Admittedly Fanny has more to suffer and therefore more time must be devoted to her; eight chapters are not too much; but a mere three (albeit long ones) to recover Tom, settle Maria, marry Julia, dispose of Mrs Norris, the Grants, Mary and Henry, and dismiss Edmund and Fanny to eventual happiness, is – though not as perfunctory as a summary makes it sound – equally not as nicely organized as the conclusion of *Emma*.

Although characters are of varying importance and of different types, the ways in which they are subordinated to the main purpose are those Jane Austen has always used: first the author's own brief comment gives essentials, then their own speech shows characteristic preoccupations, and thirdly these preoccupations are made to work on a topic of serious importance to the main theme. This is a good, simple, humorous, and essentially ironic method, capable of such variation that it is scarcely perceptible as a consistent method at all, and in Jane Austen's hands can never become a routine. This is how Jane Austen introduces Mr Woodhouse:

> Having been a valetudinarian all his life, without activity of mind or body, he was a much older man in ways than in years; and though everywhere beloved for the friendliness of his heart and his amiable temper, his talents could not have recommended him at any time. (7)

When he actually appears he is discussing the Westons, about whom we need to know just as much as about Mr Woodhouse himself –

> 'Poor Miss Taylor! – I wish she were here again. What a pity it is that Mr Weston ever thought of her!'
> '. . . You would not have had Miss Taylor live with us for ever . . . when she might have a house of her own?'
> 'A house of her own! – but where is the advantage of a house of her own? This is three times as large.' (8)

– and his next subject is Emma's match-making, and as relevant as it is characteristic in manner:

> 'I wish you would not make matches and foretel things, for whatever you say always comes to pass. Pray do not make any more matches.' (12)

Mr John Knightley appears in the same way, but with quite different effect:

> Mr John Knightley was a tall, gentleman-like, and very clever man; rising in his profession, domestic, and respectable in his private character; but with reserved manners which prevented his being generally pleasing; and capable of being sometimes out of humour. He was not an ill-tempered man, not so often unreasonably cross

as to deserve such a reproach; but his temper was not his great perfection; and, indeed, with such a worshipping wife, it was hardly possible that any natural defects in it should not be increased. (92–93)

Some of his first words, too, are about the Westons, and Mr Weston's behaviour to Frank –

'Nobody ever did think well of the Churchills, I fancy,' observed Mr John Knightley coolly. 'But you need not imagine Mr Weston to have felt what you would feel in giving up Henry or John. Mr Weston is rather an easy, cheerful tempered man, than a man of strong feelings.' (96)

– showing at once the fault of his own character and yet quite fairly pointing out the fault in Mr Weston's.

Characters who appear late in the story have extra preparation by being familiar by report long before they appear; Miss Bates, who does not come in until the nineteenth chapter, is mentioned in the first, in just the same way as the Perrys and the Coles, whom one then feels to be constantly promising to appear, by analogy with Miss Bates and Jane. The Perrys in fact never appear at all, but the Coles narrowly contrive it, since, after writing an invitation and giving a party, Mrs Coles is allowed to utter two speeches in our hearing. Such a method shows a great advance on (for example) the introduction of Mrs Palmer in *Sense and Sensibility*, who appears before we even know she exists, and that of Mrs Gardiner in *Pride and Prejudice*, who is only briefly prepared for, while Colonel Fitzwilliam is not prepared for at all. Frank Churchill, the greatest of the late-comers, is brilliantly presented. There is always the danger that a person coming so late, especially a serious character, may be an anticlimax. Frank is prepared for by lengthy false hopes, and by Emma's sympathetic apprehension on Mrs Weston's account:

Mrs Weston's faithful pupil did not forget either at ten, or eleven, or twelve o'clock, that she was to think of her at four . . . The clock struck twelve as she passed through the hall . . . She opened the parlour door, and saw two gentlemen sitting with her father – Mr Weston and his son. (189–90)

This sudden appearance takes the reader as much by surprise as it does Emma, and thus very neatly gives a new burst of interest to what has threatened to become stale, and drops a hint of Frank's irregular character before he can say a word.

Important characters are anticipated in a significant way: Jane is talked of chiefly by her devoted aunt and by Emma, both of them prejudiced in their different ways, and never by Mr Knightley and Mrs Weston, or any other rational person who approves of her, until after she has arrived, when they add a great deal to a character who cannot add much to herself. Frank, in contrast, is the object of disagreement long before he arrives, foreshadowing what he will be in person.

The proportion observed in presentation of whole scenes and whole characters extends to details of action and speech. The skill Jane Austen showed with different styles of speech in *Pride and Prejudice* is taken a stage farther here. She frequently represents secondary characters in a third-person version of their own words, which has all its personal, rhythmical and idiomatic traits, without its immediacy. This is used to subordinate characters: first, those who would otherwise be overwhelming, like Mrs Elton; second, those whose comment is of the first importance although they themselves are not –

'[Mr Woodhouse] could not see any objection at all to his, and Emma's, and Harriet's, going there some very fine morning. He thought it very well done of Mr Knightley to invite them – very kind and sensible – much cleverer than dining out. – He was not fond of dining out.' (357)

– and third, those who are really only an appropriate mouthpiece for necessary information about events, making it more interesting than the author's own statement could be.

Mr Frank Churchill did not come . . . Mr Weston was surprized and sorry; but then he began to perceive that Frank's coming two or three months later would be a much better plan; better time of year; better weather; and that he would be able, without any doubt, to stay considerably longer with them than if he had come sooner. (144)

Jane Austen's own style is hardly noticeable in *Emma*. There are few of the sharp detached comments such as she makes on everyone in *Mansfield Park*, or of the epigrammatic generalizations which she has used in earlier work. As a rule her style merges with Emma's own, and only on occasions as momentous as Mr Knightley's proposal do they part company:

What did she say? – Just what she ought, of course. A lady always does . . .

Seldom, very seldom, does complete truth belong to any human disclosure; seldom can it happen that something is not a little disguised, or a little mistaken; but where, as in this case, though the conduct is mistaken, the feelings are not, it may not be very material. – Mr Knightley could not impute to Emma a more relenting heart than she possessed, or a heart more disposed to accept of his. (431–2)

Although Emma's speech merges with her author's written style, this does not mean that the two are ever more confused than the author intended. They are not alike, but shade into each other by the same methods as have been used for different ends with the secondary characters.

The hair was curled, and the maid sent away, and Emma sat down to think and be miserable. – It was a wretched business, indeed! – Such an overthrow of every thing she had been wishing for! – Such a development of every thing most unwelcome! – Such a blow for Harriet! – That was the worst of all. Every part of it brought pain and humiliation, of some sort or other; but, compared with the evil to Harriet, all was light; and she would gladly have submitted to feel yet more mistaken – more in error – more disgraced by mis-judgment, than she actually was, could the effects of her blunders have been confined to herself.

'If I had not persuaded Harriet into liking the man, I could have born any thing. He might have doubled his presumption to me – But poor Harriet!'

How she could have been so deceived! – He protested that he had never thought seriously of Harriet – never! She looked back as well as she could; but it was all confusion. She had taken up the idea, she supposed, and made every thing bend to it. His manners, however, must have been unmarked, wavering, dubious, or she could not have been so misled.

The picture! – How eager he had been about the picture! – and the charade! – and an hundred other circumstances; – how clearly they had seemed to point at Harriet. To be sure, the charade, with its 'ready wit' – but then, the 'soft eyes' – in fact it suited neither; it was a jumble without taste or truth. Who could have seen through such thick-headed nonsense? (134)

After the first few facts which very economically set the scene, this is clearly almost all Emma, the third person representing the way her thoughts go, only the most fervent of them being in direct speech, as though her feelings grow so strong as to force her to speak them aloud. Jane Austen's comments are in the nature of stage direction – 'every part of it brought pain and humiliation', 'she looked back as well as she could' – and offer no comment on what Emma is thinking. Emma's speech is so ruled by the author's moral purpose that it is sufficient comment on itself here or anywhere else in the story, and this scene concludes with Emma saying

'But now, poor girl, her peace is cut up for some time. I have been but half a friend to her.' (137)

Emma, like Elizabeth Bennet, needs no guiding comments even when she is considering other people in the light of her own prejudice. Here she is pondering Frank's London haircut:

There was certainly no harm in his travelling sixteen miles twice over on such an errand; but there was an air of foppery and nonsense in it which she could not approve. It did not accord with the rationality of plan, the moderation in expense, or even the unselfish warmth of heart which she had believed herself to discern in him yesterday. Vanity, extravagance, love of change, restlessness of temper, which must be doing something, good or bad; heedlessness as to the pleasure of his father and Mrs Weston, indifference as to how his conduct might appear in general; he became liable to all these charges. (205)

Emma's opinion is quite sound – 'an air of foppery and nonsense' – but the next phrase – 'which *she* could not approve' – reminds us of her vanity, and introduces the typical overimpetuous opinion without proper evidence – 'which she had believed herself to discern in him *yesterday*' – this is a different kind of judgement, as 'yesterday' reminds us, from the very sound one Mr Knightley has found himself able to form without meeting Frank at all. Similarly the grand collection of faults which conclude Emma's argument is an exaggeration from inadequate evidence. The perfect balance here between Emma's own good and bad qualities never fails, and the excellence of Jane Austen's style is embodied in it. It is the result of clear thinking and a firm purpose, not of consideration of pictorial, rhetorical or musical qualities. This is equally the basis of her pervading irony, which expresses itself in so many different topics in so many different constructions that any solely technical classification is impossible; the only reliable criterion lies in its function.

6 · *Persuasion*

THIS IS JANE AUSTEN's last work in anything approaching a final form (*Sanditon* is only a fragment, with no clear plot) and is generally judged as a finished novel; in a letter to her niece, Jane Austen claimed to have 'a something ready for Publication'[1] which was what is now called *Persuasion*, but even so it is difficult to believe that in her days of health and mature judgement she would have thought these two volumes, with their imperfect plot, sketchy characters, lightly drawn scenes and their dependence on the author's narrative, could constitute a finished work. It must be judged as it stands, however, and not by what one guesses or hopes she would have done had she not died two months later. Although it is not *Emma*, or even *Pride and Prejudice*, it has deserved and got high praise, particularly from those who are not at ease with the subtleties of *Emma*.

Jane Austen's attitude to her reader and the tone she adopts towards both him and her subject is at its most assured. There is more direct narrative than ever before; she has generally preferred conversation or character to transmit information, but here she herself says a great deal (much of it witty and acute, as she always is), assuming complete agreement in her reader, but yet without being personal as she was in *Northanger Abbey*, or didactic as she was in *Sense and Sensibility*. This reveals a different intention here from in the other novels. Although *Persuasion* shows many of the skills which appeared first in its immediate precursor *Emma*, it resembles those parts of *Mansfield Park* which concern Fanny in that it is serious and even melancholy in tone. Jane Austen, here as always, is uncompromisingly moral in aim and intention, but she is no longer satirical, the broad burlesque of her early work is

1 Letter to Fanny Knight, 13 March 1817, *Letters*, p. 484.

gone, and no character even hints at the bitterness aroused by
Mrs Norris. Yet her method is not much changed: she still under-
states her points, and minor characters still reveal themselves
ironically.

The change is at the centre. Jane Austen agrees with her heroine
much more than she has ever done before, because Anne has
really no faults. Her one error which makes the story – as it makes
the majority of Jane Austen's stories – has been committed eight
years before the action starts, when she refused Wentworth; it
has been atoned for, as well, so that *Persuasion* begins where *Emma*,
Pride and Prejudice and *Northanger Abbey* are ready to leave off,
when the heroine has become wise through suffering the consequences of her own mistakes. Jane Austen has usually seen what
her heroines see, but here this is almost all one needs to see,
because Anne is just as right as her author. When Anne forms
opinions, she has no prejudices to mislead her like Emma and
Elizabeth, and so she sees quite clearly even the things that
concern her closely, like the relations growing up between the
Miss Musgroves and Captain Wentworth. No one conceals anything from her; indeed, she often hears more than she likes, and a
pleasant and wittily original kind of irony results, in which
character as well as author may share:

> On one other question, which perhaps her utmost wisdom might
> not have prevented, she was soon spared all suspense; for after the
> Miss Musgroves had returned and finished their visit at the Cottage,
> she had this spontaneous information from Mary:
> 'Captain Wentworth is not very gallant by you, Anne, though
> he was so attentive to me. Henrietta asked him what he thought of
> you, when they went away; and he said, "You were so altered he
> should not have known you again".' (60)

Anne also knows and understands all the characters, even the hero
on whom her happiness depends:

> There was a momentary expression in Captain Wentworth's
> face at this speech, a certain glance of his bright eye, and curl of his
> handsome mouth, which convinced Anne, that instead of sharing
> in Mrs Musgrove's kind wishes, as to her son, he had probably been

at some pains to get rid of him; but it was too transient an indulgence of self-amusement to be detected by any who understood him less than herself. (67)

With such perception as this to guide him, the reader needs to see less of Captain Wentworth's thoughts, although Anne and he are estranged, than he does even of Mr Knightley's, whom Emma knows so well. Consequently the heroine combines with Jane Austen as narrator after the first three chapters, which describe the family and Kellynch and prepare for the removal to Bath; they have all the point and some of the tone of *Mansfield Park*, though not even that had so long an introduction with no conversation. They fall easily into direct moral utterance –

> Though not the very happiest being in the world herself, [Lady Elliot] had found enough in her duties, her friends, and her children, to attach her to life, and make it no matter of indifference to her when she was called on to quit them. (4)

and they pass easily back again to irony:

> This friend, and Sir Walter, did *not* marry, whatever might have been anticipated on that head by their acquaintance. (5)

They continue to move as the topic requires, until a final sharp comment passes the main narrative over to Anne –

> . . . 'a few months more, and *he*, perhaps, may be walking here.' (25)

– ends one chapter, and this begins the next:

> *He* was not Mr Wentworth, the former curate of Monkford, however suspicious appearances may be. (26)

But although character and author rarely part company, Anne is not Jane Austen, and even to guess that she is more like her than any of her other heroines is wishful thinking. The skill which makes Anne a readily sympathetic heroine prohibits it. Anne's view is the true one and there is nothing left for the author to hint or the reader to guess. Anne is presented with complete propriety in direct narrative, not by ambiguous conversation as Elizabeth was or through a personality as faulty as it is self-revealing as was *Emma*. There is no place here, therefore, for that exquisite regulation of tone shown in *Emma*, for those distinctions between what events seem to be and what they are, and for whole situations to be distorted by what the heroine thinks of them. Jane Austen speaks frequently and wittily, but remains self-effacing, describing rather than qualifying Anne (as she very frequently qualified what Fanny said), yet neither she nor Anne is ever didactic, as both she and Elinor were in *Sense and Sensibility*. The author's tone is as close to Anne's as to Elizabeth Bennet's, and closer than to any other heroine's. What is more, the plot contains little that could be seen other than through Anne, so Jane Austen rarely resorts to using other, minor, characters where her heroine fails her, as she did in *Sense and Sensibility*, and on occasions even in *Emma*. This kind of interest done away with, another takes its place. Jane Austen's attitude to minor characters has mellowed. Mary and Charles Musgrove go out to dine, leaving Anne to take care of their sick son, and this is the comment:

> They were gone, she hoped, to be happy, however oddly constructed such happiness might seem. (58)

This is a much less simple reaction to imperfect and limited personalities than any in the other novels, even though none of them, though simpler, is unjust. *Persuasion* is essentially serious, like *Mansfield Park*, but its tone is more satisfactory; hence the praise for its 'construction' that it has received, since it leaves a more coherent and satisfying impression as a whole. The plot, in fact, is simple, whereas that of *Mansfield Park* is elaborate, and there is no place in it for irony. Anne Elliot, an 'elegant little woman of seven and twenty . . . with manners as consciously right as they were invariably gentle' (153), is as wise as her creator (as far as her context allows) and shows also Jane Austen's increased power by having enough mild humour of her own for Jane Austen's comment to chime with hers:

> Anne had not wanted this visit to Uppercross, to learn that a removal from one set of people to another, though at a distance of only three miles, will often include a total change of conversation, opinion, and idea. She had never been staying there before, without

being struck by it, or without wishing that other Elliots could have
her advantage in seeing how unknown, or unconsidered there,
were the affairs which at Kellynch-hall were treated as of such general
publicity and pervading interest. (42)

Jane Austen can narrate a great deal in her own voice without
hinting at either partisanship or dissociation, and can poke fun
at her heroine's small mistakes without their becoming symptoms
of larger ones, which has been her main method up to this point.
As a consequence Jane Austen's comments slide easily into Anne's:

> The sounds were retreating, and Anne distinguished no more.
> Her own emotions still kept her fixed. She had much to recover
> from, before she could move. The listener's proverbial fate was not
> absolutely hers; she had heard no evil of herself, – but she had heard
> a great deal of very painful import. She saw how her own character
> was considered by Captain Wentworth; and there had been just
> that degree of feeling and curiosity about her in his manner, which
> must give her extreme agitation. (89)

The 'proverbial fate' is clearly Jane Austen's comment, and not
what Anne would think at such a moment.

Although such a tone, and such an attitude towards Anne,
make this different from the other novels, the way Jane Austen
organizes her material, and the aspects she chooses to notice of
the material she has, remain what they have always been. Like
Emma, *Persuasion* seems to be organized by what its heroine does,
sees, and thinks; and like *Emma* it is really more elaborate than
this. A good deal of author's information is needed here, because
there are few conversations to supply facts or reveal states of mind.
Most of this necessary information is provided in the first three
chapters (rather indigestibly for some readers), and reinforced
thereafter by short, unobtrusive passages. One of the most
notable is that in which we discover how Captain Wentworth
thinks of Anne; so far we have heard only her side of the story;
we must hear his if he is to become the hero he should be:

> He had not forgiven Anne Elliot. She had used him ill; deserted
> and disappointed him; and worse, she had shewn a feebleness of
> character in doing so, which his own decided, confident temper

could not endure. She had given him up to oblige others. It had been the effect of over-persuasion. It had been weakness and timidity.

He had been most warmly attached to her, and had never seen a woman since whom he thought her equal; but, except from some natural sensation of curiosity, he had no desire of meeting her again. Her power with him was gone for ever. (61)

This is what one expects from Jane Austen, and we know by the brisk speech-rhythms at the end that this is what Wentworth thinks rather than what is actually true.[1]

Persuasion is Jane Austen's least dramatic work, both for surprising turns of plot and for method of presentation. This, however, does not give the author's narrative the predominance that might be expected. Large portions of the book are résumés or abstracts of dialogue.

They had the pleasure of assuring her that Bath more than answered their expectations in every respect. Their house was undoubtedly the best in Camden-place; their drawing-rooms had many decided advantages over all the others which they had either seen or heard of; and the superiority was not less in the style of the fitting-up, or the taste of the furniture. Their acquaintance was exceedingly sought after. Every body was wanting to visit them. They had drawn back from many introductions, and still were perpetually having cards left by people of whom they knew nothing. . . . But this was not all which they had to make them happy. They had Mr Elliot, too. Anne had a great deal to hear of Mr Elliot. He was not only pardoned, they were delighted with him. He had been in Bath about a fortnight; . . . and his first object, on arriving, had been to leave his card in Camden-place. (137-8)

This does as much in two paragraphs as the arrival of Mr Collins's letter does in as many pages in *Pride and Prejudice*; it tells all we need to know about what Bath means to the Elliots, and recalls

[1] *Persuasion* therefore looks forward, on its small scale, to George Eliot, who is at her best as narrator in just this kind of perceptive analysis, of Gwendolen Harleth, for example, among her heroines, and of Bulstrode or Rosamund Vincy among her subordinate characters. It shows how flexible Jane Austen's methods are that they may be used by a later writer for characters so different from each other, and for characters and ends that are quite outside her own range.

them to mind by using their own idioms: 'Their acquaintance was exceedingly sought after. Every body was wanting to visit them' is deliberate and telling tautology, just such as Elizabeth or Sir Walter would use. Such method concentrates all the attention on Anne, since, with very few exceptions, no one else's thoughts are perceived, and for long spaces no one else is even heard. One may suspect, however, that Jane Austen might well have revised the novel had she lived, and expanded many of these résumés into the dialogues she so obviously enjoyed.

Some of the awkwardnesses of the plot will be examined later, but one at least is a question of attitude. This is what concerns Mr Elliot and Mrs Clay. Miss Lascelles sees here Jane Austen's chronic objection to such material; sexual immorality is not comic, and 'these two could not receive full life unless they should be conceived of as comic in virtue of the part they had to play together'.[1] Whatever the cause, there is no doubt that Mrs Clay is never spoken of in any terms which would lead one to connect her with Mr Elliot; her whole connexion is with Elizabeth, and her own language – the few times that she does speak – points to nothing but herself; while we very rarely hear Mr Elliot speak at all, and certainly never to Mrs Clay.

The characters themselves have always been the absorbing thing for Jane Austen; she attends less than most other great novelists to scenery, external events, and the places where her characters live. *Persuasion* shows a new interest in these hitherto secondary matters, for their own sakes, and as a way of organizing the characters. The move to Portsmouth in *Mansfield Park* was startling, even revolutionary; such moves are an essential part of the pattern of *Persuasion*. They give Anne varied social settings, they impress the reader with a much wider world than so small a number of characters would lead one to expect, and they exemplify one of the main subjects of the novel: family ties and relationships. There are four groups of characters, those at Kellynch, Uppercross, Lyme and Bath. There is a steady development from the emotional aridity of Kellynch to the happy richness of Lyme,

[1] *Jane Austen and her Art*, p. 81.

where the sailors' families show so well the life which Anne will share after her marriage. The novel opens at Kellynch, with Sir Walter and Elizabeth Elliot, and Lady Russell, supported by Mr Shepherd and Mrs Clay. There is an immediate ironic contrast between what a home and family for Anne might be and what Kellynch actually is, and between Anne herself and her nearest relations and friends. The opening sentence states this theme, and does not, as before in Jane Austen's opening sentences, tell us what the story will be about:

> Sir Walter Elliot, of Kellynch-hall, in Somersetshire, was a man who, for his own amusement, never took up any book but the Baronetage; there he found occupation for an idle hour, and consolation in a distressed one. (3)

The Debrett entry which follows describes a bleak and rank-ridden family in the shortest, bleakest and most rank-ridden way, and significantly couples Mr William Elliot, the only other member of the family, with this aspect of it, long before he can appear. It also shows the immediate happenings from which the story develops – the decision to leave Kellynch. Sir Walter's first and chief function is to be the cause of leaving, but he seems to act in his own character, rather than to have been given that character in order to comply with the story. After this Sir Walter does and says very little, merely pointing out, in his own characteristic way, a few necessary details, such as Mrs Clay's ascendancy over himself and Elizabeth:

> 'I should recommend Gowland, the constant use of Gowland, during the spring months. Mrs Clay has been using it at my recommendation, and you see what it has done for her. You see how it has carried away her freckles.' (146)

Elizabeth is a variant on her father. She does and says very little; her function is virtually performed simply by existing: she makes a family attitude out of what, if represented by her father alone, would be mere idiosyncrasy. Anne's fault therefore in giving way to family influence at nineteen is less culpable, and her triumph in having overcome it at twenty-seven is greater. Elizabeth also shows the uneasy indifference which takes the place of affection between the sisters, an attitude elaborated by Mary at Uppercross. She provides the family reaction on subjects (such as Mrs Clay) on which Anne cannot speak to her father, and reveals herself in precisely her father's terms:

> 'If Mrs Clay were a very beautiful woman, I grant you, it might be wrong to have her so much with me; not that any thing in the world, I am sure, would induce my father to make a degrading match; but he might be rendered unhappy. But poor Mrs Clay, who, with all her merits, can never have been reckoned tolerably pretty! I really think poor Mrs Clay may be staying here in perfect safety. One would imagine you had never heard my father speak of her personal misfortunes, though I know you must fifty times. That tooth of her's! and those freckles!' (35)

'Misfortunes' – which suggests her widowhood – turns out to mean freckles, just as it would if Sir Walter were speaking.

Sir Walter and Elizabeth have two foils, Mr Shepherd and his daughter Mrs Clay. Their chief purpose is to provide the two main events of the plot: Mr Shepherd carries through the leasing of the Kellynch estate, and Mrs Clay, appearing here to demonstrate the family folly and vanity and Anne's contrasting perception, is later used to dispose conveniently of Mr William Elliot.

Both characters are as self-seeking as the Elliots, and a good deal more intelligent. Chapter III, the only one in which Mr Shepherd appears, is a lively piece of conversation, and Mr Shepherd as lively and subtle a piece of characterization in his small way as any in *Mansfield Park*. The type recalls Henry Crawford. He is provided with sense and tact, but drops easily from what is true to what he knows will please his hearer, true or not. Sir Walter objects to the idea of a tenant:

> 'I am not fond of the idea of my shrubberies being always approachable; and I should recommend Miss Elliot to be on her guard with respect to her flower-garden. I am very little disposed to grant a tenant of Kellynch Hall any extraordinary favour, I assure you, be he sailor or soldier.'

After a short pause, Mr Shepherd presumed to say,

> 'In all these cases, there are established usages which make every thing plain and easy between landlord and tenant. Your interest, Sir

Walter, is in pretty safe hands. Depend upon me for taking care
that no tenant has more than his just rights. I venture to hint, that
Sir Walter Elliot cannot be half so jealous for his own, as John
Shepherd will be for him.' (18–19)

Such third-person references as conclude this are always suspect
in Jane Austen. Unfortunately the story requires Mr Shepherd no
further when the family has left Kellynch, and he drops from sight
and memory as Jane Austen has never allowed so lively a person
to drop before. Even Mr Rushworth, who appears only in the
first half of *Mansfield Park*, stays in the reader's mind throughout
because of his situation as Maria's husband.

The same is true of Mrs Clay as of her father. In this same chapter she is a pleasure the reader expects more of, and is disappointed.
She is one of the long line of flatterers including the Steeles, Miss
Bingley and Mr Elton, and recalls in particular Mrs Norris, when
in toadying vein:

> 'I quite agree with my father in thinking a sailor might be a very
> desirable tenant. I have known a good deal of the profession; and
> besides their liberality, they are so neat and careful in all their ways!
> These valuable pictures of yours, Sir Walter, if you chose to leave
> them, would be perfectly safe . . . You need not be afraid, Miss
> Elliot, of your own sweet flower-garden's being neglected.' (18)

But even so excellent a beginning is not enough to make one believe that she is the danger both Mr Elliot and Anne think her,
despite Sir Walter's comments on the way Gowland has carried
away her freckles. The only hint of her intrigue with Mr Elliot
is that she is once seen meeting him in the street; this certainly
arouses some suspicion, but on its own it is not enough. Jane
Austen, who revealed so well the underhand intrigue between
Henry Crawford and Maria, could certainly have done better
with this.

The other Kellynch personality is Lady Russell. She is a
different case; she must be respectable and respected, for she
advised Anne to refuse Wentworth, and Anne, a sensible woman,
took her advice and never believes she was wrong to do so:

'To me, she was in the place of a parent. Do not mistake me, however. I am not saying that she did not err in her advice. It was,
perhaps, one of those cases in which advice is good or bad only as
the event decides; . . . I mean, that I was right in submitting to
her, and that if I had done otherwise, I should have suffered more in
continuing the engagement than I did even in giving it up, because
I should have suffered in my conscience.' (246)

She is a character with good principles but little idea of the motives
and feelings of others, and no wit, and is therefore both in function
and treatment rather like Sir Thomas Bertram: she is a 'late'
character, different from anything Jane Austen conceived before
Mansfield Park. Jane Austen's triumph is to get our approval for
the woman who has destroyed Anne's happiness once, and who
almost manages to do so again – however well-meaningly – when
she suggests that Anne should accept Mr Elliot; a woman who
shares the Kellynch taste for rank:

> Herself, the widow of only a knight, she gave the dignity of a
> baronet all its due; and Sir Walter . . . was, as being Sir Walter,
> in her apprehension entitled to a great deal of compassion and
> consideration under his present difficulties. (11)

Fortunately the first thing we see her do is to draw up a workable
plan of economy for getting Sir Walter out of debt, and most of
her other appearances are praiseworthy ones. One delights in her
comment on the Musgrove children – 'I hope I shall remember,
in future . . . not to call at Uppercross in the Christmas holidays'
(135) – and even when she recommends Mr Elliot as a husband her
motives and feelings are sound:

> 'I own that to be able to regard you as the future mistress of
> Kellynch, the future Lady Elliot – to look forward and see you
> occupying your dear mother's place, succeeding to all her rights,
> and all her popularity, as well as to all her virtues, . . . would
> give me more delight than is often felt at my time of life!' (159–60)

Nothing Jane Austen does with her is wrong, but one could wish
that in the later stages she could do more. She is an important link
between Kellynch and Bath, and Jane Austen means her to be,
yet at Bath, although her influence is felt and a whole perceptive

paragraph of the conclusion is devoted to her, there is only one conversation in which she appears, the one (Volume IV, Chapter V) in which she tries to persuade Anne to accept Mr Elliot.

From Kellynch the story moves to Uppercross, and to a new set of characters, who are on the whole an improvement on Kellynch, and who allow new sides of Anne's character to be revealed. In general these people are affectionate and well intentioned, though not always sensible. Mary Musgrove is a variant of Mrs Bennet, both unreasonable and amusing, but more subtle, being capable of something like logic and observation when it suits her:

> '[Henrietta] took hardly any notice of Charles Hayter yesterday. I wish you had been there to see her behaviour. And as to Captain Wentworth's liking Louisa as well as Henrietta, it is nonsense to say so; for he certainly *does* like Henrietta a great deal the best.' (77)

The first sentence is true, the second wishful thinking. Mary links Uppercross with Kellynch:

> While well, and happy, and properly attended to, she had great good humour and excellent spirits; but any indisposition sunk her completely; she had no resources for solitude; and inheriting a considerable share of the Elliot self-importance, was very prone to add to every other distress that of fancying herself neglected and ill-used. (37)

Just as she is less cold than Elizabeth, so the milieu she has chosen by marriage is less cold to Anne. Her husband is another link, the person who (apart from Lady Russell) first shows signs of appreciating Anne. Charles Musgrove has once proposed to her, and is shown to appreciate her as much as his easygoing and unperceptive nature allows; when his son dislocates his collar-bone Anne offers to stay to nurse him while Charles and Mary dine with the elder Musgroves:

> 'This is very kind of Anne, . . . but it seems rather hard that she should be left at home by herself, to nurse our sick child.' (58)

This is not much praise, but it is more than Anne has had so far. Charles's comments on Charles Hayter, who has got 'a very good living . . . in the centre of some of the best preserves in the kingdom' (217), and on Captain Benwick, who, although a reader, distinguishes himself in a rat-hunt, show that he is at heart what he ironically denies: a man 'so illiberal as to want every man to have the same objects and pleasures as myself' (218).

His parents resemble him; Anne gets wry praise from them, too: 'Well done, Miss Anne! very well done indeed! Lord bless me! how those little fingers of yours fly about!' (47) is their praise of her music; and she has more of their confidence than is discreet or desirable, particularly about the way Mary mismanages her children. Even such confidence as this is in significant contrast to Kellynch, where nobody confides in Anne at all.

A new theme appears at Uppercross, that of family affection and domestic ties, quite different from the snobbery that binds the Elliots to their cousins Lady Dalrymple and the Honourable Miss Carteret. The affection shown by the Uppercross families is limited by the limited sense of the characters, so that it shall lead up to, but not overshadow, these virtues as they appear at their finest among the naval characters. This is Mrs Croft and Mrs Musgrove, for example:

> '. . . the only time that I ever fancied myself unwell, or had any ideas of danger, was the winter that I passed by myself at Deal, when the Admiral (*Captain* Croft then) was in the North Seas. I lived in perpetual fright at that time . . . but as long as we could be together, nothing ever ailed me, and I never met with the smallest inconvenience.'
>
> 'Ay, to be sure. – Yes, indeed, oh yes, I am quite of your opinion, Mrs Croft . . . *I* know what it is, for Mr Musgrove always attends the assizes, and I am so glad when they are over, and he is safe back again.' (71)

Charles Musgrove also thinks well of his cousins the Hayters, and of Charles Hayter, the curate who wishes to marry Henrietta, although they are not polished enough to satisfy Mary; and his two sisters Henrietta and Louisa have

> that seemingly perfect good understanding and agreement together, that good-humoured mutual affection, of which [Anne] had known so little herself with either of her sisters. (41)

The neatest comment on these two is Admiral Croft's 'very nice young ladies they both are; I hardly know one from the other' (92). They become distinct from one another only when Louisa is singled out by Wentworth, and receives his lecture on resolution and independence; in following his advice she enforces its deficiencies, and at the same time becomes a source of comedy. Henrietta is chiefly useful in relation to Charles Hayter, so keeping the Kellynch snobbery – shown in Mary's disapproval – in mind throughout this section. She therefore does not appear at Bath – though she comes there to buy wedding clothes – when the Elliots themselves are before the reader and can make their own effect. Louisa, though seeming an impediment, in fact hastens Wentworth's return to Anne: the wilful obstinacy that causes her own accident at Lyme teaches him his lesson:

> He had learnt to distinguish between the steadiness of principle and the obstinacy of self-will, between the darings of heedlessness and the resolution of a collected mind. (242)

A few servants are mentioned at Uppercross, indicating that they are thought of here, whereas at Kellynch servants are merely part of the machinery of living. Dr Shirley, the rector, and the Hayter family bring in another layer of society between these servants and the one Jane Austen is concerned with; and there are significant mentions of the children, who, as in *Emma* and *Pride and Prejudice*, enrich the picture of family life, and who, as in those novels, are wisely given little part in the action, even though young Charles by dislocating his collar-bone has a direct effect on the plot.

Finally, there are the first and most important of the naval characters: Frederick Wentworth – who will be dealt with later – and Admiral and Mrs Croft. As the lessee of Kellynch the Admiral has been heard of already, and has made his splendid comment that 'the baronet will never set the Thames on fire' (32). At Uppercross we see him and his wife together, embodying the idea of happy marriage which is a central one in the novel. They are in the style of *Emma*, humorous characters who are yet respectable, whom we do not think of deriding. Though they have little to do, their important part in the conversation on sailors and their wives brings them forward – Mrs Croft especially – as models of cheerful practical sense; she elicits a smile rather by the vigorous way she speaks than by what she says; this is an exchange with Wentworth:

> '. . . how impossible it is, with all one's efforts, and all one's sacrifices, to make the accommodations on board, such as women ought to have . . . I hate to hear of women on board, or to see them on board.' . . .
> '. . . I declare I have not a comfort or an indulgence about me, even at Kellynch-hall,' (with a kind bow to Anne) 'beyond what I always had in most of the ships I have lived in; and they have been five altogether.'
> 'Nothing to the purpose,' replied her brother. 'You were living with your husband; and were the only woman on board.'
> 'But you, yourself, brought Mrs Harville, her sister, her cousin, and the three children round from Portsmouth to Plymouth. Where was this superfine, extraordinary sort of gallantry of yours, then?' (68–69)

She and the Admiral are complementary; they share the same sense and the same turns of speech, but his expressions are broader, and she is more perceptive. Jane Austen has habitually used cliché to reveal insincerity, but the Admiral's odd nautical phrases are quite apt and true. They show how Jane Austen has improved upon her early style: her right-thinking minor characters no longer have to be witty to show sense. After the one important conversation at Uppercross in which the Admiral declares 'I wish Frederick would spread a little more canvas, and bring us home one of these young ladies to Kellynch' (92), the Crofts need not appear much at Bath, though when they do it is to good purpose: the Admiral gives a humorous check when Anne wants to know what Wentworth thinks of Louisa's engagement –

> 'He does not give the least fling at Benwick; does not so much as say, "I wonder at it, I have a reason of my own for wondering at it." No, you would not guess, from his way of writing, that he had ever thought of this Miss (what's her name?) for himself.' (173)

– and Mrs Croft continues to be practical about marriage:

> 'I would rather have young people settle on a small income at once, and have to struggle with a few difficulties together, than be involved in a long engagement.' (230)

Such remarks keep Anne firmly based on the practical; Jane Austen may be idealistic in this novel, but she runs no risk of being sentimental.

From such characters it is an easy step to the last group of sailors, at Lyme: Captain and Mrs Harville and Captain Benwick. They are socially inferior to anyone who has appeared so far, and Captain Harville is lame as well as poor, 'his taste, and his health, and his fortune all directing him to a residence unexpensive, and by the sea' (97). Their function is, of course, to show the good sense and feeling of the world Captain Wentworth inhabits, and to contrast it with Anne's. They carry on the idea begun with the Admiral, of frankness – even indiscretion – as a guide to character and a token of virtue, in opposition to the correct social conduct as it is embodied in Mr Elliot. This is in striking contrast to *Pride and Prejudice* in particular, where social propriety is almost equated with virtue. Captain Harville is the personification of what Sir Walter dislikes –

> a tall, dark man, with a sensible, benevolent countenance; a little lame; and from strong features, and want of health, looking much older than Captain Wentworth (97)

– bearing out Mrs Clay's thesis on the harmful effects of work. This is all that is seen of him, yet in such a context his one long intimate conversation with Anne, about his dead sister and Captain Benwick – which brings about Wentworth's proposal – seems neither abrupt nor unlikely.[1]

Captain Benwick himself is an agreeable figure; his main use, of course, is to marry Louisa and so get her out of Captain Wentworth's way, but he also admires Anne, showing that she is still attractive, and preparing for Mr Elliot's stronger admiration. He embodies a romantic idea of fidelity – he looks melancholy,

[1] Volume IV, Chapter XI.

is quiet and retired, and reads Byron – and so shows that such an idea is neither Anne's nor Jane Austen's.

Finally, there is Bath. Although Bath is primarily the meeting-place for them all, where the differences, and misunderstandings at the other places, can resolve themselves, two new characters appear here – Mr Elliot (who, his identity unknown, has put in a short appearance at Lyme) and Mrs Smith – and a few minor ones are mentioned, of which Lady Dalrymple and Miss Carteret merely emphasize the Elliot snobbery, and Colonel and Mrs Wallis – 'the beautiful Mrs Wallis' (145) – are suspect by association with the Elliots and so little defined that they help to render their friend Mr Elliot suspect, too. Mrs Smith soon confirms the suspicion: 'Colonel Wallis has a very pretty silly wife, to whom he tells things which he had better not' (205). Mrs Smith is a difficulty; she comes too late, is obviously a convenient piece of machinery, and having too much to reveal in too little time, in a novel where by Jane Austen's standards characters say little, she talks too much. That she should be Anne's former schoolfellow as well as the widow of Mr Elliot's close friend (as she must if she is to tell all Anne must know about Mr Elliot and his opinions), this is a coincidence Jane Austen makes no attempt to disguise. Mrs Smith, dealing so much as she does in hearsay and gossip, herself contradicts the good impression Jane Austen makes for her at first:

> Anne found in Mrs Smith the good sense and agreeable manners which she had almost ventured to depend on, and a disposition to converse and be cheerful beyond her expectation. Neither the dissipations of the past – and she had lived very much in the world, nor the restrictions of the present; neither sickness nor sorrow seemed to have closed her heart or ruined her spirits. (153)

However, her cheerful disillusion – the antithesis of Captain Benwick – prevents Anne from seeming sentimental.

Mr Elliot is another difficulty. He is like Henry Crawford in having good manners but not outstanding good looks, having, in fact, the appearance and manners which in the early novels might well betoken virtue; and while she has got him Jane Austen uses him perfectly: it is her method of getting rid of him that displeases. All the hints of his relationship with Mrs Clay are consistent, but there are not nearly enough of them, and it must seem out of character for him to behave as he does, abandoning for the insignificant Mrs Clay the position in society and the place in the family which we have been brought to believe that he esteems. The conclusion of *Persuasion* shows the same passion as in *Mansfield Park* for tying up loose ends, and for very strict morality: in a novel like *Pride and Prejudice* Mr Elliot could have married Elizabeth Elliot: that he would then have been Anne's and Wentworth's brother-in-law would not have mattered, for Wickham was Darcy's. Mr Elliot is, however, generally both useful and interesting. At Lyme, his passing admiration draws Wentworth's attention to Anne's returning prettiness, thus preparing Wentworth, when he sees the faults in Louisa, to contrast them with Anne's good sense, and preparing him also to see in Mr Elliot, a cousin and intimate of the family, a powerful rival. While there is never any doubt or much anxiety about whether Wentworth will finally marry Anne, Mr Elliot's presence helps raise some reasonable apprehensions by reopening the question of overpersuasion: Lady Russell favours him, which gives Captain Wentworth some very proper misgivings. Mr Elliot himself is more subtle than any of Jane Austen's other outright villains; Wickham, for instance, can impose on Elizabeth much more easily, and Willoughby can impose on a whole family (Elinor never bothers herself with Willoughby's motives, only with Marianne's conduct). But Mr Elliot soon shows the one prevailing quality of all her bad characters – hypocrisy:

> . . . there had been a period of his life (and probably not a short one) when he had been, at least, careless on all serious matters; and, though he might now think very differently, who could answer for the true sentiments of a clever, cautious man, grown old enough to appreciate a fair character? How could it ever be ascertained that his mind was truly cleansed? (161)

It is clearly a subtle man who produces such an effect on a subtle heroine.

In *Persuasion* conduct is usually correct – these are not young people who have to learn how to behave – and conduct in small matters is not the reliable guide it was to moral qualities. Indeed, almost the opposite is true, and the naval characters (above all Captain Wentworth) point it out:

> She prized the frank, the open-hearted, the eager character beyond all others. Warmth and enthusiasm did captivate her still. She felt that she could so much more depend upon the sincerity of those who sometimes looked or said a careless or a hasty thing, than of those whose presence of mind never varied, whose tongue never slipped. (161)

This is a sensible and practical view of character, but as a way of considering a hero, unromantic: Captain Wentworth's lapses are not admirable, and do not in themselves please Anne. For instance, on the occasion when Mrs Musgrove mourns sentimentally for her worthless son:

> ...a certain glance of Captain Wentworth's bright eye, and curl of his handsome mouth convinced Anne that...he had probably been at some pains to get rid of him. (67)

If he cannot conceal trivial irritation, he is not likely, as Mr Elliot is, to be able to conceal anything worse. Wentworth, as we have seen, by no means pleases everyone. Sir Walter and Elizabeth treat him coldly, and for Lady Russell 'he was brilliant, he was headstrong. – Lady Russell had little taste for wit; and of any thing approaching to imprudence a horror' (27). It is as though Jane Austen's usual hero and heroine had changed places: Anne, like Mr Knightley, is steadily and unobtrusively right, while Wentworth, like Emma, is wrong, and just as Emma nearly ruins her chances of marriage to the right person, so does he. His personality is a development of Henry Tilney's; he has the same teasing and good-humoured wit: his reply to Mary's silly lament that they were not able to recognize Mr Elliot at Lyme recalls some of Henry Tilney's exchanges with Mrs Allen and Catherine:

> 'Putting all these very extraordinary circumstances together,' said Captain Wentworth, 'we must consider it to be the arrange-

ment of Providence, that you should not be introduced to your cousin.' (106)

Jane Austen's treatment of him is excellent: it must be difficult to introduce a man who has estranged himself from the heroine and will think ill of her, and who must yet be an agreeable character from the first. His thoughts are given after their first meeting (they have been quoted above), very much as Darcy's are given soon after he has met Elizabeth, and for the same reason: to make him intelligible and agreeable where the situation makes him the opposite. Wentworth enters by degrees: one anticipates that he will soon come when the Crofts take Kellynch; he comes to Uppercross and Anne just avoids a formal meeting at dinner, and therefore all the Miss Musgroves' reports of him come before he does; he finally appears for a moment at the cottage, where the meeting is as unostentatious as could well be – 'Her eye half met Captain Wentworth's; a bow, a curtsey passed' (59) – and thereafter he can appear easily either in conversation or as Anne sees him.

Lastly there is Anne herself. In fact, as with all the novels, it is impossible to discuss much of it without at the same time talking about the heroine, especially here, where Anne's attitude so nearly coincides with her author's: she is not so astringent as her creator, but very nearly as understanding, and very nearly contemporary. She therefore bears easily her part of the narrative and of the moral comment. Anne is always perfectly right, and known to be so from her first appearance:

> [Lady Russell] consulted, and in a degree was influenced by her, in marking out the scheme of retrenchment, which was at last submitted to Sir Walter. Every emendation of Anne's had been on the side of honesty against importance. She wanted more vigorous measures, a more complete reformation, a quicker release from debt, a much higher tone of indifference for every thing but justice and equity. (12)

This is very obvious good sense, and makes the way clear for things less obvious, like her opinions on other people:

> Anne could believe, with Lady Russell, that a more equal match

might have greatly improved [Charles Musgrove], and that a woman of real understanding might have given more consequence to his character, and more usefulness, rationality, and elegance to his habits and pursuits. (43)

The way is clear also for her analyses of the motives of people she knows little of:

> While she considered Louisa to be rather the favourite, she could not but think, as far as she might dare to judge from memory and experience, that Captain Wentworth was not in love with either. They were more in love with him; yet there it was not love. It was a little fever of admiration; but it might, probably must, end in love with some. (82)

It allows her at last to utter the kind of generalization usually the prerogative of her author:

> She was persuaded that any tolerably pleasing young woman who had listened and seemed to feel for him, would have received the same compliment. He had an affectionate heart. He must love somebody. (167)

Anne's opinions as seen here have a wider impact than any other heroine's. Analysing single incidents, she often produces a general principle of action, or an aphorism on human life and conduct:

> 'Don't talk of it, don't talk of it,' he cried. 'Oh God! that I had not given way to her at the fatal moment! Had I done as I ought! But so eager and so resolute! Dear, sweet Louisa!'
> Anne wondered whether it ever occurred to him now, to question the justness of his own previous opinion as to the universal felicity and advantage of firmness of character; and whether it might not strike him, that, like all other qualities of the mind, it should have its proportions and limits. (116)

Anne is therefore an easier character to understand than the other heroines, since her remarks are only very rarely ironically at variance with Jane Austen's, and it requires less of that mental alertness, which Jane Austen so habitually demands, to appreciate her. *Emma*'s exclamatory method of retailing thought is largely done away with because Anne's idioms and style are not clues to her meaning; there is generally little difference in style between what Anne says and what Jane Austen says, and it is sometimes both difficult and unnecessary to decide which one is speaking. Anne only once loses her judgement, and this is itself a nice piece of judgement on Jane Austen's part:

> 'You should have distinguished,' replied Anne. 'You should not have suspected me now; the case so different, and my age so different. If I was wrong in yielding to persuasion once, remember that it was to persuasion exerted on the side of safety, not of risk. When I yielded, I thought it was to duty; but no duty could be called in aid here. In marrying a man indifferent to me, all risk would have been incurred, and all duty violated.' (244)

She is, logically, right, but it would have been psychologically unlikely that Wentworth should have thought in such terms. This in its more subtle way recalls Elinor:

> Elinor scolded him, harshly as ladies always scold the impru-dence which compliments themselves, for having spent so much time with them at Norland, when he must have felt his own in-constancy. (*Sense and Sensibility*, 368)

Anne generally appears more by what she thinks than what she does. Compared with Catherine Morland, Elizabeth and Emma, and even with Elinor (who herself has not much to do), Anne is a passive heroine. Fanny is the only other heroine who does so little, but in *Mansfield Park* a great many things can happen without her, as she is not the organizing force the other heroines are. Anne has very little to do, and her actions, like her manners, are 'as consciously right as they [are] invariably gentle' (153). Her most important acts are to take charge after Louisa's fall, and to go forward deliberately to speak to Captain Wentworth at the concert when her family ignores him.

The plot of *Persuasion* is very slight, even for so short a novel, and seems slighter than it might, since we only see what immediately concerns Anne. One good reason for not developing the affair between Mr Elliot and Mrs Clay is that it would produce too much interest in which Anne had no part, just when Anne herself ought to be the most absorbing person. As it is, they are an un-satisfactory feature of the plot, for there is no good reason why they should go off together; if Mr Elliot could not marry Anne for love and the family position, he could have married Elizabeth for the family position alone, and certainly need not have gone off with Mrs Clay without either. It is not to be believed – for all Jane Austen's wit – that

> it is now a doubtful point whether his cunning, or hers, may finally carry the day; whether, after preventing her from being the wife of Sir Walter, he may not be wheedled and caressed at last into making her the wife of Sir William. (250)

The idea is entertaining – a case of two biters being reciprocally bitten – but this is the humour of earlier works, and as *Persuasion* now stands it has no place in it.

Mrs Smith is even less obviously worked into the action. It is unusual for a Jane Austen character to have only one link with the present action (as Mrs Smith has in Anne) and not be finally linked or seen in contact with many other characters.[1] Like Mrs Clay's, Mrs Smith's actions are consistent with the information given about her, but are yet not quite satisfactory. She has good reasons for concealing Mr Elliot's bad character:

> 'I considered your marrying him as certain, though he might not yet have made the offer, and I could no more speak the truth of him, than if he had been your husband.' (211)

But even so, this utterance jars against her arch exchanges with Anne just before it, and against her requests that Anne, when married, will influence Mr Elliot in her favour; these seem to spring from much less noble motives than those she professes. Mrs Smith is certainly very necessary, but she appears only in Bath, she does what she has to do, and then, like Mr Elliot, she briskly receives her deserts; this is very much less accomplished than the nicety with which Captain Benwick is introduced and delicately disposed of.

Another summary disposal is Lady Russell's:

[1] Mrs Smith's other link, with Mr Elliot, is so far in the past and so completely at an end that it cannot count.

There was nothing less for Lady Russell to do, than to admit that
she had been pretty completely wrong, and to take up a new set of
opinions and of hopes. (249)

But we never see her doing it; we never see her even receive the
news of Anne's engagement. There has been no need in the other
novels to see hostile people find out about engagements (although
Mr Bennet has to give permission for Elizabeth's), but the moral
Lady Russell has had an influence well-meaning but wrong, and
she ought to be seen to acknowledge it. No other novel ends
quite so abruptly after a proposal and acceptance, because, since
there is no doubt even as early as Chapter VII that Captain Wentworth will propose and be accepted as soon as he is in a position
to do so, there is not much in the way of explanation and understanding to be done afterwards, such as there was between Emma
and Mr Knightley or Elizabeth and Mr Darcy. Lady Russell is
the only problem.

The faults in *Persuasion* are all confined to subordinate action
and to what could be, with enlargement, a sub-plot. The pattern-
ing of the main plot is as exquisite as any of the novels. Being so
short, the book is in only two volumes, not divided, however, at
the most dramatic point (which is Louisa's fall) in the way
Mansfield Park is divided at Sir Thomas's return from Antigua,
but at the more significant one where Anne and Henrietta, accompanied by Captain Wentworth, return from Lyme to Uppercross, a point which marks the change in Wentworth's feelings
towards Anne. Chapters are as systematically arranged as ever –
a tidy twelve to each volume – and the passage of time within
them is as neatly marked as ever by the unobtrusive allusions to
seasons, weather, and – at Bath – particular days of the week.[1]
The movement is the opposite of her more usual method – seen
especially in *Northanger Abbey* and *Pride and Prejudice* – of beginning with accounts of particular days in orderly sequence, and
then broadening out to cover longer intervals in a shorter space.
Persuasion begins with whole months, retailed by significant or

[1] Mr Elliot is particularly noted as leaving on a Thursday, and a visit to the
theatre is proposed, which is on a Saturday (see Chapman's 'Chronology of
Persuasion', *The Novels of Jane Austen* (Oxford), V, p. 280).

representative incidents (Anne goes to Uppercross in September and to Bath after Christmas); and it ends at Bath by chronicling particular days, where every day has its importance, either in uniting Captain Wentworth and Anne, or in keeping them apart. Such a plan contributes to make *Persuasion* an easier book to read than *Emma* or even *Pride and Prejudice*, which both exact intense concentration from the reader in the opening chapters. *Persuasion* leads easily into the story, and gains in facility for the reader what it loses in dramatic power.

Its really new feature is its use of locality. This has already been mentioned in connexion with the characters, who are patterned and grouped by where they appear. Such use helps to prevent the confusion which must arise on first reading, partly because so many are related – like the Crofts and the Wentworths, the Elliots and the Musgroves, and the Musgroves and the Hayters – and therefore have names in common; not only surnames like the two Musgrove households, but family Christian names, like Charles Musgrove and his cousin Charles Hayter. The settings are relevant and illuminating to these characters, and are also more widely relevant to the theme of the novel itself. They do, in fact, what some of the minor characters did in other novels. Place and weather indicate Anne's state of mind, just as the references to Lady Stornaway and Mrs Fraser indicated Mary Crawford's, or as the various members of the militia indicated Lydia Bennet's at Brighton.

Kellynch, as befits its occupants, is a frigid place. An estate, simply by existing, may be relied on to make its own impression;[1] what detail is given must therefore be relevant, not merely informative, and there need be very little even of that when everyone is about to go away. What we do hear at first is artificial or petty: there is mention of a flower-garden, of carriages, and of Anne's 'favourite grove', which is even less than we hear of Norland before the Dashwoods leave it. Kellynch comes to life only with lively occupants when the Crofts arrive, with engaging

---

[1] On Jane Austen's contemporary readers, that is; there is no need, when she writes, for the labour Henry James has to bestow on his own version of the same thing, Gardencourt, in *The Portrait of a Lady*.

remarks about umbrellas, the laundry door, a chimney which
smokes, and one very pertinent one about a dressing-room:

> 'I have done very little besides sending away some of the large
> looking-glasses from my dressing-room, which was your father's
> . . . I should think he must be rather a dressy man for his time of
> life. – Such a number of looking-glasses! oh Lord! there was no
> getting away from oneself.' (127–8)

While this use of Kellynch is fairly close to the way Jane Austen
habitually uses her setting, Uppercross begins an alteration. The
two houses here are very deliberately relevant to their occupants:

> Uppercross was a moderate-sized village, which a few years back
> had been completely in the old English style; containing only two
> houses superior in appearance to those of the yeomen and labourers,
> – the mansion of the 'squire, with its high walls, great gates, and old
> trees, substantial and unmodernized – and the compact, tight
> parsonage, enclosed in its own neat garden, with a vine and a pear-
> tree trained round its casements; but upon the marriage of the young
> 'squire, it had received the improvement of a farm-house elevated
> into a cottage for his residence; and Uppercross Cottage, with its
> viranda, French windows, and other prettinesses, was quite as likely
> to catch the traveller's eye, as the more consistent and considerable
> aspect and premises of the Great House, about a quarter of a mile
> farther on. (36)

This gives the impression that the occupants of the cottage may
themselves be *less* 'consistent and considerable', which is soon
confirmed by more similar evidence. In the cottage Anne finds
Mary 'lying on the faded sofa of the pretty little drawing-room,
the once elegant furniture of which had been gradually growing
shabby, under the influence of four summers and two children'
(37); the condition is Mary's, as well as her furniture's. Such
detail has only been found before this in the Portsmouth section
of *Mansfield Park*, where its function is different. Soon afterwards
they call on the elder Musgroves,

> to sit the full half hour in the old-fashioned square parlour, with a
> small carpet and shining floor, to which the present daughters of
> the house were gradually giving the proper air of confusion by a

grand piano forte and a harp, flower-stands and little tables placed in every direction. Oh! could the originals of the portraits against the wainscot, could the gentlemen in brown velvet and the ladies in blue satin have seen what was going on, have been conscious of such an overthrow of all order and neatness! The portraits themselves seemed to be staring in astonishment. (40)

The engaging conceit   anticipating the humour of the Victorian novelists – which closes the passage is new to Jane Austen, and uses new material, even though in the old way it is strictly relevant to character, as the next sentence shows:

The Musgroves, like their houses, were in a state of alteration, perhaps of improvement. The father and mother were in the old English style, and the young people in the new. (40)

Another episode at Uppercross is new:

Her *pleasure* in the walk must arise from the exercise and the day, from the view of the last smiles of the year upon the tawny leaves and withered hedges, and from repeating to herself some few of the thousand poetical descriptions extant of autumn, that season of peculiar and inexhaustible influence on the mind of taste and tenderness, that season which has drawn from every poet, worthy of being read, some attempt at description, or some lines of feeling. . . . and after another half mile of gradual ascent through large enclosures, where the ploughs at work, and the fresh-made path spoke the farmer, counteracting the sweets of poetical despondence, and meaning to have spring again, they gained the summit of the most considerable hill. (84–85)

This retails Anne's thoughts and so reveals character; but Jane Austen has never treated nature in this 'pastoral-comical' way before, and the passage reaches a climax at 'meaning to have spring again', which clearly points to the course of Anne's own life, which is to have its own second spring. But the style slips easily back to Jane Austen's usual level and to Mary's commonplace expressions: 'Bless me! here is Winthrop – I declare I had no idea!' (85)

This all prepares the way for the treatment of Lyme which readers rightly remark. The well-known description of Lyme is unlike any other in her work, the only other thing approaching it in length being the description of Donwell Abbey (*Emma*, p. 358), which is all seen through Emma's eyes. The passage on Lyme has no immediate relevance to the matter in hand, and is unmistakably Jane Austen's own feelings, with no recourse to Anne as a mouthpiece:

> They were come too late in the year for any amusement or variety which Lyme, as a public place, might offer; the rooms were shut up, the lodgers almost all gone, scarcely any family but of the residents left – and, as there is nothing to admire in the buildings themselves, the remarkable situation of the town, the principal street almost hurrying into the water, the walk to the Cobb, skirting round the pleasant little bay, which in the season is animated with bathing machines and company, the Cobb itself, its old wonders and new improvements, with the very beautiful line of cliffs stretching out to the east of the town, are what the stranger's eye will seek; and a very strange stranger it must be, who does not see charms in the immediate environs of Lyme, to make him wish to know it better. The scenes in its neighbourhood, Charmouth, with its high grounds and extensive sweeps of country, and still more its sweet retired bay, backed by dark cliffs, where fragments of low rock among the sands make it the happiest spot for watching the flow of the tide, for sitting in unwearied contemplation; – the woody varieties of the cheerful village of Up Lyme, and, above all, Pinny, with its green chasms between romantic rocks, where the scattered forest trees and orchards of luxuriant growth declare that many a generation must have passed away since the first partial falling of the cliff prepared the ground for such a state, where a scene so wonderful and so lovely is exhibited, as may more than equal any of the resembling scenes of the far-famed Isle of Wight: these places must be visited, and visited again, to make the worth of Lyme understood. (95–96)

This makes Lyme a pleasant, even a romantic place, a setting for the pleasant characters there – in particular the Harvilles – for the first signs of Anne's returning beauty, and for Wentworth's returning admiration for her. Such praise, coming uncompromisingly from the author, makes Lyme remain a pleasant place even after Louisa's disastrous fall. The accident cannot efface the first impression either for the reader or for Anne herself:

> 'One does not love a place the less for having suffered in it, unless it has been all suffering, nothing but suffering – which was by no means the case at Lyme.' (184)

Bath is neutral ground, it serves much the same purpose as London does in *Sense and Sensibility*, as a meeting-ground, the only place where all the characters – including the new ones Mrs Smith and Mr Elliot – can mingle without incongruity.[1] It is also a place Anne does not like, either in anticipation – 'the possible heats of September in all the white glare of Bath' (33) – or in fact:

> amidst the dash of other carriages, the heavy rumble of carts and drays, the bawling of newsmen, muffin-men and milk-men, and the ceaseless clink of pattens . . . she persisted in a very determined, though very silent, disinclination for Bath. (135)

Bath is a fashionable city, and therefore suits the snobbery of the Elliots and is a significant setting for Mr Elliot, to whose character we need all such significant clues that we can get.

Being so short, *Persuasion* is divided into only two volumes, and in these two (as has already been shown) there is more of Jane Austen herself to tell the story than in any of the longer novels; there is less conversation between characters and less use of the monologue. Jane Austen's style therefore more readily recalls that of her eighteenth-century masters. Miss Lascelles finds signs of Johnson and of Boswell's rendering of him, and there are Johnsonian rhythms.[2] This need not indicate a new dependence on him, but only a more solemn subject and less dramatic treatment of it, which allows an habitual debt to appear with propriety. Such a tone for the narrative is heard in the first sentence:

> Sir Walter Elliot, of Kellynch-hall, in Somersetshire, was a man who, for his own amusement, never took up any book but the Baronetage; there he found occupation for an idle hour, and con-

[1] London has always been for novelists 'that ocean where each kind Does straight his own resemblance find'; other cities are more rarely used (although Smollett used Bath in *Humphry Clinker*).
[2] *Jane Austen and her Art*, pp. 107–11.

solation in a distressed one; there his faculties were roused into
admiration and respect, by contemplating the limited remnant of
the earliest patents; there any unwelcome sensations, arising from
domestic affairs, changed naturally into pity and contempt, as he
turned over the almost endless creations of the last century – and
there, if every other leaf were powerless, he could read his own
history with an interest which never failed – this was the page at
which the favourite volume always opened. (3)

And there follows his pedigree. This is the Johnson of *The Rambler*,
and shows a fine use of the period whose weight is satirically far
too great for the meaning which should support it: after 'changed
naturally' one naturally expects 'tranquillity', whereas 'pity and
contempt' have a finer rhythm, but their sense is bathos. The
method recalls Mrs Norris, who 'found herself obliged to be
attached to the Rev. Mr Norris . . . with scarcely any private
fortune' and who 'began [her] career of conjugal felicity with
very little less than a thousand a year' (*Mansfield Park*, p. 3). If
Persuasion had been *Pride and Prejudice*, one suspects that the
opening chapter would have been what is now Chapter III, whose
lively conversation gives over again a good deal of the information
Jane Austen's own account has already provided.

The different method of attack continues; Jane Austen passes
over whole stretches of time in her own voice:

> The party at the Great House was sometimes increased by other
> company. The neighbourhood was not large, but the Musgroves
> were visited by every body, and had more dinner parties, and more
> callers, more visitors by invitation and by chance, than any other
> family. They were more completely popular.
>
> The girls were wild for dancing; and the evenings ended, occa-
> sionally, in an unpremeditated little ball. There was a family of
> cousins within a walk of Uppercross, in less affluent circumstances,
> who depended on the Musgroves for all their pleasures: they would
> come at any time, and help play at any thing, or dance any where;
> and Anne, very much preferring the office of musician to a more
> active post, played country dances to them by the hour together . . .
>
> So passed the first three weeks. Michaelmas came; and now Anne's
> heart must be in Kellynch again. (47)

This does more than merely lead up to the fateful day on which the Crofts enter Kellynch; these are all representative and relevant details showing how Anne is thought of by her companions, and how she behaves. Elsewhere Jane Austen is aphoristic:

> 'I hope I shall remember, in future,' said Lady Russell, as soon as they were reseated in the carriage, 'not to call at Uppercross in the Christmas holidays.'
> Every body has their taste in noises as well as in other matters; and sounds are quite innoxious, or most distressing, by their sort rather than their quantity. (135)

The passage goes straight on to say how Lady Russell was not disturbed by the clatter of Bath, and so the scene is changed. It is a deliberately abrupt change, Jane Austen being concerned to make the statement about human conduct rather than simply to advance the story, which now seems to come so easily to her that she can be less concerned with it:

> . . . they walked together some time, talking as before of Mr Scott and Lord Byron, and still as unable, as before, and as unable as any other two readers, to think exactly alike of the merits of either, till something occasioned an almost general change amongst their party, and instead of Captain Benwick, she had Captain Harville by her side. (107)

The reader, accustomed to her usual precise ways, expects the author to tell him what that 'something' was; but this is not relevant and so is left out. Jane Austen in *Persuasion* is concerned with states of mind aroused by events, rather than with the events themselves. Her method here is to select what is of universal application from her material, rather than – as in *Emma* – to let the universal emerge ironically by contrast with her particular topic. She tends towards passages such as this reflection on Mrs Smith:

> . . this was not a case of fortitude or of resignation only. – A submissive spirit might be patient, a strong understanding would supply resolution, but here was something more; here was that elasticity of mind, that disposition to be comforted, that power of turning readily from evil to good, and of finding employment

which carried her out of herself, which was from Nature alone. It was the choicest gift of Heaven; and Anne viewed her friend as one of those instances in which, by a merciful appointment, it seems designed to counterbalance almost every other want. (154)

Jane Austen's style is therefore commonly more aphoristic and periodic than has been her custom: and the style extends to her characters, particularly, of course, to Anne. Anne's reflections blend easily with Jane Austen's because they are like hers:

> She felt that she could so much more depend upon the sincerity of those who sometimes looked or said a careless or a hasty thing, than of those whose presence of mind never varied, whose tongue never slipped. (161)

This refers immediately to Captain Wentworth, but is not the less universally true. She occasionally lets Anne, while still reflective, be a little less acute than herself, as in her overidealized estimate of nurses and nursing – 'a sick chamber may often furnish the worth of volumes' (156) – and she is also less given to humour:

> Prettier musings of high-wrought love and eternal constancy, could never have passed along the streets of Bath, than Anne was sporting with from Camden-place to Westgate-buildings. It was almost enough to spread purification and perfume all the way. (192)

There is another more notorious example of Jane Austen dissociating herself from her characters. She comments on Mrs Musgrove's sentimental laments for her son:

> Captain Wentworth should be allowed some credit for the self-command with which he attended to her large fat sighings over the destiny of a son, whom alive nobody had cared for.
>
> Personal size and mental sorrow have certainly no necessary proportions. A large bulky figure has as good a right to be in deep affliction, as the most graceful set of limbs in the world. But, fair or not fair, there are unbecoming conjunctions, which reason will patronize in vain, – which taste cannot tolerate, – which ridicule will seize. (68)

This shows how Jane Austen's habitual tone elsewhere in this novel has altered from what it was in the early novels; this passage to which so many have objected would probably have gone unnoticed in the sharper and lighter context of *Sense and Sensibility* or *Pride and Prejudice.*

Minor characters also share this moral tone, and especially notable are Lady Russell and Mrs Smith. Lady Russell says little in her own voice, but her opinions are given, whether by the author or herself, in the same open didactic way: this is her opinion that Sir Walter must economize:

> 'What will he be doing, in fact, but what very many of our first families have done, – or ought to do? – There will be nothing singular in his case; and it is singularity which often makes the worst part of our suffering, as it always does of our conduct.' (12)

Mrs Smith is at once more cheerful and more cynical:

> 'Call it gossip if you will; but when nurse Rooke has half an hour's leisure to bestow on me, she is sure to have something to relate that is entertaining and profitable, something that makes one know one's species better. One likes to hear what is going on, to be *au fait* as to the newest modes of being trifling and silly.' (155)

Superficially, this recalls Elizabeth Bennet; but such expression – the impersonal construction and the detached phrase 'one's species' – is a long way from Elizabeth's eagerness to laugh at her acquaintance 'whenever she can', and shows how a change of attitude produces a change of style quite apart from the requirements of character. Mrs Smith becomes a part of the theme and the main pattern of the novel by the style Jane Austen employs for her, even though she is so tenuously connected in the more obvious ways.

The weighty style and tendency to aphorism persist in Sir Walter and Mrs Clay, but with them it is devoted to the wrong subjects, subjects so patently and precisely wrong that they enrich the other serious characters by the contrast with them. This is Mrs Clay:

> 'In fact, as I have long been convinced, though every profession is necessary and honourable in its turn, it is only the lot of those who are not obliged to follow any, who can live in a regular way, in the country, choosing their own hours, following their own pursuits, and living on their own property, without the torment of

trying for more; it is only *their* lot, I say, to hold the blessings of health and a good appearance to the utmost.' (20–21)

This shows clearly that Mrs Clay is at this point essential to the novel as a whole – the beginning of her sentence seems to be leading to one of the author's own firmly held ideas of a worthy existence – whatever may happen to her later. Sir Walter is the same; here he gives the opinions on the navy which provoked Mrs Clay's discourse above:

'. . . it is in two points offensive to me; I have two strong grounds of objection to it. First, as being the means of bringing persons of obscure birth into undue distinction, and raising men to honours which their fathers and grandfathers never dreamt of; and secondly, as it cuts up a man's youth and vigour most horribly; a sailor grows old sooner than any other man; I have observed it all my life. A man is in greater danger in the navy of being insulted by the rise of one whose father, his father might have disdained to speak to, and of becoming prematurely an object of disgust himself, than in any other line.' (19)

Jane Austen seems to have found that the extensive and brilliant conversations which are so obviously lacking were less to her purpose in this novel; she has here a large number of characters whose speech and behaviour is 'consciously right'. Even Sir Walter and Elizabeth may be relied upon to say the right thing –

There was little to distress them beyond the want of graciousness and warmth. – Sir Walter made no objection, and Elizabeth did nothing worse than look cold and unconcerned. (248)

– while Mr Elliot is to be distrusted on the very grounds that he *is* 'consciously right':

That he was a sensible man, an agreeable man, – that he talked well, professed good opinions, seemed to judge properly and as a man of principle, – this was all clear enough. He certainly knew what was right, nor could she fix on any one article of moral duty evidently transgressed; but yet she would have been afraid to answer for his conduct. (160)

There are therefore none of the superb accounts of talk and actions – although plenty of social gatherings occur where they could take place – that there are in *Emma*. Conversation when given is usually significant of the theme and of the character actually speaking, and does comparatively little to advance the action, to throw light on other characters, or to give information about the plot, as it has usually done hitherto.

In *Persuasion*, Jane Austen's last completed work (if finished it actually is), she has turned away from her customary interest: the effect of moral standards on the individual in his relations with the society in which he lives; and turned away from what have been her two greatest strengths: her power to let the individual reveal himself by what he does and says in the company of others – that is, by commonplace but significant details of action and speech – and her power to produce from such details an ordered whole which is shaped by and at the same time justifies those moral standards which she puts forward. If she had lived to write more, and if she did not intend to revise this novel into something more like her others, *Persuasion* shows that Jane Austen was moving towards a more introspective kind of writing, towards a study of the individual and of his moral growth within himself, rather than within his society.

Bibliography

In this selective bibliography I have included, besides the writings cited in the foregoing chapters, others which I have found particularly important, whether for their intrinsic value or for the profitable disagreement which they provoke.

I WORKS BY JANE AUSTEN

✓*The Novels of Jane Austen*, ed. R. W. Chapman, five volumes, third edition 1933, fifth impression 1953.

Jane Austen's Letters, ed. R. W. Chapman, second edition, reprinted and corrected 1959.

II OTHER WORKS

✓AUSTEN-LEIGH, J. E. *A Memoir of Jane Austen*, 1870: ed. R. W. Chapman, 1926.

AUSTEN-LEIGH, W. and R. A. *Jane Austen: her Life and Letters*, 1913.

BOWEN, E. 'Jane Austen', in *The English Novelists*, ed. D. Verschoyle, 1936.

BRABOURNE, LORD. *The Letters of Jane Austen*, 1884.

BRADBROOK, F. W. *Emma* (a critical study), 1961.

BRADLEY, A. C. 'Jane Austen', in *Essays and Studies of the English Association*, II, 1911; reprinted in *A Miscellany*, 1929.

British Critic. Reviews of *Sense and Sensibility*, May 1812; of *Pride and Prejudice*, February 1813; of *Emma*, July 1816; of *Northanger Abbey* and *Persuasion*, March 1818.

BROWER, R. A. *The Fields of Light*, 1952.

CECIL, LORD DAVID. *Early Victorian Novelists*, 1934.

✓CECIL, LORD DAVID. 'Jane Austen' (the Leslie Stephen Lecture, 1935); reprinted in *Poets and Storytellers*, 1949.

CHAPMAN, R. W. 'Jane Austen: a Reply to Mr. Garrod', in *Essays by Divers Hands*, 1931.

CHAPMAN, R. W. 'Jane Austen's Text', *Times Literary Supplement*, 13 February 1937.

✓CHAPMAN, R. W. *Jane Austen: Facts and Problems*, 1948.

CHAPMAN, R. W. *Jane Austen: a Critical Bibliography*, 1953.

Critical Review. Reviews of *Sense and Sensibility*, February 1812; of *Pride and Prejudice*, March 1813.

DUFFY, J. M., JR. 'Emma: the Awakening from Innocence', *E.L.H.*, XXI, 1954.

DUFFY, J. M., JR. 'Moral Integrity and Moral Anarchy in *Mansfield Park*', *E.L.H.*, XXIII, 1956.

ELTON, O. *A Survey of English Literature, 1780–1840*, Vol. I, 1924.

FORSTER, E. M. *Abinger Harvest*, 1936.

GARROD, H. W. 'Jane Austen: a Depreciation', In *Essays by Divers Hands*, 1928.

Gentleman's Magazine. Review of *Emma*, September 1816.

✓LASCELLES, M. *Jane Austen and her Art*, 1939.

LEAVIS, F. R. *The Great Tradition*, 1948.

LEAVIS, Q. D. 'A Critical Theory of Jane Austen's Writings', *Scrutiny*, X, 1942, and XII, 1944.

LEWES, G. H. 'The Novels of Jane Austen', *Blackwood's Magazine*, July 1859.

LEWIS, C. S. 'A Note on Jane Austen', *Essays in Criticism*, IV, 1954.

LIDDELL, R. *Some Principles of Fiction*, 1955.

MANSFIELD, K. 'Jane Austen', in *Novels and Novelists*, ed. J. M. Murry, 1930.

✓MUDRICK, M. *Jane Austen: Irony as Defense and Discovery*, 1952.

Quarterly Review. Reviews of *Emma* (by Sir Walter Scott), October 1815; of *Northanger Abbey* and *Persuasion* (by Archbishop Whately), January 1821.

RALLI, A. 'Jane Austen', *Critiques*, 1927.

SADLEIR, M. 'A Footnote to the Northanger Novels', *Edinburgh Review*, CCXLVI, 1927.

SAINTSBURY, G. *A History of Nineteenth-Century Literature*, 1896.

SHANNON, E. F. '*Emma*: Character and Construction', *Publications of the Modern Language Association of America*, LXXI, 1956.

WOOLF, V. *The Common Reader*, 1925.

WRIGHT, A. H. *Jane Austen's Novels: a Study in Structure*, 1953.

Index

The principal reference to each subject is given first, separated from other references by a semicolon. The titles of Jane Austen's novels are abbreviated as follows:

NA *Northanger Abbey*
SS *Sense and Sensibility*
PP *Pride and Prejudice*
MP *Mansfield Park*
E   *Emma*
P   *Persuasion*